VISIONS OF PRIVACY:
POLICY CHOICES FOR THE DIGITAL AGE

Edited by Colin J. Bennett and Rebecca Grant

As the world moves into the twenty-first century, cellular systems, high-density data storage, and the Internet are but a few of the new technologies that promise great advances in productivity and improvements in the quality of life. Yet these new technologies also threaten personal privacy. A surveillance society, in which the individual has little control over personal information, may be the logical result of deregulation, globalization, and a mass data-processing capacity. Consumers report increasing concern over erosion of personal privacy even as they volunteer personal information in exchange for coupons, catalogues, and credit. What kind of privacy future are we facing? In *Visions of Privacy: Policy Choices for the Digital Age*, some of the most prominent international theorists and practitioners in the field explore the impact of evolving technology on private citizens. The authors critically probe legal, social, political, and economic issues, as each answers the question, How can we develop privacy solutions equal to the surveillance challenges of the future?

COLIN J. BENNETT is Associate Professor in the Department of Political Science at the University of Victoria.
REBECCA GRANT is Associate Professor in the Faculty of Business at the University of Victoria.

Studies in Comparative Political Economy and Public Policy

Editors: MICHAEL HOWLETT, DAVID LAYCOCK, STEPHEN MCBRIDE, Simon Fraser University

Studies in Comparative Political Economy and Public Policy is designed to showcase innovative approaches to political economy and public policy from a comparative perspective. While originating in Canada, the series will provide attractive offerings to a wide international audience, featuring studies with local, sub-national, cross-national, and international empirical bases and theoretical frameworks.

Published to date:
1 **The Search for Political Space: Globalization, Social Movements, and the Urban Political Experience**
   Warren Magnusson
2 **Oil, the State, and Federalism: The Rise and Demise of Petro-Canada as a Statist Impulse**
   John Erik Fossum
3 **Defying Conventional Wisdom: Free Trade and the Rise of Popular Sector Politics in Canada**
   Jeffrey M. Ayres
4 **Community, State, and Market on the North Atlantic Rim: Challenges to Modernity in the Fisheries**
   Richard Apostle, Gene Barrett, Peter Holm, Svein Jentoft, Leigh Mazany, Bonnie McCay, Knut H. Mikalsen
5 **More with Less: Work Reorganization in the Canadian Mining Industry**
   Bob Russell
6 **Visions of Privacy: Policy Choices for the Digital Age**
   Edited by Colin J. Bennett and Rebecca Grant

EDITED BY COLIN J. BENNETT AND
REBECCA GRANT

Visions of Privacy:
Policy Choices for the
Digital Age

UNIVERSITY OF TORONTO PRESS
Toronto Buffalo London

© University of Toronto Press Incorporated 1999
Toronto Buffalo London
Printed in Canada

ISBN 0-8020-4194-9 (cloth)
ISBN 0-8020-8050-2 (paper)

Printed on acid-free paper

Canadian Cataloguing in Publication Data

Main entry under title:

Visions of privacy : policy choices for the digital age

(Studies in comparative political economy and public policy)
Selected papers from the Visions of privacy conference, held at the
University of Victoria, May 1996.
Includes bibliographical references and index.
ISBN 0-8020-4194-9 (bound)   ISBN 0-8020-8050-2 (pbk.)

1. Privacy, Right of – Congresses.   2. Data protection – Congresses.
I. Bennett, Colin J. (Colin John), 1955– .   II. Grant, Rebecca A.
III. Series.

JC596.V57 1999   323.44'83   C98-931874-5

University of Toronto Press acknowledges the financial assistance to its
publishing program of the Canada Council for the Arts and the Ontario Arts
Council.

This book was published with the assistance of the Social Sciences and
Humanities Research Council (Canada), the University of Victoria, and the
Office of the Information and Privacy Commissioner of British Columbia.

Contents

Preface

This book has its origins in a conference. On 9–11 May 1996 the Office of the Information and Privacy Commissioner of British Columbia together with the University of Victoria hosted an international conference entitled 'Visions for Privacy in the Twenty-first Century: A Search for Solutions' in Victoria. The conference featured an impressive range of experts, officials, and advocates. Representatives from privacy and data protection agencies from several countries were present, as were many of the world's privacy activists. The conference offered the opportunity for intensive interdisciplinary and international debate about the extent and nature of surveillance in the twenty-first century and the range of solutions to address the threats to privacy posed by such surveillance.[1]

Most of these essays were originally offered as papers at this conference, and we would like to thank the authors for their cooperation and patience throughout the preparation of this volume. We also gratefully acknowledge the support of the sponsors of the Visions for Privacy Conference: the Social Sciences and Humanities Research Council of Canada, the University of Victoria, the Chief Information Officer of British Columbia, the Credit Bureau of Vancouver, Equifax Canada, American Express, BC Tel, Stentor Telecom Policy Inc., Mytec Technologies, and the *Privacy Journal*. We also acknowledge the work of the other members of the conference organizing committee, David Flaherty, Lorraine Dixon, and Murray Rankin, and the conference coordinator, Sandra Kahale. During the editing process, we were fortunate to have the research assistance of two students at the University of Victoria, Ritu Mahil and Aaron Hokanson. The encouragement and expertise of Margaret Williams and Virgil Duff at the University of Toronto Press were also crucial. Of course, none of these efforts would have been possible without the enthusiastic support of the Information and Privacy Commissioner of British Columbia, David Flaherty, and his staff.

NOTE

1 One manifestation of the collective resolve of the conference participants was the signing of a document which demonstrated their abiding commitment to the use of protective measures and technologies.

VISIONS OF PRIVACY:
POLICY CHOICES FOR THE DIGITAL AGE

Introduction

COLIN J. BENNETT and REBECCA GRANT

The overriding theme of this book is whether the privacy solutions of the past are equal to the surveillance challenges of the future. When most of the world's privacy legislation was written, in the 1970s and 1980s, privacy invasions were national in character, discretely connected to an identifiable individual or set of individuals, perpetuated more often by agencies of the state than by private corporations, and generally more connected to the practices that surrounded independent, 'stand-alone' databases. Now personal information is dispersed and accessible from a multitude of remote locations. It is collected, matched, traded, and profiled as part of the routine engagement with both public and private institutions. It moves openly across borders. It knows fewer national or organizational attachments. There is a new landscape for privacy protection policy.[1]

This new landscape has been shaped by trends in technological, economic, and political domains. Technologically, the privacy problem is exacerbated by the exponential pace of digitization applying to personal information in the form of text, sound, and video; the increase in access, transmission, and retrieval speed for ever more comprehensive personal data files; and the emergence of digital communications networks on a global dimension. These trends parallel movements towards deregulation that are breaking down traditional economic sectors as well as barriers between 'public' and 'private' organizations. At the same time, increasingly sophisticated techniques for market segmentation enable target marketing based on the profiling and matching of transactional data. Within our political and administrative institutions, officials continue to find increasingly creative methods to collect and process personal data to attain their policy goals, including the more effective delivery of services and conduct of law enforcement.

We make no assumption, however, about the causes of the privacy problem. It is clearly rooted in wider social forces often captured by the term 'modernity.' The bundle of technological, economic, and political factors that constitute late capitalism clearly need to be interrogated if this one issue is to be thoroughly understood. But we leave those questions to the growing body of sociological literature that has been generally concerned with the origins and causes of surveillance.[2] From our vantage point, the privacy problem has its roots in structural conditions – such as bureaucratic organization, globalized capitalism, and technological sophistication – as well as in human agency. Privacy problems arise when technologies work perfectly and when they fail. They arise when administrative, political, and economic elites have worthy motives and when they do not. They arise through both human fallibility and infallibility.

This book is not directly intended to raise public awareness about the privacy issue. The chapters do, of course, contain plenty of empirical evidence of privacy risks in a variety of technological, organizational, and national contexts. But these various issues are more than adequately addressed in the body of more popular and polemical literature on the subject.[3] Moreover, the world's privacy and data protection commissioners have now produced an impressive body of analytical work on the privacy implications of new technologies and organizational practices. This work alone is testament to the increasingly variegated range of privacy 'issues' with which these agencies have to deal, including the use of identification numbers, smart cards, video-surveillance, intelligent vehicle highway systems (IVHS), geographic information systems, computer matching and profiling, call management services, genetic databases, drug testing, and a range of intrusive practices on the Internet.[4]

Neither do we make any assumptions about the meaning of the term 'privacy.' It is an almost customary feature of any analysis of privacy to begin with a disclaimer about the inherent difficulty, perhaps impossibility, of defining exactly what 'privacy' is and of disaggregating its various dimensions. Successful attempts have probably been made to specify the various roles that privacy may perform within modern political systems.[5] A useful distinction can also be made between privacy as an intrinsic or aesthetic value, or the 'restriction of personal information as an end in itself,'[6] and privacy as an instrumental or 'strategic' value where the aim is perhaps to ensure that the 'right data are used by the right people for the right purposes.'[7] For our purposes, it would be misleading and confining even to try to provide a general definition of 'privacy' to focus the analysis. All definitions, to some extent, are based on questionable assumptions about individualism and about the distinction between the realms of civil society and the state. Many gloss over essential cultural, class-related, or gender differences. More than thirty years of semantic and philosophical analysis leaves us with the overwhelming sense that privacy is a deeply and essentially contested concept.[8]

We would insist, however, that the protection of privacy is not simply an individual problem that is challenged by an array of social forces. Along with Priscilla Regan, we would contend that privacy serves 'not just individual interests but also common, public, and collective purposes.'[9] It has value beyond its usefulness in helping the individual protect and promote his or her identity and integrity. Philip Agre puts the point this way: 'On this view, privacy is not simply a matter of control over data; it also pertains to the regimentation of diverse aspects of everyday life through the sociotechnical mechanisms by which data are produced.' [10] Our starting assumptions are similar. Privacy protection has ceased to be a solely legal issue of human rights and civil liberties. It is a problem for *public policy*. Our aim is to present and evaluate the available approaches and instruments to resolve this policy problem, given this new and unsettled landscape.

The Policy Legacies

The collection, storage, processing, and dissemination of personal information has been a complex public policy in most Western societies since the late 1960s. It has rarely become politicized, in the sense that politicians have tried to court public opinion and electoral favour through anti-surveillance (or pro-privacy) positions. Nevertheless, privacy has over time assumed the characteristics of a policy sector: a set of statutory instruments; a community of privacy agencies that possess a range of regulatory, advisory, educational, and quasi-judicial responsibilities; a circle of legal experts; a group of journalists ready to publicize abuses of personal information; a small but important network of private sector lobbyists and consultants; a growing academic community from law, social science, computer science, and business faculties; and public officials in national governments and international arenas such as the European Union (EU), the Organization for Economic Cooperation and Development (OECD), Council of Europe, and others.

Over time, international harmonization efforts, intensive attempts at cross-national learning, as well as the imperatives of increasingly global communications networks have motivated a process of international policy convergence.[11] This process has now progressed to such an extent that there is a broad international consensus, at least among the industrialized countries, about what it means for an organization to pursue privacy friendly policies. It means that an organization

- Must be *accountable* for all personal information in its possession
- Should *identify the purposes* for which the information is processed at or before the time of collection
- Should only collect personal information with the *knowledge and consent* of the individual (except under specified circumstances)
- Should *limit the collection* of personal information to that which is necessary for pursuing the identified purposes
- Should not use or disclose personal information for purposes other than those identified, except with the consent of the individual (*the finality principle*)
- Should *retain* information only as long as necessary
- Should ensure that personal information is kept *accurate, complete, and up to date*
- Should protect personal information with appropriate *security safeguards*
- Should be *open* about its policies and practices and maintain no secret information system
- Should allow the data subjects *access* to their personal information, with an ability to amend it if necessary

These principles appear (obviously in different form) in national data protection legislation, in international agreements, in voluntary codes of practice, and in the first national privacy standard published by the Canadian Standards Association.[12] They express a basic and common understanding of how the responsible organization should treat the personal data that it collects, stores, and processes, and how then it should mediate its relations with the individuals with whom it comes into contact, be they clients, consumers, suspects, or students. The historical and cultural sources of concerns about privacy may differ in interesting and dynamic ways, but the definition of what it means to be 'responsible' has increasingly converged.

Differences remain. The convergence process has not yet extended to the United States, Australia, and Canada, whose policies still rely on a combination of statutory protections for the public sector and self-regulation for the private. Although data protection law has been passed in jurisdictions such as New Zealand and Hong Kong, it is still very much a European phenomenon. Of course, intricate regulatory questions about the scope of coverage, about the powers of enforcement agencies, and about tricky definitional problems continue to exercise the policy community. These aside, an observer of the privacy protection movement in the 1980s would have concluded that a consensus existed among most experts about the fundamental requirements of a privacy protection policy: a statutory codification of the fair information principles, an application to *every* organization that processes personal data, and oversight and enforcement by an independent data protection agency. These conditions were seen by many as both *necessary and sufficient* for the implementation of privacy protection policy.

The late 1980s and 1990s, however, have seen an increasing tendency for analysts to question this assumption and to suggest potentially superior means by which privacy can be safeguarded in the increasingly networked social and economic environment of the future. These new approaches include privacy-enhancing technologies (PET) to permit secure and anonymous personal data transactions, market approaches to encourage self-regulation, global privacy solutions, and a greater role for social movements and privacy advocacy. Such approaches supplement the more traditional role of the privacy and data protection agencies that administer and oversee the data protection laws of the advanced industrial world.

So when we examine the 'privacy tool kit' in the late 1990s, several choices appear, perhaps all of which are necessary and none sufficient. These solutions might be summarized by the exhortations: *apply the principles, build privacy in, factor privacy into business practices, think privacy globally, and protest surveillance out.*

These are the potential paths to privacy protection in the next century that are discussed in the essays written for this volume. The five approaches are not mutually exclusive, even though the existing literature generally treats them as if they were. There is a certain amount of rhetoric about the need for a 'mosaic of solutions.'[13] On the other hand, there has yet to be a serious treatment of how these approaches relate one to another and of the extent to which incompatibilities of interests and resources might turn the mosaic into a confusing and irreconcilable set of strategies. This book addresses the conditions that will facilitate each of these approaches to privacy protection. *Visions of Privacy* suggests that the book presents some very different authors writing from various national, disciplinary, and organizational perspectives. It also denotes an inherent and inescapable plurality of solutions.

The Fair Information Principles: In Need of Application, Expansion, or Revision?

In most advanced industrial states, the fair information principles are codified in law and overseen and enforced by small data protection agencies, such as the Office of the Information and Privacy Commissioner of British Columbia. David Flaherty, the current commissioner and one of the central figures of the modern privacy movement, begins this collection by reflecting on thirty years of privacy advocacy in his capacities as an academic historian and now as a commissioner. He reminds us that privacy has been challenged throughout recorded Western history, from diverse ideological sources and with the use of the latest technologies. He also reminds us that people have and always will search for privacy, even though we will balance that value against other competing interests in different ways and to different degrees. For Flaherty, the fair information principles approach institutionalizes that balance in procedural terms. There is little wrong with the principles, but they must be applied more widely to new technologies such as video-surveillance, as well as to organizations in the private sector that are currently largely unregulated in North America. Flaherty's conclusion that 'I have never met a privacy issue that could not be satisfactorily addressed by the application of fair information principles' is an argument with which many of the essays in this volume take issue.

Gary Marx, for example, would not disagree with the assertion that privacy is a perennial and central human right. He insists, however, that a data protection model may have been appropriate for the database forms of surveillance in the past, but it leaves unregulated the means by which data are collected in the first place. New surveillance methods probe 'more deeply, widely, and softly' than traditional methods. The data protection model offers no criteria for deciding whether a given means of data collection or extraction is ethically acceptable. The traditional principles, and by extension the laws, codes, and international agreements on which they are based, simply regulate what can be done with personal data once they are collected. Marx, therefore, offers an expanded set of ethical principles together with a checklist of possible questions to determine the moral basis of surveillance practices.

Charles D. Raab is not so critical of the fair information principles doctrine, but he does ask some penetrating questions about what it means to 'balance' privacy against other public and private interests. Data protection advocates and officials have generally accepted the need for balance. Yet balance is an ambiguous term. Raab explores the various interpretations of this term in both the abstract and with relation to the 'systems of balance production' that may be manifested in the day-to-day work of data protection authorities as they try to weigh the public good of surveillance practices against the private harm to individuals.

Visions of Privacy-Enhancing Technology: Can One 'Build Privacy In'?

Information and communications technologies have traditionally been regarded as threats to privacy. The modern privacy movement arose in large part because of the employment of computers to store vast quantities of information held hitherto in 'manual records.' Some commentators, however, see in electronic technologies the opportunity to promote privacy. The concept of 'privacy-enhancing technologies' has entered the lexicon of the privacy movement.

PET take a variety of forms, however. For Janlori Goldman 'technologies of privacy offer a potent strategy for turning upside down the existing power imbalance.' Against the backdrop of an American privacy protection policy that is reactive, incoherent, fragmented, and inadequate, the systems she calls 'individual empowerment technologies' offer much potential. The interactive nature of contemporary communications technologies (including of course the Internet) offers more refined, immediate, and transparent methods to empower individuals to control their personal information and to make informed and participatory decisions about the conditions under which they will interact with certain organizations. One possible model is the Platform for Internet Content Selection (PICS) filter that is currently used to allow people to block access to obscene material on the Internet, but which could also be adapted to introduce privacy standards into the Internet environment. For Goldman these techniques can only be successfully applied within a general policy framework that reflects the fair information practices.

Ann Cavoukian, Information and Privacy Commissioner in the province of Ontario, shares Goldman's view to a significant extent. Focusing on health-related personal information, Cavoukian regards technological protections not just as a desirable add-on, but as a necessary condition for effective privacy protection within an increasingly interactive and networked realm. Her vision for privacy consists of a convergence of fair information principles with the initial technological design: 'The systems design and architecture should translate the essence of these practices into the language of the technology involved.' Cavoukian offers two examples of PET – blind signatures and biometric encryption – to illustrate this potential.

Also writing about medical privacy issues, Robert Gellman, an independent information consultant in Washington, DC, and former counsel to the Subcommittee on Government Information of the House of Representatives, is more sceptical. Within a context of a broader discussion about the identity of the decision makers for privacy protection, Gellman argues that privacy choices can be made at three levels: the personal, the legislative, and the technical. How the problem is framed (as a personal, legal, or technical issue) can predetermine the policy outcome. Technical solutions have their place, he says, but they do not always address the misuse of records from inside an organization or the problems created by linking personal data from separate sources. Like many of the essays in this volume, Gellman's exposes a dilemma. Privacy-enhancing technologies are best applied within a policy framework that outlines the privacy principles. On the other hand, many legislative proposals, such as those introduced in the early 1990s in the United States to protect medical privacy, were uniformly weak in considering PET as part of this framework: 'Legislation is not especially suitable for mandating technological applications of this sort.'

Visions of Privacy in the Private Sector: Is It in the Interests of Business?

The early data protection laws, especially in North America, were inspired by fears of an omniscient and centralized 'Big Brother' state. Privacy protection now occupies a prominent place on the political agendas of Canada and the United States, a fact one can attribute to the increasing range of intrusive practices perpetrated by the private sector. Indeed, trends towards deregulation, the contracting out of government services, and privatization have made it increasingly difficult to determine where the public sector ends and the private begins. The application of privacy rules within a competitive economic environment, however, raises interesting questions about the extent to which privacy protection is, or can be made to be, in the interests of the corporate sector. The North American response to private sector data protection issues has so far been to rely on an assumption that if consumers are concerned about personal privacy, their concerns will be reflected in complaints and a preference for businesses with more privacy-friendly practices. Voluntary codes of practice (based on the OECD *Guidelines* of 1981) have been the typical manifestation of the corporate response.[14]

Mary Culnan and Robert J. Bies argue that privacy protection can build a bond of trust between the corporation and its customers. Recent scandals about proposed uses of personal data for marketing purposes illustrate how consumers perceive some practices to be inherently privacy invasive. Culnan's and Bies's research suggests that these concerns stem from beliefs about procedural fairness, which are operationalized through fair information principles, and particularly through the principles of knowledge and consent. Firms are more likely to retain existing customers and attract new ones if they can implement fair information principles, create a culture of privacy within their organizations, and build a climate of trust. Whether in traditional or online environments, they contend, 'It is in the bottom-line interest of marketers to observe fair information practices.' This argument predicts a growing tendency to promote privacy for competitive advantage and market-based privacy solutions as the norm.

James Rule and Lawrence Hunter, however, argue that neither a faith in the market potential of privacy, nor legislated solutions are sufficient. They propose the creation of a property right over the commercial exploitation of personal information. This right would not constrain the collection and compilation of data from people with whom an organization already has dealings. It would define the conditions for secondary acquisition of personal information for any commercial purpose and would require the express consent of the data subject for any release of personal data; without such consent there would be no release. The approach would give individuals the right to charge royalties on the sale or exchange of personal data. This might promote the development of 'informational intermediaries' or 'data rights agencies,' which would seek to enroll clients on the promise of collecting royalties for the commercial use of their data and on the expectation of collecting an agreed commission. Rule and Hunter do not claim that this proposal will cure all privacy ills. They do propose it as an effective new instrument in the privacy toolbox.

René Laperrière agrees with Rule and Hunter that privacy legislation does not seem to reduce the collection and flow of personal information. Laperrière bases this assessment on a critique of the data protection legislation in Quebec, the only jurisdiction in North America that has regulated the private sector. Laws embodying fair information principles do not establish criteria to determine what types of data banks are legitimate; they contain numerous exemptions that facilitate exchanges, and they do not address adequately the problem of discrimination. The central problem, according to Laperrière, is the privatization of public power. Excessive surveillance by business is just one manifestation of a system of corporate power that has become progressively removed from social controls. Quebec's 1993 privacy law, he concludes, has done little to redress the balance in favour of individuals.

Visions of Global Solutions: Can Purely National Solutions Suffice?

A fourth approach to the issue of privacy examines the dilemmas of building international standards for personal data protection within an increasingly international environment for personal data communications. Globalization forces business to use computer and telecommunications networks that can transfer data instantaneously around the globe, including data on individual customers, employees, suppliers, investors, competitors, and so on. The globalization of international data traffic has the potential to undermine national efforts to protect the privacy of citizens.

This is not a new issue. The debate over transborder data flows began in the late 1970s and inspired two early international instruments from the OECD and the Council of Europe that were designed to harmonize data protection policy and to force those without appropriate safeguards to pass equivalent legislation.[15] Neither instrument was particularly successful. Consequently, from 1990 until 1995, the countries of the European Union (EU) negotiated a general directive on the 'Protection of Individuals with Regard to the Processing of Personal Data and on the Free Movement of Such Data' designed to harmonize all European laws and to facilitate the free flow of personal information around the single market. Article 25 of the directive stipulates that personal data should not be transferred outside the EU unless the receiving jurisdiction can guarantee an 'adequate level of protection.'[16]

Priscilla Regan and Joel Reidenberg explore the prospects for the globalization of privacy standards through the EU directive. Regan examines the politics behind the development of the directive and the reaction in the American corporate sector, for which several aspects of this directive are problematic. Intensive lobbying by some U.S. business interests, alongside their European counterparts, shaped the contents of the directive in some key respects. This experience suggests that one will see continued resistance to legislated privacy solutions in the United States and in other non-European countries. Regan also predicts continuing attempts to internationalize standards for personal data protection, such as the initiative that has just begun through the International Standards Organization (ISO).[17]

Joel Reidenberg argues that, while responses in the United States have so far been confusing and incoherent, the European data protection directive will promote obligatory standards for personal data protection in the United States (and elsewhere). The overwhelming desire for predictability in the Global Information Infrastructure (GII) will inspire a 'workable consensus on satisfying fair information practice obligations for international data flows.' Reidenberg contends that a new contractual model based on the liability of the data exporter might minimize conflicts over transborder data flows. He also speaks favourably of the potential for privacy standards, registration to which can promote guarantees of conformity in practice and help satisfy the requirement in the European directive that any professional rules and codes of practice must be 'complied with' in the receiving jurisdiction.

Visions of Privacy Advocacy: Can the Issue Be Politicized?

This bring us full circle from the personal and historical reflections of a current privacy commissioner to those of two front-line privacy advocates. John Westwood and Simon Davies consider the extent to which the privacy problem can become more politicized. Some have contended that privacy will rank with the environment as a 'quality-of-life issue.' What is the potential for a 'politics of privacy'? What role can social groups – civil liberties groups, consumer associations, and the media – play in advancing the issue?

Despite intense activity among a relatively confined policy community of advocates, officials, and academics over the past thirty years, privacy protection has never been an issue that has captured the attention of the mass public in an enduring way. It rarely, if ever, is mentioned in election campaigns. The fate of elected politicians rarely, if ever, depends on their commitment to the issue. Indeed, the opposite is more often the case in a prevailing climate of neo-conservative economics, law-and-order agendas, and pressures to save public money by fighting welfare fraud and the like.

John Westwood, of the British Columbia Civil Liberties Association (BCCLA), analyses five case studies in which his association has been involved: the development of an interactive pharmaceutical database (PharmaNet), the videotaping of police calls, drug testing in the workplace, mandatory criminal record checks, and data matching of records of welfare recipients. The record of the BCCLA in lobbying for better privacy protection is mixed on these issues. Westwood draws a number of lessons about the conditions under which privacy can be successfully politicized on the basis of his experiences of life in the 'privacy trenches.'

This collection of essays concludes with an overview of the modern privacy movement by Simon Davies, the director-general of Privacy International. From his unique position, Davies analyses the sources, organizational frameworks, and objectives of modern privacy organizations in different countries. He also describes how the Internet has provided a potent instrument with which to mobilize against surveillance practices and galvanize the international privacy movement. There is also growing evidence of direct action against excessive surveillance in countries such as Britain.

This book appears at a critical juncture in the history of the modern privacy movement. The end of the millennium marks a clear point at which to evaluate the progress of this movement to date and the likely trends in the next century. More critically, however, the rapid changes in the use and distribution of information technology are raising a bewildering variety of new surveillance issues that demand that advocates and analysts reassess whether the solutions of the past are indeed equal to the challenges of the future.

NOTES

1 Philip E. Agre and Marc Rotenberg, eds., *Technology and Privacy: The New Landscape* (Cambridge: MIT Press, 1997).
2 See David Lyon, *The Electronic Eye: The Rise of Surveillance Society* (Minneapolis: University of Minnesota Press, 1994); Oscar H. Gandy, Jr, *The Panoptic Sort: A Political Economy of Personal Information* (Boulder: Westview Press, 1993); David Lyon and Elia Zureik, eds., *Computers, Surveillance and Privacy* (Minneapolis: University of Minnesota Press, 1996).

3 For example, Ann Cavoukian and Don Tapscott, *Who Knows: Safeguarding Your Privacy in a Networked World* (Toronto: Random House, 1995); Simon Davies, *Big Brother: Britain's Web of Surveillance and the New Technological Order* (London: Pan Books, 1996); Jeffrey Rothfeder, *Privacy for Sale: How Computerization Has Made Everyone's Private Life an Open Secret* (New York: Simon and Schuster, 1992).

4 Most privacy and data commissioners now have web sites on which papers on these and other privacy issues can be found. These can be accessed through the 'Politics of Information' site created at the University of Victoria by Jason Young and Colin Bennett (www.cous.uvic.ca/poli/456/privres.htm).

5 See Alan F. Westin, *Privacy and Freedom* (New York: Atheneum, 1967), 32–9; David H. Flaherty, *Protecting Privacy in Surveillance Societies* (Chapel Hill: University of North Carolina Press, 1989), 8.

6 James Rule, *The Politics of Privacy: Planning for Personal Data Systems as Powerful Technologies* (New York: Elsevier, 1980), 22.

7 Paul Sieghart, *Privacy and Computers* (London: Latimer, 1976), 76.

8 For an excellent anthology of the philisophical literature, see Ferdinand D. Schoeman, ed., *Philosophical Dimensions of Privacy: An Anthology* (Cambridge: Cambridge University Press, 1984).

9 Priscilla M. Regan, *Legislative Privacy: Technology, Social Values and Public Policy* (Chapel Hill: University of North Carolina Press, 1995), 221.

10 Philip Agre, 'Introduction,' in Agre and Rotenberg, *Privacy and Technology*, 18.

11 Colin J. Bennett, *Regulating Privacy: Data Protection and Public Policy in Europe and the United States* (Ithaca: Cornell University Press, 1992), ch. 3; see also the re-evaluation of the convergence thesis in 'Convergence Re-visited: Toward a Global Policy for the Protection of Personal Data?' in Agre and Rotenberg, eds. *Technology and Privacy: The New Landscape* 99–123.

12 Canadian Standards Association, *Model Code for the Protection of Personal Information* (Rexdale, ON: CSA, 1995).

13 Cavoukian and Tapscott, *Who Knows?*, 180.

14 See Privacy and American Business, *Handbook of Company Privacy Codes* (Hackensack, NJ: Privacy and American Business, 1994); and Colin J. Bennett, *Implementing Privacy Codes of Practice: A Report to the Canadian Standards Association* (Rexdale, ON: CSA, 1995).

15 Organization for Economic Cooperation and Development, *Guidelines on the Protection of Privacy and Transborder Flows of Personal Data* (Paris: OECD, 1981); Council of Europe, *Convention for the Protection of Individuals with Regard to the Automatic Processing of Personal Data* (Strasbourg: Council of Europe, 1981).

16 European Union, *Directive 95/46/EC of the European Parliament and of the Council on the Protection of Individuals with Regard to the Processing of Personal Data and on the Free Movement of Such Data* (Brussels: Official Journal of the European Communities L281, 24 Oct. 1995).

17 Colin J. Bennett, *Prospects for an International Standard for the Protection of Personal Information: A Report to the Standards Council of Canada* (Ottawa: Standards Council of Canada, 1997; available at www.cous.uvic.ca/poli/iso.htm).

PART 1

ETHICAL AND VALUE CHOICES

1

Visions of Privacy: Past, Present, and Future[1]

DAVID H. FLAHERTY

In selecting the theme of 'Visions of Privacy for the Twenty-first Century' for our 1996 conference, my colleagues and I were largely taking advantage of the imminence of the millennium. But I increasingly regard that thematic choice as very fortuitous, because it allows a privacy advocate to move beyond the short-term perspective and to think at least several years into the future and, indeed, into the past as well. Let me develop the perspectives that I wish to bring to this issue of privacy protection in the foreseeable future by starting first with the past, before reflecting as well on other phases of my own development and experience as a privacy advocate.

A Historical Perspective: The Puritans in Seventeenth-Century New England

Although I am a historian, I have never written about the history of privacy, except in my first book, completed as a doctoral dissertation thirty years ago.[2] Ironically, I wrote then about a surveillance society created by English Puritans in seventeenth-century New England and how they failed, at least over time, to create the ideal 'City upon a Hill' for the eyes of all the world to behold.[3] Of course, Puritan New England was an impressive effort at surveillance and social control, especially for a pre-industrial age, but the attempt foundered on the shoals of resistant human nature, the incapacity of law enforcers to achieve the lofty goals of the legislature, and the process of generational change from the time of the Founding Fathers of the 1630s.

What I remember so vividly from when I began my research on the early Puritans in the fall of 1964, inspired by the contemporary and historical research on privacy then being directed by Professor Alan F. Westin of Columbia University, is that I expected to be able to demonstrate that the Puritans did not care about or value personal privacy, because its achievement was inimical to the collective religious goals of the hardy band of reformers who founded the colony of Massachusetts Bay, in particular, in the late 1620s. On the contrary, I learned that they indeed cared about personal privacy in its various forms, whether solitude, intimacy, anonymity, or reserve. As we do today, the Puritans sought to balance this concern for a private life with other competing values such as survival, religiosity, and the fate of the community at the hands of an intolerant God. Westin's example encouraged me to take a very broad view of the meaning of privacy, far beyond our contemporary emphasis on regulating the collection and use of personal information or the data protection component of protecting privacy.[4] Thus, I looked at the early modern concern for privacy in terms of architecture and town planning, family and community life, religious practices, social legislation, and law enforcement. I will reflect on this broad approach again later in this essay.

As a young graduate student, I found it very difficult to try to understand the mindset of the early Puritans, who were essentially English men and women transported to a hostile wilderness in very small numbers. In particular, I had to learn to distinguish between the broad collectivist goals of the society and what motivated individual men and women, young and old, as they went about the conduct of their daily lives with the usual range of competing values, including the desires for solitude, intimacy, and community. Of course, ensuring survival itself was at the forefront of their existence for many years. The wilderness was literally a hostile environment. But I also observed people wanting to have their own land and to live on it (displaying a strong sense of private property), to build their own houses, and seeking to achieve a balance among collective, familial, and individual existences. In Canada today 23 per cent of the population comprises people who live alone, a choice that was simply not practical in early Massachusetts.[5]

My interpretation of the evidence is that individuals in Puritan society did strive for and achieve personal privacy in the form of solitude, intimacy, anonymity, and reserve. Anonymity was of course the most difficult to achieve in North America until the substantial urbanization of the modern era, although even the metropolis of Boston, with a population of only about ten thousand persons as late as 1700, permitted the achievement of some anonymity despite the aspirations of local authorities to strong social control.[6]

The early Puritans cared about personal privacy, broadly encompassed, in ways quite different from our own forms of concern. One purpose of achieving solitude, for example, was for prayer and contemplation. Solitude was also readily achievable in early America, because there were few people, and they lived in a relatively large amount of space. One's ability to get away from other people, at least temporarily, was considerable in comparison with modern urban life in Europe, South Asia, and North America. There was also a great emphasis on social organization in the form of families and communities in early America, in part because it facilitated survival, communal living, and the avoidance of sin. The Puritans actually enacted laws that made it a crime to live alone; not surprisingly, these laws were essentially unenforced.[7]

Pre-twentieth-century English-speaking persons further protected their privacy by enforcing a strong sense of reserve in interpersonal communications. We can perhaps appreciate this even more because our own social mores have moved so far, indeed perhaps too far, in the opposite direction. There is considerable pressure on us in all aspects of our lives to be more open with everyone about our feelings and states of mind. In some quarters, to maintain a sense of privacy about aspects of one's existence is viewed as anti-social. The colonial Puritan equivalent was mandatory public confession at church services for Saints (those who had undergone a conversion experience and been accepted as full church members).[8] We even have the spectacle of television programs that permit individuals to achieve the compulsory fifteen minutes of fame by publicizing, or accusing others of, the most egregious kinds of misbehaviour. Privacy advocates generally believe that such persons have no idea of the consequences of their actions for their own lives and the lives of others.

The Current Achievement of Surveillance Societies

Let me turn from the Puritans to a more pessimistic perspective. My 1989 book, fortuitously in a way, addressed the many issues associated with the protection of privacy in surveillance societies.[9] Some readers were surprised that I was not writing about the Soviet Union or communist China, but about the United States, Canada, Sweden, the Federal Republic of Germany, and France. I have absolutely no doubt, technically or politically, that a true surveillance society can now be achieved, anywhere in the modern industrial world, if that is what the population, or its leadership, wants. In some ways, certain retirement communities in North America with their ordered existence and seemingly excessive security are prime examples of surveillance societies in miniature. Regrettably, the public and politicians have too little appreciation of the tools at their disposal as they rise up against, or respond to, the latest perceived threat to the public good. Whatever the social problem, it appears to them that there is a technological solution at hand.

The risks posed by pedophiles to young children and adolescents are a good case in point. The criminal conviction of a junior hockey coach in early January 1997 for sexually abusing a young player has set off a clamour for protection. Criminal record checks of hockey coaches and volunteers are only a first step. All hockey dressing rooms and showers could be monitored by cameras. Anyone in a position of power over a child or young person could be prohibited from being alone with him or her, under any circumstance, and monitoring could be conducted by cameras and electronic emitting devices that would notify the authorities if two persons with contraindicated emitting devices were alone together. We already have the practice in North America of animals being permanently identified by implants under their skin. Tracking technology will certainly be improved enough to allow a parent, or a spouse, to always know where a child or a lover is and, in an advanced enough system, who they are with. If telephone calls already can follow us from location to location in order to deliver a message, comparable satellite technology should soon allow us to track the movements of persons who concern us. Using it for known stalkers might in fact be a positive example of surveillance.

As I was writing this essay, two articles in the 11 January 1997 issue of the *Economist* made my point about surveillance. The headlines read as follows: 'Telemedicine. Big Sister is watching you,' and 'Big Brother. The all-seeing eye. The spread of automated surveillance systems will soon mean that a person's every movement on foot and by car can be tracked, day and night.' The first article describes actual uses of telemedicine in various parts of the rural United States, which allow health care professionals to interact with patients using a computer keyboard, close-up cameras, data transmission facilities, and a television screen. Similar experiments are under way in many countries, especially those with a very limited supply of medical specialists. The article does not even discuss the possible privacy implications, despite the scary headline. Thus, telemedicine has all of the appearances of being a benign form of surveillance that most of us will welcome in due course. Being able to consult a physician without leaving one's home or office appears to be a positive good, if fair information principles and practices are followed.

The automated surveillance systems described in the second *Economist* article include remote cameras, security cameras, computerized databases of digital photographs, and closed-circuit television (CCTV). Such systems are in place in Britain in local authorities, schools, housing estates, hospitals, banks, garages, retailers, and most shopping malls, and on streets and roads. The article states:

> Britain now has more electronic eyes per head of population than any other country in the world, one-party states included. The movement of all traffic in the City of London, twice bombed by the IRA, is monitored by a ring of 90 cameras which record the licence plates of every vehicle entering and leaving its inner square mile. Any vehicle which does not leave the area within a specified time automatically triggers an alert. Licence numbers are checked against other databases such as those of stolen cars. Some cameras deployed there are so advanced that they can read the words on a cigarette packet from 100 m.[10]

The British public's fear of street crime makes it quite tolerant of such expansive surveillance, and there is some evidence of falling crime rates, such as for mugging and car theft, in inner-city areas covered by cameras. The *Economist* concludes, however, that 'the way in which CCTV is operated should disturb anyone who values civil rights ... At the very least, the Home Office should issue national guidelines on protecting privacy and civil rights ... Technological fixes alone cannot solve complex social problems.'

There are certainly positive advantages to newer forms of surveillance technology. Nursing homes can keep track of elderly patients who would be at serious risk if they wandered off the property; a lost driver can use geo-positioning to find his or her way to the appropriate location. Machines can deduct tolls from cars with transponders as they move along high-speed toll roads.

But as some of these examples have indicated, we are faced with an unthinking acceptance of surveillance technologies and monitoring practices with insufficient appreciation of the kinds of surveillance societies that we are in the process of constructing. This is perhaps the most powerful point for me to emphasize as we approach the millennium. Does anyone want to live in a society without privacy, especially in public places, where anonymity has been the norm for more than a hundred years? In my view, it is essential to be level-headed and non-apocalyptic about such matters. In my visits to public bodies in British Columbia as Information and Privacy Commissioner, I always question the need for surveillance cameras, especially those linked with storage devices, and I have yet to find a camera in a hospital entrance or corridor, a parking lot, an income assistance office in a remote location, throughout prisons, or in police stations that I did not conclude was justifiable and appropriate in the circumstances.[11] However, I am also well aware that surveillance cameras are a technology in search of an application, driven by commercial imperatives.[12] Their implementation, in my view, must only occur on the basis of a balancing of competing values rather than the fact that they are available and give the appearance of having a deterrence effect.[13] The reality is that unthinking policy makers are easy prey for promoters of an application of an innovative technology highly invasive of individual privacy that gives some 'promise' of fixing a social problem.

Contemporary Privacy Regulation

Let me now turn to some brief reflections on what I have learned about data protection in more than four years as the Information and Privacy Commissioner for British Columbia.[14] The real privacy problems for individuals, I conclude, are more serious and threatening than I had feared ten years ago, even just in the public sector. The driver is an unprecedented sequence of technological innovations in data processing and software developments, which shows no signs of abating. Whether enhanced surveillance of individuals and/or their transactions is an accidental or conscious product of such changes, the negative consequences for personal privacy are the same. The interesting connection is the role of political will to operationalize such technology when it is available for the public sector. I think that experience in Quebec, Ontario, and now British Columbia and Alberta confirms the utility of having official privacy watchdogs in place. Their presence definitely raises the profile of privacy as a public issue and makes politicians and senior public servants more circumspect about blindly opting for surveillance technology. Such managers of change become easier to persuade to conduct privacy impact assessments of innovations that they are contemplating.

In British Columbia I am more and more persuaded of the importance of holding the head of a public body ultimately responsible for privacy protection. He or she is paid to minimize political controversy in a political culture where public expressions of concern for privacy in the face of ongoing privacy disasters are not viewed as positive signs. For whatever reasons, British Columbia has the benefits of media and interest groups that supplement, and in many cases stimulate, the barks of the official privacy watchdog. When politicians and public servants are warned that a particular practice challenges privacy interests, they tend to be responsive in seeking to fashion practical solutions. Opposition politicians and political parties play a similar role.

Wishing to claim objectivity for my judgments and recognizing that I can hardly do so, I nevertheless do think that the Canadian model of privacy commissioners is a reasonably effective one, even if not perfect. Speaking about my own office, we serve as an ongoing source of privacy expertise, oversight, goading, warning, complaint handling, and auditing for a vast array of public bodies from the Ministry of Children and Families, to the Greater Vancouver Mental Health Services, to a hospital in a small town. We receive briefings on a particular new or old program in order to help ensure that it is privacy friendly. We review all draft legislation from a privacy perspective. We encourage public bodies to have policies in place to ensure transparency and openness in data collection and data use. I lead site visits to several dozen public bodies each year in order to check on actual practices.[15] It helps a great deal that most privacy problems are not that complicated, if the political and bureaucratic will exists to fix them. Most do not involve rocket science so much as the application of common sense and informed choice to take specific steps to protect the privacy interests of individuals. What my office offers is an ongoing source of privacy expertise and heightened sensitivity in order to reduce unnecessary trampling on a fundamental human right.

Although I do have regulatory authority as Information and Privacy Commissioner, I use it mainly to win agreement on my recommendations that are normally arrived at by joint deliberations with authorities that keep my colleagues and myself sensitive to the demands of daily bureaucratic life and the reality of service delivery to the public. I think we have also acquired the reputation of not being extremists in pursuit of the virtuous goal of privacy protection. We promote pragmatic, cost-effective solutions that can be introduced incrementally. Our willingness to adopt such an approach reflects, I think, our maturation as a group of professionals seeking to promote statutory goals by working with public bodies. It also reflects my views on how best to achieve the goals of data protection.[16] My power on any issue is also effectively limited in our democratic society by the fact that the legislature can in fact do almost anything it wants to invade personal privacy by law or regulation, despite my best advice to the contrary. Only an aroused public can seek to mitigate this Achilles heal of data protection. I have experienced my losses in this regard, most notably over the introduction of expensive and intrusive criminal record checks for anyone who works with children. The orders that I issue usually have a privacy component in terms of allowing or prohibiting the disclosure of personal information under section 22 of our act. Although my decisions are subject to review by the Supreme Court of British Columbia, this happens infrequently. Mr Dooley said a hundred years ago that the U.S. Supreme Court follows the election returns.[17] I read the newspapers and am aware of the political currents, although at the end of the day I realize that I have a job to do either as Information Commissioner or Privacy Commissioner that is non-political in the strictest sense of the word.

Finally, I am of the view that the application of privacy protection is a matter for specialists, such as the persons in my office. The general public, the legislature, and the public service should be able to depend on our assistance and presence in jointly fashioning solutions. The 'problems' look a lot more complicated to the uninitiated than they do to professionals with a set of available solutions that we continue to apply and reapply in new venues. The public should expect privacy solutions and warnings from us, just as it has right to depend on comparable results from other specialist authorities.

Some Lessons of History for Privacy Today

My earlier point about the surveillance ideology of the Puritans is that privacy has always been under challenge throughout recorded Western history, much as it is today from government and technology. The second historical lesson is that it is almost impossible, in practice, to steal privacy completely from individuals, except in Orwellian, fictional societies and in totalitarian and authoritarian states or settings, such as prisons, which attempt to outlaw the achievement of privacy as contrary to the public, collective good.[18] My visits to provincial prisons across British Columbia have reminded me that relative deprivation of privacy is one of the most serious consequences of incarceration, although most prisoners in this province still have the luxury of access to a private room. One thinks about the attempts of vigilant Chinese neighbours today to monitor the menstrual cycles of women of childbearing years in order to achieve population control by limiting pregnancies.[19] I have read with some interest about the efforts of governments in places like the former East Germany or Singapore to regiment the intimate details of private lives, because I have every expectation that they have failed and will continue to fail. Again, one can only be impressed by the dedicated efforts of the Nazis and the Stasis in this regard and continue to worry whether complete adoption of the latest surveillance technologies would not permit them to achieve their abhorrent goals. But the informed observer knows that both the Nazis and Stasis used the best technology available to them to monitor people, including early computers and advanced recording devices, but still failed to achieve a complete surveillance society.[20] The Holocaust Museum in Washington, DC, features a Hollerith machine used in the 1930s to try to identify and keep track of Jews in German-controlled territory. One trusts that the Stasis will be similarly commemorated in Germany.

I conclude that privacy is and always has been under attack in the Western world from either surveillance ideology or technology or both. This is ably demonstrated by work on the history of technology.[21] The telegraph, the telephone, and the camera, in their turn, were each viewed as highly invasive of personal privacy. Thus, one of the goals of liberal democratic societies has been to legitimize concern for personal privacy by constitutional and legal means at points where the individual can no longer control his or her preservation of privacy because of competing goals. Thus, for example, there was an emergence of concern about government data banks in the late 1960s and 1970s, when governments first took serious advantage of mainframe computers for routine administrative purposes.[22] Vance Packard wrote about the United States as *The Naked Society* in the early 1960s.[23] In 1974 a French writer published a book with the arresting title of *La Fin de la vie privée*.[24] In essence, the death of privacy has been widely predicted and anticipated, especially by futurists, but that fateful day has yet to arrive. The basic lesson of my own personal 'history' of work on privacy during the past thirty years is that there are always new challenges to privacy from ideology and myriad forms of technology, except that today the ideology is more capitalism and less religious belief than it was several hundred years ago. I also am persuaded that the work of privacy advocates in warning about the potential for invasion of privacy in the public and private sectors has had the highly beneficial consequence of persuading proponents to seek to ensure that an application is privacy friendly. Nevertheless, much work remains to be done to achieve societal control of invasive practices.

The corollary point, which I can only assert rather than fully explicate, is that concern for privacy in various aspects of life is fundamental to human existence as one understands it historically and as one assesses the nature of contemporary life in the Western world.[25] Valuing privacy in its various forms is a very basic component of the lives of each and every one of us. Much as I continue to troll, in North America, for individuals who literally do not care about personal privacy, it is rare to find anyone who can make a persuasive case for himself or herself (upon interrogation). Where we differ is in the extent to which we are prepared to grant privacy priority over other human rights, values, and interests when a competitive environment exists. Someone without assets, a job, and a place to live is not in a position to place a high value, in practice, upon his or her privacy. But even the most ardent opponents of welfare fraud in a province like British Columbia are unwilling to take away from those on income assistance the final vestiges of privacy remaining to them, at least not so far. For such targeted groups, the surveillance power of the state is used so extensively to monitor them by collecting and matching data that it amazes me that a few individuals can still successfully perpetrate such fraud on the state, thus leading to more surveillance of everyone receiving state benefits. To qualify for income assistance is to sacrifice one's personal privacy in dramatic ways, because there is almost nothing about your life that the state does not wish to know or be informed of if your personal situation changes. The fact that such data collection is sanctioned by a democratic legislature does not make it less egregious in terms of its impact on the privacy of individuals. Ironically, high tax rates make a substantial proportion of citizens unsympathetic to the privacy claims of the less privileged.

The most encouraging point that I can make about the future in British Columbia, or North America for that matter, is that people are going to continue to search for privacy, especially in their personal and family lives. People want to live in houses and apartments of their own, and they strive to have physical space around them by a wide variety of means. I acknowledge that I can be accused of advancing a bourgeois conception of privacy that can sometimes be hostile to feminist, communitarian, and/or social democratic goals for society. There is no doubt that the enjoyment of wealth and income facilitates the achievement of the most privacy, until one reaches a point of prominence where one can only achieve isolation and solitude on occasion, although the feats of Jacqueline Kennedy Onassis and Pierre Trudeau in protecting their private lives are commendable and exceptional. One of the prices of fame or notoriety in modern society is the loss of privacy, especially in public places where most of us enjoy anonymity. The greater one's exposure in the public life of a society, the less privacy one can continue to claim and enjoy. The life and death of Diana, Princess of Wales, epitomizes such a fate.

Perhaps I can make the point about the importance of privacy even more effectively for some readers by reminding them of the importance of intimate friends, including partners and family, to the achievement of privacy. To value and enjoy intimacy is to achieve a form of personal privacy that is protected by the desires of individuals rather than by the rules of the state. In fact, I would argue that the state only needs to intervene legally for the preservation of privacy and to limit its own activities in those realms of existence where the value is at imminent risk of disappearance. This, of course, explains our preoccupation with data protection, as a key form of privacy, since the advent of large-scale automation in the 1960s in the public and private sectors. Such concerns are even more urgent now in light of the Internet, electronic commerce, and the World Wide Web. The technological environment for the protection of privacy has rarely been so unpredictable and so much out of the control of any nation state.

Thus, as I look forward into the twenty-first century, I do so as an optimist about the future of privacy, at least in the West, because it has survived as a value at least since the advent of recorded history in Greek and Roman times. I regret that being an optimist does not guarantee me the results that I wish for.

The Need for an Expansive Approach to the Preservation of Privacy

Although I earn my living as an official data protector in British Columbia by helping to implement an act, first passed by the legislature in 1992, that regulates the 'collection, protection and retention of personal information by public bodies' in order 'to protect personal privacy,'[26] I am of the view that concern for the preservation of privacy at the dawn of the twenty-first century is going to require a more expansive effort at maintaining and encouraging all forms of privacy for individuals, not just enhancing data protection. This will require both individual and societal efforts in a wide variety of spheres of existence.

It is my considered judgment, for example, that Canadians outside the province of Quebec are essentially bereft of explicit constitutional and legal protection for their personal privacy. Canada's Charter of Rights and Freedoms unfortunately does not explicitly grant us a right to privacy, as do the constitutions of Quebec, California, and Florida, for example, or the European Convention on Human Rights. The efforts of the Canadian judiciary, especially the Supreme Court of Canada, to develop a judicially recognized, common law right to privacy are admirable. Nevertheless Parliament and provincial legislatures need to go further for the next century. In 1991 Bruce Phillips, the Privacy Commissioner of Canada, and I were unsuccessful with our testimony before the Special Joint Committee of Parliament on a Renewed Canada with respect to entrenching a constitutional right to privacy for Canadians.[27] Canadians should have the same rights as Americans, especially those living in states with an explicit right to privacy in their constitutions, to make any constitutional and legal argument that they wish in order to protect what they perceive to be legitimate privacy interests, broadly construed. Despite documented efforts in that direction, Canadian courts have not been given the incentives and the tools to value protection of privacy more highly than is currently the case.[28]

By enhanced legal protections for privacy that venture beyond the patchwork quilt of statutory and common law protections currently available to residents of a province like British Columbia, I am thinking especially of a real Privacy Act for the province, beyond the weak reed currently available to us from the 1960s.[29] British Columbians require a true tort of invasion of privacy that would address the classic components of privacy identified by William Prosser, the distinguished torts scholar.[30] Residents of British Columbia, for example, are largely unaware that such highly invasive practices as drug testing are only barely regulated or covered under current federal and provincial 'privacy' legislation, especially for the private sector. It is only a form of technological lag that has drug testing less rampant in the United States than in Canada, but expanded genetic testing awaits all of us. We need additional, more meaningful protections for unauthorized invasions of our physical and territorial space by eavesdropping and surveillance techniques that can include infra-red binoculars, extremely high-powered cameras and viewing lenses, helicopters, airplanes, and satellites. Protection must include responsive sanctions for perpetrating illegitimate intrusions.

One need only visit retail stores that specialize in supposed security devices to realize the extraordinary capacity to invade the privacy of our fellow citizens that is currently available. It is already commonplace for individuals to tape record conversations with others, in person or over the telephone, using surreptitious means. As the costs of miniaturization, automation, and telecommunications continue to drop exponentially, the incentives to apply such nefarious forms of invasion of privacy will further proliferate and reveal an additional area where the state must intervene to help the citizenry protect threatened interests. I suspect that in the twenty-first century offices like that of the Privacy Commissioner of Canada and the provincial equivalents will have to be given enhanced statutory responsibility to receive complaints from the public about very broadly defined invasions of personal privacy, in effect, to become true privacy commissioners. They should also be given proactive auditing powers to monitor all forms of surveillance.

But I am not a fan of solely bureaucratic and statutory solutions for the invasion of privacy, broadly defined. Individuals have to fend for themselves wherever it is possible to do so. Individualism, which is at the intellectual root of concern for personal privacy in Western societies, has to become more strongly activated in defence of one's privacy interests. In this sense, it is beneficial that Canadian governments are increasingly downloading various responsibilities to provinces, municipalities, and then families and individuals. To the fullest extent possible, individuals should be free to choose how much privacy they want in various facets of their respective lives and then decide how best to achieve it. To my mind, this means that data protection is thus the area most requiring state intervention, as I argue elsewhere in this essay, because the person who gives his or her data to the public or private sectors essentially loses control over them. For the rest, individuals have at least some freedom to choose between an urban or a rural environment, a private home as opposed to an apartment house, to live with or without companions and roommates, to choose a solitary occupation as opposed to a crowded shopfloor, to walk in Stanley Park in Vancouver as opposed to Robson Street, to stay home alone at night or to go out with or in crowds. I am perhaps exaggerating the extent of actual choice available to most people in the West but, if individuals rank concern for their privacy high among their list of values, these are examples of some of the considerations that they normally must reflect on in making lifestyle choices.

There is no sentient human being in the Western world who has little or no regard for his or her personal privacy; those who would attempt such claims cannot withstand even a few minutes' questioning about intimate aspects of their lives without capitulating to the intrusiveness of certain subject matters. We all have some level of concern about the preservation of our privacy. Ironically, it sometimes requires temporary deprivation of privacy, such as being in the hospital or living, working, and travelling in too close quarters with others, to remind each of us of how much we need privacy in our daily lives. Given the excessive urbanization of our societies, the achievement of real solitude is increasingly problematic. As population numbers continue to soar, the problem of achieving physical privacy so visible in the very crowded public and private conditions of Hong Kong or other Chinese cities that have a very high population density will become much more commonplace. Chicago and New York are not much different for the less affluent.

My own sense is that in the twenty-first century it will become even more expensive and difficult than it already is to enjoy a modicum of privacy in one's residence, workplace, and daily activities. The flight from crowding out into suburban and rural spaces will become an even stronger motivator for individuals, a trait that the relatively wide-open spaces of British Columbia will facilitate, at least outside the lower mainland. The free-standing home, so beloved by middle-class Canadians, will become even less achievable than it is now in the most expensive real estate markets in Canada: Vancouver and Victoria.

What will become of the right to enjoy privacy for the poor and the underprivileged, categories that are currently expanding in most jurisdictions? To be poor by any definition is already to enjoy less privacy, in any form except perhaps anonymity, than the more comfortable among us and to be subject to a substantial degree of state surveillance and intrusiveness in order to obtain state benefits. It is not unlikely that all beneficiaries of the state in the twenty-first century will be subjected to mass monitoring through numerous interlocked, relational databases developed to further inhibit fraud and, of course, facilitate one-stop service for consumers of government services. Unique forms of identification for those receiving state benefits will also be in place. Because of the technological protection for privacy that they make possible, 'smart cards' for single or multiple purposes are a positive innovation. However, that same technology can also be used for additional surveillance and monitoring, if fair information principles and practices are ignored or overridden.[31]

Expanded Privacy Protection: The Critical Need to Regulate the Private Sector for Data Protection

There is one major area in which Parliament and the Legislature of British Columbia have to act almost immediately to ensure that residents of this province have the tools at hand to ensure the protection of their own information in the next century. Although I realize that other authors in this volume will address this issue in greater detail, the matter is so urgent for me as an official data protector that I need to close this essay on this point. I am referring in particular to the collection, use, and retention of personal information by bodies (primarily organizations and companies), not covered by the Freedom of Information and Protection of Privacy Act. These include telephone companies, banks, trust companies, credit unions, employer associations, labour unions, transportation and telecommunication companies, large and small retailers, grocery stores, pharmacies, direct marketers, telemarketers, credit reporting bureaus, insurance companies and brokers, physicians, dentists, lawyers, accountants, therapists, psychologists, travel agencies, charitable organizations, associations, churches, hotels, investment dealers, the media, and video rental shops. I consciously present such a long list to indicate to readers the extent to which the private sector in Canada is almost completely unregulated, except by market forces, when it comes to the use and reuse of our personal information. Quebec, by contrast, has had legislation in place mandating fair information practices for the private sector since 1 January 1994. Every member country of the European Union has similar legislation in place, as do New Zealand, Hong Kong, and Hungary.[32] When the EU's directive on data protection enters into effect in the fall of 1998, Canadian companies and organizations will be unable to move personal information about customers, members, or employees in or out of the European Union because Canada and most of its provinces do not have adequate or equivalent data protection legislation in place.[33] Contractual solutions may be available as a second-level solution. Nevertheless, it is an embarrassment that Canada has weaker protections for privacy as a human right than does the European Union. As the EU directive mandates, Canadians require oversight agencies in place for all sectors of society.

Concern for privacy is a fundamental human right that requires state intervention. The private sector continues to insist that market forces and self-regulation will be satisfactory to protect the interests of consumers; continued progress in this regard is to be encouraged. The Canadian Standard Association's *Model Code for the Protection of Personal Information*, promulgated on the basis of a number of years of consultation in 1996, is a laudatory achievement, and every 'private sector' organization in the country should subscribe to it on a voluntary basis and customize its general rules to particular business and organizational activities.[34] The only segment of the private sector that could be excluded from such regulation would be purely private uses of personal data for non-commercial purposes in manual or automated forms, a distinction usually recognized in existing state legislation. Thus, any proposed data protection regime should not apply to private diaries, private correspondence, private lists, and the like. Media activities protected under the Charter of Rights and Freedoms would also be excluded from such a data protection regime.

It is sometimes said that consent cures all in the field of privacy protection. Thus, a commercial enterprise will justify its own uses of our personal information by asking us to consent to receive a service of some sort. Too many people have no idea of the ramifications of agreeing to a service, such as signing up for a credit card with a commercial bank. On the basis of a simple signature, one is allowing a corporation to do almost anything it wants to do with our personal information, especially because the applications of such practices as data profiling of customers are not transparent to the average customer. Improved transparency and meaningful consent forms are, however, only two potential solutions to this problem. The large Canadian banks are in the vanguard of progress on this score, as indeed they ought to be, given the massive amounts of personal data that they hold.

Some years ago Professor James Rule, a sociologist from the State University of New York, advocated a royalty system that would require private companies using our personal information for any purpose beyond direct servicing of our accounts to pay a royalty per transaction.[35] Professor Kenneth C. Laudon of New York University's Stern School of Business has now developed the notion of a national information market that could allow our personal information to be bought and sold.[36] Such practices are no longer impractical, thanks to developments in technology, database management, and the monitoring of transactions. It is now possible for such detailed monitoring of transactions to take place that will allow us to charge for what are essentially invasions of our privacy. Although I have a congenital dislike for the notion that one should be allowed to sell one's privacy to the highest bidder, almost everything else is for sale in our capitalistic societies. In this case, in fact, we have been giving away our personal, private information for free, because we were not smart enough to insist on payments for its use at the outset.

A system of royalty payment would have particular application in fields such as direct marketing and credit reporting in which almost all commercial enterprises, from American Express to Mastercard to Hertz car rentals, are now engaged. Our personal information has increasing commercial value, and it is time that we are paid for its use – and stop having to pay for prohibiting its use, such as not wanting to have a telephone number listed in the phone book. Such a royalty system, plus the widespread adoption of privacy-enhancing technologies, should make a substantial contribution to the preservation of our privacy in the next century, especially as a supplement to ensuring enforceable legal rights in both the public and private sectors.

The Adequacy of Fair Information Practices

'Fair information practices' (FIP) is an attractive concept. It originated almost simultaneously in both the United Kingdom and the United States in the early 1970s. U.S. labour lawyers, who since the New Deal had become accustomed to the idea of fair labour practices, provided the inspiration. FIP have become central to state and national data protection laws in at least twenty-five countries. This much is common knowledge.

The problem with FIP today is whether they remain adequate for the next century. At the international conference on privacy in Montreal in September 1997, the Australian privacy expert Roger Clarke questioned me publicly on this point. I take his question very seriously and respond that, if FIP prove to be inadequate in any general or particular way, then they should be modified, adjusted, and supplemented as required. In my view, the entire history of the implementation of data protection since 1970 consists of such pragmatic adaptation to actual experiences with innovations in information technology.

Based on my experience in doing research and writing about data protection issues and in five years of direct experience as a privacy commissioner, I have never met a privacy issue that could not be satisfactorily addressed by the application of fair information practices, broadly defined, to include such critically important notions as transparency of data collection and processing to the affected public, the need-to-know principle for personal data sharing, and the crucial importance of audit trails to monitor compliance during and after data transfers, as required. My fallback position would be to ransack the literature and practice of privacy and data protection for new ammunition for the protection of a valued human right.

NOTES

1 I am grateful to Pam E. Smith and Colin Bennett for comments on drafts of this essay.

2 David H. Flaherty, *Privacy in Colonial New England* (Charlottesville: University Press of Virginia, 1972).

3 John Winthrop, 'A Model of Christian Charity,' (1630) in *The Puritans: A Sourcebook of their Writings*, Perry Miller and Thomas H. Johnson, eds. (New York: Harper Torchbook, 1963), vol. 1, 198–9.

4 See Alan F. Westin, *Privacy and Freedom* (New York: Atheneum, 1967).

5 Statistics Canada, *Market Research Handbook* (Ottawa: Statistics Canada 1995) (Table 6-3 – Private Households by Size of Household, by Province, 1991), 219.

6 See David H. Flaherty, 'Crime and Social Control in Provincial Massachusetts,' *Historical Journal* 24 (1981), 339–60.

7 Flaherty, *Privacy in Colonial New England*, 175–9.

8 Emil Oberholzer, Jr, *Delinquent Saints: Disciplinary Action in the Early Congregational Churches of Massachusetts* (New York: Columbia University Press, 1956).

9 David H. Flaherty, *Protecting Privacy in Surveillance Societies: The Federal Republic of Germany, Sweden, France, Canada, and the United States* (Chapel Hill: University of North Carolina Press, 1989).

10 'Big Brother. The all-seeing eye,' *Economist*, 11 Jan. 1997, 53.

11 Having learned during a site visit to the new Vancouver Public Library that it operates thirty-two video-surveillance cameras inside the building, I have launched an investigation of the practice. At the very least, staff and the public have to be notified of the filming that is going on, and there must be written policies in place with respect to the use and disposition of the resulting records.

12 See Nigel Waters, 'Street Surveillance and Privacy,' presented at the Privacy Issues Forum, Christchurch, New Zealand, 13 June 1996.

13 On this latter point, see the U.S. empirical evidence presented by Robert Ellis Smith in *Privacy Journal*, April 1997.

14 My essay on 'Controlling Surveillance,' in *Technology and Privacy: The New Landscape*, Marc Rotenberg and Philip Agre, eds. (Cambridge: MIT Press, 1997), provides greater detail on such matters by comparing the findings of my 1989 book with my BC experience.

15 See David H. Flaherty, 'The BC Cancer Agency: Results of a Privacy Check-Up' (1997; available at http://www.oipcbc.org).

16 See Flaherty, *Protecting Privacy in Surveillance Societies*, Conclusion.

17 Finley Peter, Dunne, 'The Supreme Court's Decisions.' *Mr Dooley's Opinions* (New York: R.H. Russell, 1901): http://www.ican.net/~fjzwick/dooley/dooley6.html In Jim Zwick, ed., *Anti-Imperialism in the United States, 1898–1935.* http://www.ican.net/~fjzwick/ail98-35.html (July 1996).

18 See Margaret Atwood, *The Handmaid's Tale* (Toronto: McClelland and Stewart, 1985).

19 Stephen W. Mosher's *A Mother's Ordeal: One Woman's Fight against China's One-Child Policy* (New York: Harcourt Brace, 1993) recounts how members of the Women's Federation in a factory kept track of the menses of their female workers to facilitate enforcement of the one-child policy in China. The name, means of contraception, and expected date of menstruation appeared on a large blackboard in a conspicuous place; at the onset of menstruation, the woman was expected to place a check mark next to her name (p. 264).

20 For a useful description of the work of the Ministry of State Security (Stasi), see Tina Rosenberg, *The Haunted Land: Facing Europe's Ghosts after Communism* (New York: Random House, 1995), 289–305.

21 David J. Seipp, *The Right to Privacy in American History* (Cambridge: Harvard University Program on Information Resources Policy, 1978).

22 See David H. Flaherty, *Privacy and Government Data Banks: An International Perspective* (London: Mansell, 1979).

23 Vance Packard, *The Naked Society* (New York: Mackay, 1964).

24 Gerald Messadie, *La Fin de la vie privée* (Paris: Calmann-Levy, 1974).

25 Barrington Moore, Jr, *Privacy: Studies in Social and Cultural History* (Armonk, NY: M.E. Sharpe, 1984).

26 Freedom of Information and Protection of Privacy Act, Revised Statutes of British Columbia, 1996, c. 165. The text of the act and my orders under it can be found at the web site of my office (www.oipcbc.org).

27 I testified as an academic and consultant to Mr Phillips. See also David H. Flaherty, 'On the Utility of Constitutional Rights to Privacy and Data Protection,' *Case Western Reserve Law Review* 41/3 (1991), 831–55.

28 For the contrary U.S. experience, see Ellen Alderman and Caroline Kennedy, *The Right to Privacy* (New York: Knopf, 1995).

29 Philip H. Osborne, 'The Privacy Act of British Columbia, Manitoba and Saskatchewan,' in *Aspects of Privacy Law: Essays in Honour of John M. Sharp*, Dale Gibson, ed. (Toronto: Butterworths, 1980), 73–110.

30 William Prosser, 'Privacy,' *California Law Review* 48 (1960), 383, 392–8.

31 See David H. Flaherty, 'Privacy and Identity,' presented at Conference on Smart Card Technologies: New Policy Frameworks, Regulation, Data Protection, New Technology Advance and Policy Issues, 16–17 Oct. 1996, London, U.K; also Flaherty, 'Provincial Identity Cards: A Privacy-Impact Assessment,' Victoria, 26 Sept. 1995. Both papers are available at my website (http://www.oipcbc.org).

32 See Wayne Madsen, *Handbook of Personal Data Protection* (New York: Stockton, 1992).

38   David H. Flaherty

33 See Spiros Simitis, 'Foreword,' in Paul M. Schwartz and Joel R. Reidenberg, *Data Privacy Law: A Study of United States Data Protection* (Charlottesville, VA: Michie, 1996), v–xi.
34 Canadian Standards Association, *Model Code for the Protection of Personal Information* (Rexdale, ON: CSA, 1996). Available at their website (www.csa.ca).
35 See James P. Rule's essay in this volume.
36 Kenneth C. Laudon, 'Markets and Privacy,' *Communications of the ACM 39/9* (1996), 92–104.

2

Ethics for the New Surveillance

GARY T. MARX[1]

It's a remarkable piece of apparatus.

F. Kafka, *The Penal Colony*[2]

I find the information age to be a healthy thing ... the more you know about somebody else, the better off everybody is.

Owner of personal data base company

In 1928 Justice Louis Brandeis wrote in the Olmstead case 'discovery and invention have made it possible for the government, by means far more effective than stretching upon the rack to obtain disclosure in court of what is whispered in the closet. The progress of science in furnishing the government with means of espionage is not likely to stop with wire-tapping.' His haunting and prescient words clearly apply today, as the line between science and science fiction is continually redrawn and private sector databases join those of government as a cause of concern.

New technologies for collecting personal information, which transcend the physical, liberty-enhancing limitations of the old means, are constantly appearing. They probe more deeply, widely, and softly than traditional methods, transcending barriers – whether walls, distance, darkness, skin, or time – that historically protected personal information. The boundaries that have defined and given integrity to social systems, groups, and the self are increasingly permeable. The power of governmental and private organizations to compel disclosure, whether based on law or circumstance, and to aggregate, analyse and distribute personal information is growing rapidly.

We are becoming a transparent society of record such that documentation of our history, current identity, location, and physiological and psychological states and behaviour is increasingly possible. With predictive profiles there are even claims to be able to know individual futures. The collection of information often occurs invisibly, automatically, and remotely – being built into routine activities. Awareness and genuine consent on the part of the data subject may be lacking. The amount of personal information collected is increasing. New technologies have the potential to reveal the unseen, unknown, forgotten, or withheld. Like the discovery of the atom or the unconscious, they surface bits of reality that were previously hidden or did not contain informational clues. People are in a sense turned inside out.

To be alive and a social being is to automatically give off signals of constant information – whether in the form of heat, pressure, motion, brain waves, perspiration, cells, sound, olifacteurs, waste matter, or garbage, as well as more familiar forms such as communication and visible behaviour. These remnants are given new meaning by contemporary surveillance technologies. Through a value-added, mosaic process, machines (often with only a little help from their friends) may find significance in surfacing and combining heretofore meaningless data.

The ratio of what individuals know about themselves, or are capable of knowing, versus what outsiders and experts can know about them has shifted away from the individual. Data in diverse forms from widely separated geographic areas, organizations, and time periods can be easily merged and analysed. In relatively unrestrained fashion new (and old) organizations are capturing, combining, and selling this information or putting it to novel internal uses. Of particular importance are recent developments in electronic (audio, visual, telemetric), biochemical, and database forms of information collection. The increased availability of personal information is a tiny strand in the constant expansion of knowledge witnessed in the past two centuries and of the centrality of information to the working of contemporary society.

Computer databases, video cameras, drug testing, and work monitoring are routine. They are being joined by new means that may become equally prevalent in coming decades: DNA screening and monitoring for insurance and employment, personal electronic location monitoring devices via implanted chips, Internet monitoring devices that keep a record of what one has viewed and for how long, 'intelligent' highway systems, 'smart cards' that contain extensive personal information, satellites, and 'smart homes' in which data flows (whether electricity, communications, or energy) into and out of the home are part of the same monitored system.

Broadening the Principles of Fair Information Practice

Some of the essays in this volume are informed by the principles of fair information practice that received widespread public notice in the United States in 1973 when drafted by the U.S. Health Education and Welfare Department and that form the basis of the 1981 OECD *Guidelines* as well as most national legislation.[3] The recent *Code for the Protection of Personal Information* from the Canadian Standards Association has expanded these principles to include: (a) accountability; (b) identifying purposes; (c) consent; (d) limiting collection; (e) limiting use, disclosure, and retention; (f) accuracy; (g) safeguards; (h) openness; (i) individual access; and (j) challenging compliance.[4] In offering publicity, complaint, and compliance mechanisms these standards are clearly an advance over the minimalist standards of the earlier period.

This model has generally been seen as appropriate for the database forms of surveillance up to the 1980s.[5] One concern of the conference at which the essays in this book were presented was to ask whether this model still applies with recent changes such as those involving cross-border data flows and the spread of Internet usage. A related question is whether the model is (or ever was) adequate for other forms of the new surveillance – not just those that are only computer based. The information superhighway is not the only road into or out of people's lives.

I argue that this model is not adequate and that a more encompassing framework is needed. For example, the conventional principles offer no criteria for deciding whether a given means of data collection is ethically acceptable. Nor do they give adequate attention to the actual process of extracting the data. This is because the collection of the data entered into computers is usually not at issue – most often this involves biographical facts or sales transactions. Such is not the case for urine drug testing, the polygraph, or hidden video cameras. Yet this issue will become more important for computers. As we move from data entered into a computer by an operator at a terminal to remote automatic entries based on visual, auditory, and biometric forms of data, questions over the appropriateness of the initial data collection will become increasingly important.

The essence of the fair information practice code involves informed consent and unitary usage and non-migration of the data. These are essential, but they are of little help with respect to the appropriateness of the original goals, nor do they adequately cover the broader context within which the data are collected.

My concern in this chapter is to offer a broader set of ethical principles for all forms of technological personal data collection and use, not just those involving computers.[6] The fair information principles need to be located within a more general framework. They are not sufficient for many of the new technologies and uses.

Information technologies are controlled by laws, organizational policies, etiquette, and various protective counter-technologies. These control efforts imply ethical assumptions that are often unstated. Many persons feel a sense of discomfort in the face of indiscriminate drug testing, hidden video cameras, electronic work monitoring, and the collection and marketing of their personal information – even as they favour responsible behaviour, efficiency, economic growth, and credit card-aided consumption. But what is there about the new information technologies that is troubling? By what standards should we conclude that a given practice is right or wrong?

My initial goal as a social scientist is to understand the factors that can generate unease across a variety of contexts. I argue that at an abstract level there are shared expectations in American, and perhaps to a degree more generally in Western and industrial-capitalist cultures, whose violation underlies the discomfort experienced in the face of new information technologies.

I seek to identify the major normative factors that would lead the average person to feel that a surveillance practice is wrong or at least questionable. I differentiate various elements of the surveillance setting which require ethical analysis. Table 2.1 lists twenty-nine questions to be asked the reader. These questions involve the tactic used, the data collection context, and the goals. Without claiming that they are morally equivalent, I argue that the more one can answer these questions in a way that affirms the underlying principle, or a condition supportive of the principle, the more ethical the use of the tactic is likely to be.

In general the emphasis here is on the watchers rather than the watched, on avoiding harm rather than doing good,[7] on the individual not the group, and the short rather than the long run. This chapter suggests an ethic for those who carry out the surveillance or data collection. It assumes that under appropriate conditions they may have a right to do this, but they also have a duty to do it responsibly. Reciprocally, those subject to legitimate surveillance may have duties as well (for instance, not to distort the findings), even as they also have rights not to be subjected to some forms of surveillance.

Let us begin the analysis by making a distinction between (a) the *means* (instrument) of data collection, (b) the *context and conditions* under which the data are gathered, and (c) the *uses or goals* to which the data are put. There is a temporal sequence here as we start with the means and then move to collection and use. These may of course overlap (as when a system of retinal eye pattern identification, which persons consent to automatically, results in access or its denial). But they are often distinct. A given means such as video can be used for a variety of goals, and a given goal such as drug testing can be accomplished in a variety of ways. Means and goals apart, the conditions under which these appear also show enormous variation. The ethical status can vary from cases in which the means, the context, and the use are all abhorrent to those in which they are all acceptable or even desirable, to varying combinations. Ethical analysis needs to consider all three factors. Beyond different value priorities and interpretations, disagreements in evaluation often involve persons emphasizing one rather than another of these elements.

The Means of Data Collection

Are there some means of personal information collection that are simply immoral? Torture is the obvious case. Other techniques that many observers find unethical include the polygraph with its tight-fitting bodily attachments,[8] manipulation, and questionable validity; a drug test requiring a person to urinate in front of another; and harming or threatening friends or relatives of a suspect in order to obtain information. Similarly, most persons recoil at the thought of certain coercive bodily intrusions such as pumping the stomach of a suspect believed to have swallowed evidence or removing a bullet from the body for ballistics matching (practices that the courts have generally prohibited). In contrast, the non-consensual collection of hair, blood, and fingerprints has greater acceptability.

For many moral theorists and much of society, lying, deception, and manipulation are a cluster of means that in and of themselves are ethically questionable.[9] These come together in the case of undercover tactics. Such means (unlike many other surveillance means) always present a moral dilemma. This is not to suggest that under certain conditions and for certain ends they may not on balance be appropriate. But no matter how compelling the latter, this does not alter the fact that in our culture neither lying and trickery, nor physical force and coercion, are morally preferred techniques.

TABLE 2.1
Questions to Help Determine the Ethics of Surveillance

A   *The Means*

1 *Harm.* Does the technique cause unwarranted physical or psychological harm?
2 *Boundary.* Does the technique cross a personal boundary without permission (whether involving coercion or deception or a body, relational, or spatial border)?
3 *Trust.* Does the technique violate assumptions that are made about how personal information will be treated such as no secret recordings?
4 *Personal relationships.* Is the tactic applied in a personal or impersonal setting?
5 *Invalidity.* Does the technique produce invalid results?

B   *The Data Collection Context*

6 *Awareness.* Are individuals aware that personal information is being collected, who sells it, and why?
7 *Consent.* Do individuals consent to the data collection?
8 *Golden rule.* Would those responsible for the surveillance (both the decision to apply it and its actual application) agree to be its data subjects under the conditions in which they apply it to others?
9 *Minimization.* Does a principle of minimization apply?
10 *Public decision making.* Was the decision to use a tactic arrived at through some public discussion and decision-making process?
11 *Human review.* Is there human review of machine-generated results?
12 *Right of inspection.* Are people aware of the findings and how they were created?
13 *Right to challenge and express a grievance.* Are there procedures for challenging the results or for entering alternative data or interpretations into the record?
14 *Redress and sanctions.* If the individual has been treated unfairly and procedures violated are there appropriate means of redress? Are there means for discovering violations and penalties to encourage responsible surveiller behaviour?
15 *Adequate data stewardship and protection.* Can the security of the data be adequately protected?

TABLE 2.1   *(Concluded)*

16 *Equality–inequality regarding availability and application:*
   i Is the means widely available or restricted to only the most
     wealthy, powerful, or technologically sophisticated?
   ii Within a setting, is the tactic broadly applied to all people or
      only to those less powerful or unable to resist?
   iii If there are means of resisting the provision of personal informa-
       tion are these equally available or restricted to the most
       privileged?
17 *The symbolic meaning of a method.* What does the use of a method
   communicate more generally?
18 *The creation of unwanted precedents.* Is it likely to create precedents that
   will lead to its application in undesirable ways?
19 *Negative effects on surveillers and third parties.* Are there negative effects
   on those beyond the data subject?

C   *Uses*

20 *Beneficiary.* Does application of the tactic serve broad community goals,
   the goals of the object of surveillance, or the personal goals of the data
   collector?
21 *Proportionality.* Is there an appropriate balance between the importance of
   the goal and the cost of the means?
22 *Alternative means.* Are other less costly means available?
23 *Consequences of inaction.* Where the means are very costly, what are the
   consequences of taking no surveillance action?
24 *Protections.* Are adequate steps taken to minimize costs and risk?
25 *Appropriate vs inappropriate goals.* Are the goals of the data collection
   legitimate?
26 *The goodness of fit between the means and the goals.* Is there a clear link
   between the information collected and the goal sought?
27 *Information used for original vs other unrelated purposes.* Is the personal
   information used for the reasons offered for its collection and for
   which consent may have been given, and do the data stay with the
   original collector, or do they migrate elsewhere?
28 *Failure to share secondary gains from the information.* Are the personal
   data collected used for profit without permission from, or benefit to,
   the person who provided them?
29 *Unfair disadvantage.* Is the information used in such a way as to cause
   unwarranted harm or disadvantage to its subject?

There is a folk morality that underlies judgments made about the collection of personal information. A popular expression claims, 'If it doesn't look right that's ethics.' When the means do not look right, I hypothesize, the act of collecting personal data is likely to involve saying 'yes' to one or more of the following questions:

1 Does the act of collecting the data (apart from its use) involve physical or psychological harm?
2 Does the technique produce invalid results?
3 Does the technique cross a personal boundary without permission (whether involving coercion or deception or a body, relational, spatial, or symbolic border)?
4 Does the technique violate trust and assumptions that are made about how personal information will be treated (for example, no secret recordings)?

To the extent that one or more of these concerns are present the means as such raise ethical concerns. Although distinct, these factors can of course be related (for example, in crossing a personal boundary the betrayal of trust can cause harm, as may relying on invalid data). In spite of the fact that some data collection or surveillance means are inherently undesirable, most contemporary disputes do not involve the means as such, rather they involve the context and the ends. Ethical disagreements and problems are more likely to be found in the conditions around the data collection and/or in the use of the data than with the means. There is also an accelerating effort to develop 'softer' and more valid technologies for which the answer to some of the four questions posed above is 'no.'

My argument reflects a more general perspective on ethics that stresses contexts rather than behaviour or a technology as such. We often tend to act as if the material technology or behaviour and their moral evaluation were one, instead of seeing the latter as a social construct whose application largely depends on the setting, not the technology or the behaviour in and of itself.[10] For example, contrast a weapon used to hunt food as against one used in the commission of a crime, or a location-monitoring device carried by a skier as a protection against avalanches, as against surreptitiously applying such a device to a person's car. Similarly omnipresent video-surveillance, even in bathrooms, is not treated as an inappropriate invasion of privacy in prison for security and safety reasons, although in most other settings it would be.

The Data Collection Context

With respect to the context, we ask how the technique is applied and in what social setting. Simply having a means that is morally acceptable is not sufficient justification for taking action. We also need to attend to the context of its application and then to its use.

A distinction here can be made between, first, the actual collection of the information and, second, the broader conditions surrounding this. In the first case we are again concerned with the presence of harm, invalidity, unwarranted border crossings, and violations of trust. At the most general level, these represent disrespect for the dignity of the person. In this case we assume that it is possible to collect the information in an ethically acceptable fashion that *avoids* these four conditions. We draw attention to the discretion surveillers have to behave within or beyond ethical bounds in their use of such a means.

Data Collection Harm

With respect to harm during the process of information collection, tactics such as interviews, psychological tests, drug tests, and searches can be done to minimize or maximize discomfort. Examples include intentionally inflicting pain in drawing blood (for example, in the mandatory AIDS tests required of those in prison and the military), a gender mismatch in a strip search, an invasive video-surveillance as in a department store changing room, or a stressful application of the polygraph.

Invalidity

Validity here refers to whether the tactic is applied correctly and measures what it claims to measure. Some questions here include who has warrant to claim whether or not it is valid, how hazy data should be interpreted, and what the costs are to those using invalid technologies. Situations in which invalid readings result (whether out of malevolence, incompetence, good faith errors, faulty machines, or unaccounted-for confounding factors) are obviously unfair and wasteful (not to mention the liability issues involved in wrongful application and use). There must be means to verify results. It must not be assumed that fallible humans can design and operate infallible machines (or, given their complexity, even that machines are infallible).

The issue of validity as a principle is not publicly disputed. Privately surveillers are sometimes indifferent to validity because the means are seen as a deterrent scare tactic, or because those assessed are believed to be guilty or undeserving anyway, even if the test does not reveal it this time. Individuals may not discover the invalidity, and the cost of increasing validity may be deemed to be too great.

Lack of validity may apply to an individual case, as with the switching of a positive for a negative drug test or factors that can confound a drug test such as taking a prescription medicine or eating poppy seeds. Problems of validity can apply to a broad group; for example, when a large number of false readings result because of faulty lab procedures (as in an unfortunate navy case) or data entry errors (as with the case in a small New England town when all the credit records were deemed bad). A pattern of systematic errors is particularly troubling, because it then amounts to the institutionalization of unfairness.

Border and Trust Violations

The law recognizes the validity of a reasonable expectation of privacy and the 'right to be let alone.' Yet judges apply this inconsistently, depending on the offence (for example, in drug cases the standard is less stringent, and its legal meaning is vague). Under what conditions are individuals likely to feel that personal borders have been violated and/or that their information has been inappropriately gathered or treated?[11] On the basis of interviews, observation, court cases, and mass media accounts, I hypothesize that this is likely to involve one or more of the four following conditions.

The first occurs when a 'natural' border protective of information is unreasonably breached. The restriction here is on the senses. The assumption is that what you can 'normally' or 'naturally' see or hear when your presence is not hidden, you are entitled to perceive, although not necessarily to share. However, tools that extend the senses require special permission or notice.

There are several distinct categories here:

1 Clothes that protect parts of the body from being revealed (nakedness)
2 Observable facial expressions or statements or behaviour, as against inner thoughts and feelings
3 The assumed non-observability of behaviour behind walls, closed doors, darkness, and spatial distance

4 Skin and bodily orifices that serve respectively as protective shells or gates into the body
5 Directed communications such as a sealed letter, telephone, and E-mail messages that are sent to a particular person with physical protections intended to exclude consumption by other than the addressee (for example, contrast expectations here with an open message on a bulletin board or yelling to someone across the room).

The second condition is when a social border assumed or expected to be protective of information is breached. This involves expectations about social roles such as a doctor, lawyer, or member of the clergy who violates confidentiality, a family member or friend who reveals secrets, or a bureaucrat who fails to destroy confidential records when that is required.

This dimension alerts us to the relationship between the data collector and the data subject. Thus, formal means of data collection are generally more appropriate in impersonal settings (where there are few expectations of trust) than in settings where individuals have close personal relations. Contrast, for example, the extensive formal monitoring of those working in the impersonal setting of financial institutions with the use of video cameras, drug tests, and the polygraph on children or spouses within a family.

A third condition occurs when a temporal or spatial border is breached which separates information from various periods or aspects of one's life. This involves assumptions about the compartmentalization or separation of elements of personal biography, including the past and the future and information in different locations. Even though the individual may have no clear interest in protecting any single aspect (age, education, religion, education, or occupation), the picture significantly changes when a mosaic can be created from many diverse pieces. The sum becomes much greater than the individual parts. This overlaps with the first condition in the sense that before linked computers there were 'natural' barriers to combining this information even when it was publicly available.[12] More abstractly physical barriers and time were traditionally similar in working against the aggregation of information. The presumed ability to simultaneously access and link the past, present, and predicted future alter the traditional meaning of time and the information protection it offered.

A fourth condition occurs when interaction and communication, which are thought to be ephemeral and transitory like a river, are captured through hidden video or audio means. This is believed to encourage candour and intimacy. Similarly, we assume that things that are discarded in the garbage will in fact disappear and not be claimed by information scavengers. This is the 'short shelf-life assumption.' Other factors being equal, things that are said and the material artefacts of our personal life should not have a continued life after use.

Borders have legitimate and illegitimate crossing points and interstitial and grey areas. Information collected in a public setting such as a street or park is different from that in a private setting. Even there, being invited in the front door is very different from breaking it down or sneaking in the back. Sitting on a park bench and leaning to overhear what two people whispering to each other are saying is different from listening to a soapbox orator. However, the public–private place distinction may become hazy as when a person on a public street looks in the window of a home, or loud music or cooking smells from a home go beyond it.

Awareness and Consent

Personal border crossings and trust are related to, and even defined by, whether (a) individuals are aware that personal information is being collected and by whom and for what purpose and, if so, (b) whether they agree to the collection and subsequent uses of the data. These are difficult concepts because no one can be fully aware of all the possible consequences of the act of data collection, nor of subsequent uses.[13] In the same way 'consent' is always conditioned by the range of choices and their relative costs and benefits.

To consent implies being aware; the converse, however, is not necessarily true. Whether or not consent is sought is perhaps the most important ethical question with respect to the collection of personal data. Of course there are social roles that implicitly grant the right to transcend personal boundaries without consent, such as police and emergency medical personnel (if in principle under controlled and accountable conditions) and cases where the presence of awareness or consent would defeat a legitimate purpose, as in undercover or audio or video recordings in criminal justice investigations and/or cases involving the defendant, but in conventional settings the failure to inform, or a coercive lack of choice, is of a different order.

There are also degrees – such as full awareness that a tactic may be used versus knowing that it will be used but not in precise detail where and when (for example, location of a hidden camera or whether there is a monitor or recorder behind a known camera). A nice example of the joining of being informed with consenting are some Internet web pages that tell users that 'cookies,' a program that charts what the individual views, enters a user's hard drive and may be activated or blocked as the user chooses. The check-off option offered by some magazine subscription services with respect to not having one's personal information reused is another.

Taking information without consent may also be seen to violate an implied right the individual has to control his or her personal information. This could either be in the form of traditional property rights or, at the other extreme, insurance that undue coercion is not brought to bear, as reflected in the protection against self-incrimination in the Fifth Amendment of the U.S. Constitution.

One component of justice is fair warning – providing people with information about the rules, procedures, rewards, and punishments they are subject to. Beyond showing respect for the person, full disclosure can be a means of shaping behaviour, as individuals know they will be assessed and may behave accordingly (for example, paying bills on time to avoid being automatically identified in a database as a bad credit risk). Openness regarding data collection can also help bring accountability to the data collectors and more responsible behaviour on their part as a result. In that regard it is similar to a supervisor walking behind and monitoring workers, instead of having this done secretly via remote computer. The knowledge of who is doing the monitoring can be a constraint on how it is done.

We can also ask if consent has the quality of 'opting in' or 'opting out.' In the latter case individuals are told that if they give their permission their individual data will be collected. In the former individuals are told that their data will automatically be collected unless they request that it not be. Those with an interest in gathering the data strongly prefer the latter system of opting out – that is, requiring persons to ask that they not be included. To be sure that is better than offering no choice at all. But because many persons will be ignorant of the possibility of opting out or not want to take the time, not remember, or be unaware of the potentially negative consequences of providing personal data, 'opting in' is preferable.

The concept of consent of course can be very problematic, given the role of culture in shaping perceptions and the fact that choice always occurs within situations that are not fully free or within the making of the person choosing. For example, the meaning of choice with respect to agreeing to take a drug test is very different in a one-industry town from what it is in a setting where one can find equivalent work in which not all employers require such a test.[14]

In flying on a domestic Canadian airline, I saw the following sign:

Notice: Security measures are being taken to observe and inspect persons. No passengers are obliged to submit to a search of persons or goods if they choose not to board our aircraft.

Rather than spend days in the car or on the train, I chose to fly and 'agreed' to be searched. Most persons would do the same. But to claim the choice is somehow voluntary as the sign suggests is disingenuous in the extreme. The situation is the same for signs in some federal buildings in Washington, DC, which warn 'in entering here you have agreed to be searched.' In a related example during the controversy over the caller-ID service a telephone company representative said, 'When you choose to make a phone call, you are choosing to have your phone number released.' Choice, to be meaningful, should imply some genuine alternatives and refusal costs that are not wildly exorbitant.

We also need to ask 'consent to what?' Thus, a mass marketing executive reported at a conference a few years ago, 'The data isn't out there because we stole it from them. Someone gave it away, and it's out there for us to use.' In a legal sense that is true. But the element of 'giving it away' was not a wilful choice in the obvious sense. Rather the data became available indirectly as a result of taking some other action such as a mail order purchase. At the time if individuals were to be asked if they agree to have their personal information used for marketing purposes (as is the case with some purchases), there would be far less 'out there' waiting for specious disclaimers about its non-theft.

We can also ask, 'Who consents?' Thus, when children follow the advice of a television clown telling them to hold their telephone receivers in front of the TV while a remote signal sent through the television set activates the phone sending its number over an 800–line, they have acted voluntarily. But they did not know that this was to be used for direct mail candy marketing, and, even if they did, the 'consent' of small children obtained by a clown on TV seems specious.

This can also be approached by asking, 'Who's informed and who needs to consent?' In phone transactions it is now common to be told, 'This conversation may be recorded to insure quality service.' The employee is informed and may have consented. For the customer only the first reasonably applies (although in choosing not to hang up an implicit consent is offered, but again this can be a specious choice given the need for information or a service). Given the complexities and competing values, the absence of informed consent is not automatically a sign of unethical behaviour, but situations where it could be offered, and is, are clearly morally preferable to those where it is not.

None of the principles offered here are unconditional. With the complexities and competing values, the absence of informed consent is not automatically a sign of unethical behaviour (although situations where it could be offered, and is, are clearly morally preferable to those where it is not). Thus, the law and morality set limits on what can be agreed to (for example, limits on selling one's vote or selling oneself into slavery or agreeing to live in substandard housing for reduced rent). Similarly to inform people of an outrageous tactic does not justify it. Neither a technology's potential, nor publicizing its use or consent should be sufficient to define a reasonable expectation of privacy, though they relate to it.

Even if the data gatherer does not offer a formal choice, it may be possible to have the equivalent of choice by using a counter-technology to block the collection of personal information (assuming one is aware of the collection). If devices to prevent the unwarranted collection of personal information are widely available but nevertheless not used, then there is a sense in which persons do choose to release their private information. Yet that is not the case if such means are very expensive or difficult to use. An element of choice may also be present when privacy becomes commodified such that persons can choose by payment or compensation the level of privacy they desire.[15] Yet it is still important that privacy thresholds be available below which no one falls.

Minimization

One aspect of harm and crossing possibly perilous personal borders involves going farther than is required or than has been publicly announced (and perhaps agreed to by the data subject). Here we ask does a principle of *minimization* apply to the collection of personal data?

Such a principle requires that one should go no farther than is necessary for the task at hand, in spite of temptations and incentives to go beyond. Granted that many of these tactics by their very nature cross personal boundaries and may subject the person to feelings of embarrassment, shame, and powerlessness, we can still ask, 'Was this done in a professional manner and only to the extent necessary to obtain the informational end, or does it go beyond that?' For example, is wiretapping applied in a categorical way such that all communications are listened to, or only those pertaining to the focused goal? If federal minimization rules are followed regarding wiretapping it will be only the latter. If a conversation is not relevant or involves parties not of legal interest, it is not to be monitored (of course this also offers a way of neutralizing it if one can assume that the rules will be followed). A related example is the very precise time and place limits of search warrants.

In contrast many private sector data gatherers face no such limits. As an 'insurance' policy, data collectors often favour gathering more information rather than less, because they can never be sure that sometime in the future they might not need it or that a new way of using it might not be discovered. Consider large retail chains that routinely ask customers, even cash purchasers, for their name and phone number. Only recently have models become available to mine their detailed retail transaction data for marketing purposes. Other examples of extraneous data collection are the unrelated questions about lifestyle and social circumstances that accompany warranty forms. Medical samples taken for employment purposes may be analysed for conditions for which informed consent has not been given.

The potential to go too far is also found among the systems operators for many networked computers. For example, some interactive computer games or other services that involve using software at a company's web page give the company the opportunity to explore everything in a user's computer. There may be valid reasons for doing this (for example, to see if a player has stolen or misused files), but there is no justification for looking at other unrelated files. In the same way, providers of telephone and E-mail services may need to monitor communication to be sure their systems are working, but listening to conversations or reading E-mail beyond what may be technically required for service reasons is wrong. Yet the temptation can be great.

The Social Setting

The second aspect of the conditions of data collection involves the broader social context, rather than the direct application of the tactic as such. I identify six procedural or enabling conditions and four general conditions involving the social setting. Given the absence of the former, or the presence of negative values for the latter, problems are more likely to occur. The opposite does not make a tactic ethical, but does increase the likelihood of ethically acceptable outcomes.

Some procedural conditions include:

1 *Public decision making.* Was the decision to use a tactic arrived at through some public discussion and decision-making process? For example, are the conditions of computer and telephone work monitoring of reservation and telephone receptionists jointly developed through a management–union or workers' council committee? Is the introduction of a new technology for delivering unlisted phone numbers, as caller-ID initially was, subject to broad review via citizen input and a regulatory commission or simply offered by technological fiat? Is a decision to introduce video cameras onto highways and public streets discussed by the city council?

2 *Human review.* Is there human review of machine-generated results? This is vital given the acontextual nature of much of the data the technology generates and the possibility of hardware and software failure. Generally individuals as interpreters of human situations are far more sensitive to nuance than are computers, even if they are much more expensive. [16]

3 *The right of inspection.* Are people aware of the findings and how they were created? Fundamental aspects of procedural justice include being entitled to know the evidence and, as the next condition suggests, to challenge it. The right to see one's file is related to a broader principle that holds that absent extreme conditions, there should be no secret personal databases in a democratic society.

4 *The right to challenge and express a grievance.* Are there procedures for challenging the results or for entering alternative data or interpretations into the record?

5 *Redress and sanctions.* If the individual has been treated unfairly and procedures are violated, are there appropriate means of redress and, if appropriate, for the destruction of the record? Are there means for discovering violations and penalties to encourage responsible surveillance? Unlike Europe and Canada where there are official data commissioners who may actively seek out compliance, in the United States it is up to individuals to bring complaints forward. But in order for that to happen individuals must first be aware that there is a problem and that there are standards.

6 *Adequate data stewardship and protection.* Can the security of the data be

adequately protected? There must be standards for who has access to the data and audit trails, for whether and when data are to be updated, for how long they are to be kept, and the conditions under which they are to be destroyed.

Finally four more general questions deal not with a given individual, but with broader social consequences:

7 *Equality–inequality regarding availability and application.* This involves four questions:
   i Are the means of data collection widely available or restricted to only the wealthy, powerful or technologically sophisticated?
   ii Within a setting, is the tactic broadly applied to all people or only to those less powerful or unable to resist?
   iii Even in settings where differential application is appropriate, would the surveillers (both those responsible for the decision to use a technology and those who actually apply it) have enough confidence in the system that they would willingly submit to it themselves if the situation were reversed?
   iv If there are means of resisting the unwanted acquisition of personal information (whether technically, economically, or legally) are these equally available or restricted to the most privileged?

The first question applies particularly to conflict and hierarchical settings and relates to Kant's principle of universalism or consistency which asks, 'Would it be acceptable if all persons or groups used the tactic?' The democratization of surveillance as a result of low cost and ease of use can introduce a healthy pluralism and balance (as well as reciprocal inhibitions in use for fear of retaliation). On the other hand, it can also help create a more defensive and suspicious society with an overall increase in anxiety-generating and resource-consuming surveillance.[17]

We can also apply a principle of consistency which asks whether the tactic is applied to everyone (which is different from asking what if everyone applied it). Here we ask about equality within a setting – Is the tactic (particularly if it is controversial) applied to all or only to some (usually those lower in status)? For example, are executives drug tested and are their phone and E-mail communications subject to monitoring just as other employees? If a bitter pill must be swallowed on behalf of some presumably greater good, it seems administratively easier and fairer if all share the cost, rather than the least privileged or those least able to resist. If there is inequality we need to ask whether the rationale for differential applications is clear and justifiable.

Finally, we need to consider (in the absence of being able to just say 'no') whether there are means available that make it possible for people to maintain greater control over their personal information and if so, how widely available these are. Some means such as providing a false name and address when the request is irrelevant (as with paying cash for consumer electronics) or free anonymous E-mail forwarding services are available to anyone. In other cases privacy may come with a price tag – as with the purchase of a device for shredding records, having an unlisted phone number, or possessing the technical skill to encrypt one's E-mail or telephone communications.

8 *The symbolic meaning of a method.* What does the use of a method communicate more generally? Some practices simply look morally objectionable because they violate a fundamental principle such as respect for the dignity of the person. Something much broader than the harm to a particular individual may be involved. There is a sense in which a social value is undermined, and the community as a whole may be harmed.[18] This also has major implications for political action. As Priscilla Regan observed until privacy infringements are defined as social, rather than simply individual, violations, the political will for strong privacy legislation will be lacking.[19]

9 *The creation of unwanted precedents.* Is it likely to create precedents that will lead to its application in undesirable ways? Even if a new tactic seems otherwise acceptable, it is important to apply a longer range perspective and consider where it might lead. The social security number which has become a de facto national identifier, which the U.S. Congress clearly did not intend when it was created, is an example.

10 *The negative effects on surveillers and third parties.* Are there negative effects on those beyond the data subject? For example, what is the impact on the personality of a professional watcher or infiltrator? Super electronic sleuth Harry Caul in the film *The Conversation* is suggestive. Over the course of his professional career Caul becomes paranoid, devoid of personal identity, and desensitized to the ethical aspects of surveillance. In another example, there is some evidence that police who use radar guns in traffic enforcement have higher rates of testicular cancer. Audio- and video-taping may record the behaviour of suspects, as well as that of their family and friends. Tac-

tics rarely stand alone, and their possible implications for persons beyond the data subject need to be considered.

Uses of Surveillance Data

Let us move from the tactic itself and the social context in which information is collected to its actual use. The first two may be ethically acceptable even though the uses to which the data are put are ethically unacceptable. One approach is to adopt a principle of proportionality in which means and ends stand in appropriate balance. For example, one does not use a sprinkling can to put out a house fire, nor a sledge hammer to crack open a nut. The danger is that the more important the goal, the greater may be the acceptance of means that are less than ideal.[20] This principle encourages us to think comparatively about means. Where a less than ideal means is preferred we need to ask, 'Are other less costly means available?' Where they are not, and the costs of the favoured means are great, we need to ask, 'What are the consequences of taking no action?'

Obtaining consensus on either the importance of the goal or the cost of the means is not an easy task in a heterogeneous society. I am not suggesting that the ends should justify the means, but in other than extreme cases, they are certainly relevant to a consideration of the means. Where means involve significant risks and costs, the case needs to be affirmatively made for why their use is appropriate given the goal and for the steps that are taken to minimize costs and risks.

Another related approach is to consider the type of goal and who benefits from achieving the goal. Thus, it is easier to justify crossing a personal border when the goal serves the community rather than the personal goals of the data gatherer. For example, a recent requirement that prospective air passengers provide personal identification or submit to X-ray body searches in order to fly is undertaken for broad community-serving goals. This action is also intended to serve the presumed goal of the individual flyer. Equivalent surveillance undertaken by a merchant is morally much less compelling because it directly benefits neither the community nor the individual. Similarly a ban on smoking in public places in which the goal is to protect non-smokers seems easier to justify than a ban on employees smoking outside of work, in which the goal is to lower company health care costs.

In considering goals, it is easier to identify relatively non-controversial positive goals such as productivity, health protection, and crime prevention than it is to assess their relative importance.[21] It is often more difficult to identify questionable goals, because by their very nature they are less likely to be publicized (for example, DNA insurance exclusion examples based on future predictions). Questionable goals may involve an effort to force an employer's morality, politics, or opposition to unions onto employees, circumvent established procedures, or engage in an unreasonable quest for profit or strategic gain on the part of personal data-mongering entrepreneurs.

The grey area here is large, even if cases at the extremes are clear. For example, is use of a pulmonary lung test (to determine whether employees comply with a company's non-smoking policy) a necessary health and cost-saving measure good for both the company and the employee? Or is it a wrongful crossing of the boundary between work and non-work settings?

In considering goals, we also need to be alert to the possibility that the publicly stated goals may mask other less desirable goals. Even when that is not the case, moral worth must be sought in the consequences of the use beyond the good intentions of those applying the technology.

To help in assessing the 'use' issue the following questions need to be asked. Other factors being equal, the first response suggests an ethical use and the second an unethical use.

1 *Appropriate versus inappropriate goals.* Are the goals of the data collection legitimate? Are they publicly announced? Consider the following contrasting cases: drug testing school bus drivers versus junior high school students who wish to play in the school band; a doctor asking a female patient about her birth control and abortion history in a clinical setting versus asking this of *all* female employees (as one large airline did) without indicating why the information was needed; asking about the religious beliefs and practices of prospective clergy versus asking this of prospective factory workers.

2 *The goodness of fit between the means and the goal.* Is there a clear link between the information sought and the goal to be achieved? How well a test measures what it claims to (for example, drug and alcohol use, miles driven, or location) can be differentiated from second-order inferences made about goals only indirectly related to the actual results of the measurement. As we move from the direct results of a measure that is immediately meaningful given the goal (for example, a drug test to determine if a person has abided by the conditions of his or her parole), to more remote inferences about goals, questions may arise.

For example, some research suggests that drug tests may not be associated with the employment performance behaviours they are presumed to predict. In that regard a test for transportation workers that directly measures reflexes is preferable to a more inferential drug test.

3 *Information used for original versus other unrelated purposes.* Is the personal information used for the reasons offered for its collection and for which consent was given? Do the data stay with the original collector, or do they migrate elsewhere? For example, the results of medical tests undertaken for diagnostic and treatment purposes may be sold or otherwise obtained by potential insurers, pharmaceutical companies, and employers, to be then used for their own goals, or by a polygraph examiner for a national defence agency who uses the extensive personal data he collects to decide who to date.

Using data for unrelated purposes may violate the individual's expectations of full disclosure and data security. When information is used without the data subject's permission for other purposes, we need to ask was this done with prior planning by the original gatherers or by others who bought, found, stole, or deceptively obtained the data? For the original collectors, there is a responsibility to both keep their word and protect confidentiality.

4 *Failure to share secondary gains from the information.* Are the personal data collected used for profit without permission from, or benefit to, the person who provided them (or at least participated in their generation)? This implies a private property defence of personal information and contrasts with a definition based on universal human or democratic citizenship rights. To sell another person's information without asking him or her and without letting the supplier share in the gain might even be seen as a kind of theft. The issue of ownership of personal information raises novel copyright issues, for example, involving the sale of information about a person's purchases or a clone of the person's cell structure.

5 *Unfair disadvantage or harm.* Is the information used in such a way as to cause unwarranted harm or disadvantage to its subject? There is much room for debate over whether these occur and are warranted or unwarranted. Yet some major types can be identified and extreme examples are easy to find:

  i An unfair strategic disadvantage or advantage with respect to a situation in which there is a conflict of interest (e.g., a bugged car sales waiting room that permits the seller to learn a customer's concerns and maximum payment).

ii Unfairly restricting social participation as in denying someone an apartment, insurance, or employment on the basis of information that is invalid, irrelevant, acontextual, or discriminatory (e.g. not hiring someone because their DNA suggests that they have a better than average chance of developing a serious illness in the future or not to rent to someone because of their ethnic background).

iii The unwarranted publication or release of personal information that causes embarrassment, shame, or otherwise puts a person in a negative light. The emphasis here is on the subjective harm the individual experiences as a result of the release of confidential information, apart from its validity.[22] U.S. state laws that protect against the 'tort' of privacy invasion apply here. Direct, tangible, material harm can more easily be determined than subjective harm involving embarrassment, shame, stigma, humiliation, and the creepy feeling of being invaded.[23]

iv A feeling of betrayal of confidence. The failure to maintain confidentiality and security or use information only as promised applies here. This can involve friends telling something they should not, violations of professional confidentiality, or a phone company revealing unlisted numbers through a new service such as caller-ID or malicious acts (whether by data custodians or transgressors) such as informing persons that medical tests for HIV were positive when that was not the case.

v Intrusions into solitude. An important element of privacy is the right to be left alone in a busy world. The indiscriminate traffic in personal information may result in unwanted mass marketing intrusions via telephone, mail, E-mail, or face-to-face solicitations.

vi Manipulation and/or propaganda appeals based on hand-tailored and very specific messages designed for narrow-casting, segmented marketing. Such messages may be more effective than general broadcasting aimed at an undifferentiated mass market. Consider, for example, a candy company's mailing advising diet workshop participants of a special discount offer.

vii Use of communication resources without permission, such as sending unsolicited faxes or calling a cellular phone number (which requires the recipient to pay) or flooding an E-mail address with unwanted messages.

Given the variety of tactics for extracting personal information and the conditions under which they are applied, an ethics of surveillance must be very general. Categorical imperatives mandating prohibition, or use, are difficult to defend. It is unrealistic to expect a general principle to apply equally in all contexts and across all technologies. But we can talk in relative terms and contrast tactics, situations, and uses as being more or less ethically acceptable depending on the interplay of the factors discussed.

The questions asked here about the means, data collection, context, and use offer an ethical guide for assessing surveillance tactics. The more the principles implied in these questions are honoured, the more ethical the situation is likely to be, or conversely the fewer of these present, the less ethical the surveillance. I intend this additive approach as a sensitizing strategy and do not suggest that equal moral weight necessarily be given each factor. But hopefully they do touch the major ethical elements.

There are no simple evaluative formulae for the varied and complex situations in which personal data are collected and used. Suggesting an ethic for a particular tactic such as computer databases or drug testing can be worthwhile in offering more focused guidelines, but it is also important not to ignore the commonalities and to see the broader social picture. Regardless of the tactic, one hopes asking the twenty-nine questions in Table 2.1 (which summarize the argument) will yield better results than ignoring them.

The twenty-nine questions in Table 2.1 summarize the argument of this essay. They should be asked when considering the ethics of any surveillance activity. They can help answer the question, 'Is the surveillance right or wrong?' Although each of these questions implies broader normative justifications, I have not taken this further (beyond space and my own limitations) because the analytic distinctions and hypothesized empirical factors offered here are a necessary first step before a more formal ethics of surveillance is possible (if ever). This essay is about the societal norms that I believe both do and should inform an ethics for surveillance. More systematic empirical research and a more rigorous and consistent set of arguments supporting or attacking the above is welcome.

Yet underlying these questions are a cluster of value justifications. The most overarching and important is the Kantian idea of respect for the dignity of the person. When the self can be technologically invaded without permission and often even without the knowledge of the person, dignity and liberty are diminished. Respect for the individual involves not causing harm, treating persons fairly through the use of universally applied valid measures, offering meaningful choices, and avoiding manipulation and coercion. These in turn depend on being adequately informed. Viewing personal information as something the participant has a property right in (not unlike a copyright) can be an independent justification, but autonomy over the use of one's information also shows respect for the person. Another major value is trust and its implications for community. When trust is violated through deception or the failure to honour agreements and implied contracts in data collection, the value of community is undermined.

Conclusion: Twilights or Dawns?

These technologies require new cultural standards and public policies. The technologies offer wonderful possibilities. Yet they are also reminiscent of Franz Kafka's short story 'In the Penal Colony,' in which a prison officer invents a sophisticated machine for punishing inmates. The story ends with the officer being killed by the machine he created. There is no guarantee that hard-won rights will stay won or be extended in the face of continual social and technical change – absent knowledge, wisdom, and vigilance.

Former U.S. Supreme Court Justice William O. Douglas has written that the U.S. Constitution and the Bill of Rights 'guarantee to us all the rights to personal and spiritual self-fulfillment. But the guarantee is not self-executing. As nightfall does not come at once, neither does oppression. In both instances, there is a twilight when everything remains seemingly unchanged. And it is in such twilight that we all must be most aware of change in the air – however slight – lest we become unwitting victims of the darkness.'[24] We are in such a period now with respect to new information technologies.

There is the possibility of becoming an even more stratified society based on unequal access to information in which individuals live in glass houses, while the external walls of large organizations are one-way mirrors. There is a significant (and perhaps growing gap) between the capabilities of the new surveillance technologies and current cultural, legal, and technical protections. Powerful social and psychological forces work against any easy assumptions that a decent society is self-perpetuating. The masthead of a black civil rights era newspaper in Sun Flower County, Mississippi, reads: 'Freedom Is a Constant Struggle.' This heralds an important truth. There are no permanent victories in democratic society. As past and contemporary events of this century indicate, liberty is fragile.

NOTES

1 This article draws from a forthcoming book tentatively entitled *Windows into the Soul: Surveillance in an Age of High Technology*. A more developed statement regarding the new surveillance and its expression in the maximum security society can be found in chapter 8 of Gary T. Marx, *Undercover: Police Surveillance in America* (Berkeley: University of California Press, 1988). See also the discussions in James Rule, *Private Lives and Public Surveillance* (London: Allen Lane, 1973); Michel Foucault, *Discipline and Punish: The Birth of the Prison* (New York: Vintage, 1977); Kenneth Laudon, *The Dossier Society: Value Choices in the Design of National Information Systems* (New York: Columbia University Press, 1986); Roger Clarke, 'Information Technology and Dataveillance,' *Communications of the ACM* 31/5 (1988); David Lyon, *The Electronic Eye: The Rise of Surveillance Society* (Minneapolis: University of Minnesota Press, 1994); David Lyon and Elia Zureik, eds., *Computers, Surveillance and Privacy* (Minneapolis: University of Minnesota Press, 1996); and Oscar Gandy, *The Panoptic Sort* (Boulder: Westview Press, 1992). I am grateful to Hugo Bedau, Richard Leo, Helen Nissenbaum, Greg Ungar, Mary Virnoche, and Lois Weithorn for their critical reading and suggestions.
2 Franz Kafka, 'In the Penal Colony,' from *Complete Short Stories of Franz Kafka*, ed. by Nathan N. Glazer (London: Allen Lane, 1983), 140.
3 U.S. Department of Health, Education and Welfare, *Computers, Records and the Rights of Citizens* (Washington, DC: HEW, July 1973). Organization for Economic Cooperation and Development (OECD), *Guidelines on the Protection of Privacy and Transborder Flows of Personal Data* (Paris: OECD, 1981).
4 Canadian Standards Association, *Model Code for the Protection of Personal Information* (Rexdale, ON: Canadian Standards Association, 1996; available at www.csa.ca). See also, Colin J. Bennett, *Implementing Privacy Codes of Practice: A Report to the Canadian Standards Association* (Rexdale, ON: CSA 1995).
5 For related discussions see David H. Flaherty, *Protecting Privacy in Surveillance Societies* (Chapel Hill: University of North Carolina Press, 1989); Colin J. Bennett, *Regulating Privacy: Data Protection and Public Policy in Europe and the United States* (Ithaca: Cornell University Press, 1992); Priscilla M. Regan, *Legislating Privacy: Technology, Social Values and Public Policy* (Chapel Hill: University of North Carolina Press, 1995); and H. Jeff Smith, *Managing Privacy: Information Technology and Corporate America* (Chapel Hill: University of North Carolina Press, 1994).

6 Our discussion is based on conventional domestic settings in a democratic society for those with full adult citizenship rights. In situations of extreme crisis such as war, when dealing with very different countries or cultures, children, the ill, the incompetent, or those juridically denied certain rights such as prisoners, a different discussion is needed, and the lines in some ways will be drawn differently. That, however, does not negate the value of the principles to be discussed here as ideals that should apply more broadly, other factors being equal.

7 The fact that something is not bad does not necessarily make it good. The idea of doing good is implicit in calling for appropriate goals. But given the moral component of both means and ends, a good goal is never enough, any more than is a good means apart from its use.

8 This becomes even stronger when the polygraph is applied in such a fashion as to intimidate, as recommended by some early instructional manuals.

9 See Sissela Bok, *Lying: Moral Choice in Public and Private Life* (New York: Pantheon, 1984).

10 However, Winner notes there are conditions under which some technologies clearly have political and social (and by indirection, ethical) implications. For example, the decision to use nuclear power will of necessity imply central-ization and higher levels of security. Langdon Winner, *The Whale and the Reactor: A Search for Limits in an Age of High Technology* (Chicago: University of Chicago Press, 1988).

11 Here we emphasize the meaning of an invasion of privacy as the ability to take something from persons rather than the ability to impose something upon them (e.g., communication, sound, smells, or tactile sensations).

12 Helen Nissenbaum offers a useful conceptualization of this problem of privacy in public, in 'Toward an Approach to Privacy in Public: Challenges of Information Technology,' in *Ethics and Behavior* 7, no. 3 (1997), 207–19.

13 An important issue is specification of when awareness, awareness and consent, or neither ought to apply.

14 In the former there may be no choice but to follow Arlo Guthrie's words in *Alice's Restaurant* to 'walk in' and get 'inspected, detected, infected, neglected and selected.' This of course can be mischievously defined as choice.

15 See James Rule and Lawrence Hunter, 'Towards Property Rights in Personal Data,' in this volume.

16 For example, in an early Massachusetts computer matching case a list of those on welfare was compared with a list of those with more than $5,000 in the bank (the cut-off point for being on welfare). Those on both lists had their welfare payments automatically terminated with no further checking. Among cases inappropriately cut off were a woman whose money was

legally held in trust to be used for her funeral expenses and a student who had temporarily deposited his student loan money in his mother's account while waiting for school to start. See Jake Kirchner, 'A History of Computer-Matching in the Federal Government,' *Computerworld*, 14 Dec. 1981, and G. Marx and N. Reichman, 'Routinizing the Discovery of Secrets: Computers as Informants,' *American Behavioral Scientist* 27, no. 4 (April 1984), 423–54.

17 In a related fashion it might also be argued that the more expensive and difficult to use that a technology is, the greater the disincentives to use it and the less frequent its use. From this perspective the real problems begin when tactics become widely available (as with miniature voice- or motion-activated audio or videotape recorders hidden in familiar objects).

18 We have emphasized how surveillance may cause unjustified harm to the individual. As well we should give some consideration to the reverse – the abuse or erroneous use of surveillance data that helps an undeserving individual. For example, a police chief in a small town (in an anti-surveillance move) erased his son's record of drunk driving from the computer. However, the latter is much less likely to come to public attention and seems to have less moral bite (i.e., the cost of unfairly helping someone does not seem as great as unfairly hurting them). In zero-sum situations these are related (altering data so that a less deserving person gets a job denied a more deserving person). But much of the time the harm is to an impersonal mass and the damage done is symbolic and diffused. It offends shared values. The social costs of having a bad driver on the road can be great but are likely to be more distanced and not initially centred on harm to a particular person.

19 Regan, *Legislating Privacy*, 220–31.

20 In simplified form, combining degree of importance for goals and risks/cost for means suggests four types. The moral implications of using a costly means for an unimportant or undesirable goal, or a non-costly means for an important goal, are clear. What is more difficult and interesting are cases where the goal is very important and the means very costly.

21 Rather than goals other justifications may emphasize claimed 'rights' to the data involving property, contracts, self-defence and the freedoms of the Bill of Rights or legitimacy as a result of following fair information practices.

22 This could be greatly elaborated. Consider, for example, the harm from a pseudo-personalized mass mailing that congratulates persons assumed to be parents on their child's first birthday in an effort to sell them things one-year-olds need (this is based on their doctor's selling information about their pregnancy). How does a couple who had a miscarriage that is not reported feel when they automatically receive such solicitations? Such insensitive mailings (an actual case) can cause a particular kind of harm. Or consider a

mass mailing to recently retired persons advising them of the advantages of cremation over burial. Certainly this is not an issue to run to the barricades over, but it does suggest the kind of subtle manners question that the purchasers of databases ought to consider.

23 Here we need to separate embarrassment caused by an invalid result (e.g., having an alarm go off by mistake as one walks through a detection device in a store or library) from accurate results. But even the latter can be troubling if confidentiality is due and is not respected. One of the grounds on which non-public figures can sue for privacy invasion in the United States is if the information puts them in an unfavourable public light, even if true.

24 M. Vrofsky, ed., *The Douglas Letters* (Bethesda, MD: Odler and Odler, 1987).

3

From Balancing to Steering:
New Directions for Data Protection

CHARLES D. RAAB

Privacy protection[1] in law and practice involves a balance between competing values in order to achieve a result that safeguards individual privacy while also accommodating other important social, political, or economic ends. The first quarter-century of data protection laws and regimes has established this doctrine by underwriting privacy claims while tempering their force with limitations, exemptions, and countervailing precepts that reflect a concern for other values, public interests, and policies.

Thus, data protection regimes aim to restrain certain data practices, which, if given free rein, could otherwise serve as a charter for privacy-invasive developments of commerce or public administration, but they also limit the extent to which privacy can be safeguarded. Although privacy protection legislation is based on a conception of human rights that is supported by international conventions and treaties, the right to privacy is not seen as a value that takes precedence over all uses of personal information. Indeed, privacy costs are often underemphasized in the light of the benefits that are held to accrue, whether to individual consumers or to citizens generally, from the more intensive exploitation of their own and others' personal information.

A shadow is also cast across the practical field of privacy policy-making and implementation by the ambiguity and contested meanings of 'privacy.' This unclarity makes it difficult to insert privacy considerations into policy discourses in which the primacy of security, public interest, efficiency, and other objectives – albeit similarly vague – is asserted. Moreover, individuals and whole societies or cultures often vary in what they understand to constitute a private life or a private sphere and disagree about where the boundary should be drawn between privacy and legitimate state or societal purposes. Therefore, data protection is as inherently political a policy area as any other – for example, health care, education, or the economy – by virtue of these conflicts of value and of interests whose resolution involves settlements that can only be regarded as provisional.

It is likely that the doctrine of 'balancing' will remain at the centre of privacy policy for a long time to come, yet its premises and their practical implementation have rarely been closely examined in the many years since Rule and his colleagues criticized its ambiguity and imprecision in the work of Westin and Miller.[2] These objections remain broadly cogent. Can we be certain about what 'balancing' means and about what it can mean? Does it obscure or interfere with other ways of regulating in the privacy field? We may know what gets balanced against what, although the substantives that are involved can be constructed in different ways, with crucially different implications, as will be shown below. But what do privacy regulators,[3] data users, or data subjects do when they balance privacy against other important interests, and how do we, or they, know when a balance has been reached? There are no clear-cut answers to these questions, but they should be asked lest 'striking a balance' or 'getting the balance right' remains a *mantra* rather than a practical philosophy for decision making in difficult circumstances where fundamental issues are at stake.

This chapter seeks to bring some of these matters into clearer focus by holding the 'balancing' paradigm up to closer scrutiny and by pointing up other, and perhaps better, decision-making descriptions and prescriptions that incorporate but surpass it. It concludes that regulators' activities can be understood in terms of wider frameworks of control in which, alongside the application of sanctions, balancing often constitutes steering towards a preferred privacy outcome, and that 'balancing' as such is an inadequate normative conception.[4] Steering towards privacy would imply that deflections require to be legitimated, rather than the other way round. It might base itself on the premise that data processing should be minimized and justified, and that data users should reconsider whether personal identities need to be collected at all in order to fulfil commercial and governmental objectives.

The 'Balancing' Paradigm

That the doctrine of 'balance' constitutes the prevailing model for privacy protection needs no elaborate demonstration. The laws upon which the decisions of privacy regulators are based already embody balances that were struck in the legislative or other official processes through which they were enacted. The 1981 Council of Europe Convention, one of the fundamental international documents on data protection, is a case in point. Privacy protection had to be reconciled with another right, the free flow of information across borders. This right to information was seen as 'a principle of fundamental importance for individuals as well as nations. A formula had to be found to make sure that data protection at the international level does not prejudice this principle.'[5]

Because the latter principle was incorporated in human rights instruments, the Council of Europe Convention restricted it 'only to the extent strictly justified for the protection of other individual rights and freedoms, in particular the right to respect for individual privacy.'[6] The solution was to establish a common core of minimum data protection principles in all countries subscribing to the Convention, so that these countries could then mutually renounce restrictions on data flows across borders. This would remove the threat posed to the free-flow principle by any kind of trade protectionism masquerading as a special concern for privacy.

A further instance is the European Union's 1995 'Directive on the Protection of Individuals with Regard to the Processing of Personal Data and on the Free Movement of Such Data.'[7] This registers, in the title's final clause, a change from the first draft of the Directive in 1990 that reflects the European policy context within which data protection operates. It is crucial to note, however, that the balancing here refers more to a utilitarian objective, related to the EU's single-market aim to establish freedom of movement of goods, services, persons, and capital across borders, than to any human rights-related freedom of information principle. Differences in the level of privacy protection afforded by different member states were seen as an obstacle to the free flow of personal data in various economic activities and that would 'distort competition and impede authorities in the discharge of their responsibilities under Community law.'[8]

The directive therefore aimed to bring the level to equivalence across the states, thus – as in the Council of Europe Convention – preventing further inhibitions of free movement on grounds of privacy protection. An interesting, and very different, further balance was built into the framework of the directive regarding the special treatment of the media through exemptions made at the discretion of member states.[9] This controversial provision – Article 9 – acknowledged that the value of individual privacy competed with another fundamental freedom; it thus held the competing freedoms in some form of balanced relationship, although striking a balance in the legislative translation of Article 9 has been notoriously difficult.

These examples illustrate the complicating fact that, at several levels or in various dimensions of a system, data protection is intended to be balanced, either with a different fundamental right or with important processes and policies in the economy, society, or polity. The right to privacy, therefore, comes into conflict with other, equally grand, human rights and freedoms such as those concerning information, life, or liberty. In a different vein, privacy also contends on the policy landscape of 'high politics' which involves matters close to the heart of state sovereignty, such as policing, counter-terrorism, anti-fraud activities, and foreign policy. But it may also cut across policy areas of lesser grandeur, such as health care and education, or across commercial practices, such as banking and retailing, in which very sensitive personal details are sometimes gathered.

Finally, privacy is also weighed in the scales against particular procedural objectives or criteria of performance in the practices of firms or governments that may be reflected not only in the drafting of laws and policies,[10] but also in the operations of organizations that come within the sights of privacy regulators. Balancing in this case forms part of day-to-day decision making at a level that most closely affects the activities of data users and the rights of data subjects. It is also built into the descriptions that privacy commissioners give of their own job, that of ensuring the implementation of the law.

Where the privacy regulator is also an information commissioner with responsibilities in the field of public access to information, the 'balancing' task is, of course, inherently prescribed in the role. Thus, the Ontario commissioner observes that 'one of the challenges facing the Information and Privacy Commissioner is to uphold the separate values of privacy and access and strike the proper balance, when necessary, between the public's right to know and an individual's right to confidentiality of personal information.'[11] The reflections of the British Columbia Information and Privacy Commissioner indicate the acute dilemma of such a role. On the one hand, he writes that 'the primary role of a data protection agency is the actual articulation and advancement of the privacy interests at stake and requiring defence in a particular setting.'[12] Thus, he now regards it as naive to balance privacy against other values and purposes because 'the balance within government is automatically struck so much against the privacy interests of individuals that it is a wonder we have any privacy left.'[13] On the other hand, he confesses that his dual responsibilities have meant that he has 'occasionally sacrificed the privacy interests of individuals in the pursuit of greater openness,'[14] and he subscribes to an approach that features a pragmatic, non-confrontational search for consensus in negotiations.

But even where there is no such dual mandate involving two fundamental rights, examples of a 'balancing' stance, embracing the mundane as well as the grand, are legion. Thus, the director general of the Swedish Data Protection Board wrote: 'To be taken seriously, the Privacy Commissioner must use common sense when applying her authority. Consequently, a goal for the operation is to strike the correct balance between the privacy interests of the individual and legitimate opposing public interests.'[15] The Federal German Data Protection Commissioner agreed with this: 'It goes without saying that not only data protection concerns must be taken into account when making decisions. We must seek to strike a balance acceptable to all concerned between the interests in, for instance, security, the control of expenditure, an efficient administration, and data protection.'[16]

A further illustration is the New Zealand privacy commissioner's remark: 'In the conduct of my office I am required not only to have regard to the information privacy principles but also to have due regard to the protection of important human rights and social interests that compete with privacy, including the general desirability of a free flow of information and the recognition of the right of Government and business to achieve their objectives in an efficient way.'[17] Another comes from the Australian privacy commissioner's observation about offices like his: 'They serve as a promoter of the case for good privacy practice, as a moderator of unreasonable demands for data made by organizations ... and, on occasions, will be found articulating the public interest case for overriding absolute privacy protection.'[18]

However, the 'right balance' in each case, as adjudged by policy makers or by privacy regulators, might result in less or more privacy. The nature of the predicament of deciding in complex and dynamic circumstances was identified by the United Kingdom Data Protection Registrar: 'In the field of privacy there is always a balance to be struck between the rights of the individual and the legitimate requirements of organizations for information. Perhaps more importantly for every individual a balance has to be struck between convenience and confidentiality, between privacy and public interest. *The difficulty is that the point of balance is different for different individuals; and it changes.'*[19]

Whether this is a problem – implying a possible solution – or simply an inherent property of the privacy field, or perhaps an opportunity to move closer to the goal of privacy protection, can be debated. In the case of data protection, as in other regulatory and quasi-judicial processes, balancing is a question of finding a solution that is acceptable within a particular society or political system at a particular time, given a particular configuration of information activities. This involves interpretations of rules and vague principles, as well as their application to specific cases or practices; the difficulty that regulators have encountered in deciding on the practical meaning of 'fair processing' and related principles is one illustration of the contested nature of these decisions. Yesterday's balance might not be today's; what is acceptable in one country might not do in another. Technological change often renders old balances obsolete. There may be many different points of view to be taken into the balance on each issue, not just two. Moreover, the importance of the anti-privacy values or interests may be variable and disputed, so that data users and data subjects might disagree strongly on whether a particular compromise constitutes a balance between their points of view. The problem of 'weighting' will be considered at greater length below. However, if regulators are meant to be privacy watchdogs, they must bark and bite, not balance. To modify the old saying: dogs balancing on their hind legs do not do it well; should we marvel that they do it at all?

The Position and Exercise of 'Rights'

The reconciliation that balancing connotes holds contrasting values, interests, policies, objectives, or rights in some tension.[20] It is realist in the sense that it recognizes the established legitimacy of purposes that might conflict with privacy, and in that it acknowledges that there should be practical constraints placed upon any pursuit of privacy as a privileged value. However, it is important to question the implicit assumption that a right can always be balanced against other interests, which means that in any given instance the claim to the right might be disallowed. In the public-opinion survey literature, privacy 'fundamentalists' favour laws and regulatory action to reinforce privacy rights; they are distinguished from 'pragmatists,' who weigh up, in each instance, the advantages of revealing personal details against the dangers in the light of the available safeguards.[21] Fundamentalists arguably would reject this form of balancing in principle, whereas pragmatists might only reject particular compromises that seem, in each instance, to undercut privacy.

Pragmatists appear to outnumber fundamentalists. However, this can have no bearing on the question whether fundamentalism better protects privacy for all by supporting the right to privacy and bolstering a strong legal regime, whereas a data protection system based on pragmatic settlements might leave unprotected those who are less able to exercise pragmatism in their own relations with organizations of data users. Moreover, a system that relied on pragmatism rather than on the clear establishment of privacy rights would have data users, and perhaps regulators as well, gearing their practices and decisions to the standards deemed acceptable to the pragmatic majority. Not only might this standard fluctuate, but it could also be overly influenced by the data users themselves, whose persuasive and well-financed arguments – in short, their power position – would shape the parameters of pragmatism. This would amount to giving people only the privacy they want (or could be persuaded to want), rather than what they ought to have as determined by some external rights-based criterion of privacy protection that stood as the basis for public policy on the grounds that privacy is a collective good and not just an individual one, conducive only to personal autonomy.[22]

Such an outcome is not to be rejected out of hand, for it might be the only workable solution in practice,[23] and the satisfaction of wants commands respect as one criterion of good government and a healthy economy. Controversially, however, it corresponds to a rational actor or intelligent consumer conception of data subjects as persons who know what they want and can weigh up the consequences of exchanging their data for benefits. For this model to work – privacy as individual choice – there must be, at least, a high degree of transparency in the processing of data and an easy availability of information about these processes, so that data subjects can in fact make such determinations. To the extent that data users sustain their end of this bargain with data subjects, the quality of data protection may be improved in terms of adherence to the fair information principles, including consent and specification of purpose. But whether rational actor models are valid may be questioned, as might data subjects' capability, unaided, to effect such a combination of understanding and control.

The advocacy of privacy rights, on the other hand, is often an argument that the right should be established as fundamental. Dworkin's discussion is important in this context. He argued that there are two models that governments can use in defining moral rights. One involves 'striking a balance between the rights of the individual and the demands of the society at large ... a mistake on one side is as serious as a mistake on the other. The course of government is to steer to the middle, to balance the general good and personal rights, giving to each its due ... this middle policy will ensure that errors on one side will balance out errors on the other over the long run.'[24]

But, Dworkin asserted, although the appealing metaphor of balancing personal claims against the public interest is well established, it is a false model, and the problem is in the metaphor. He argued that taking rights seriously involves one or both of two ideas: one concerns the dignity of human beings; the other concerns equality, which 'supposes that the weaker members of a political community are entitled to the same concern and respect of their government as the more powerful members have secured for themselves, so that if some men have freedom of decision whatever the effect of the general good, then all men must have the same freedom.'[25]

Following from this, a government that protects a right 'simply pays a little more in social efficiency than it has to pay,' whereas to invade the right is 'worth a great deal of that coin to avoid.'[26] A right cannot be restricted simply on grounds of societal cost or inconvenience, unless the threat to society is very grave indeed: 'If someone has a right to something, then it is wrong for the government to deny it to him even though it would be in the general interest to do so.'[27] Moreover, such a right is claimed on non-utilitarian grounds; whether or not it would lead to social betterment, for example, is beside the point in any defence of rights.[28] In Dworkin's view, balancing is only appropriate in governmental choices between competing individual rights claims and not between one such claim and the supposed right of the majority.

Applying this argument to privacy, the right is fundamental if it is necessary for human dignity or equality. Both these objectives, and particularly the first, are well established in philosophical as well as legal discourse on privacy. Therefore, an objection to the way balancing in data protection is normally construed is that the other side of the equation typically involves social utilities such as governmental efficiency or the maintenance of law and order (in which distinctions between infractions that pose very different degrees of threat are often glossed over), or other personal utilities such as access to goods and services, as in the pragmatist's calculation or in the privacy regulator's decision process. On Dworkin's grounds, these criteria give insufficient warrant for a balancing process. Looking at it another way, it may be inferred from the prevalence of this model of balancing that privacy is not always taken seriously as a fundamental right in data protection systems and as a goal of public policy. This is arguably too bleak a conclusion, but the onus of proof is on the other side that to relinquish a rights claim in pursuing a pragmatic strategy of accommodating other interests or policies is not to give a hostage to the fortunes of politics, government, and commerce. Privacy protection may be in danger of becoming absorbed into the conceptual framework of consumerism, where it is just one among other criteria such as value for money, wholesomeness, convenience, and the like. In this light, the practical necessity of transmuting privacy rights into the operational inventory of fair information principles can be seen as assisting this absorption unless participants bear in mind what the principles represent.[29]

The Concept of 'Balance'

At the heart of these issues lies the concept of 'balance' itself. Let us explore it. 'Balance' is an ambiguous term, both as a verb and as a noun; dictionary definitions include many shades of meaning which have different implications for action.[30] There are also technical meanings of balance or equilibrium in cybernetics and systems theory and in the arts. Social scientists have used it, but they have also criticized its use as an analytical tool, in part because of the chequered career of systems theory and functionalism in the social sciences.[31]

Machlup's argument offers insights into the case of balancing privacy, although his context is the field of economics. He criticized economists' confusion of 'equilibrium' as a valid methodological device in abstract theory with its operational use in characterizing concrete situations and with its service as a political value judgment in connoting, for instance, the goodness of harmony.[32] Equilibrium describes a condition in which certain interrelated variables of particular magnitudes are so adjusted that, in the model they constitute, there is no inherent tendency to change. If a new variable is added or something happens to change a magnitude, then the balance is upset and a new one is sought.

However, Machlup claimed that this theoretical construct cannot be observed in the real world, which has far more variables and interrelations than the abstract model. An empirical subset of phenomena can be arranged as a balance sheet, as in trade flows. But this merely means that the sums are equal on both sides of the line, and to call it 'equilibrium' would require linkage to a more elaborate range of variables and interrelations on a theoretical plane. Nor should an observed stability in something over a long time – prices, for example – be confused with equilibrium, or fluctuations be confused with disequilibrium; the latter, for example, might simply reflect rapidly changing balances. Moreover, our judgments of situations as 'good' or 'bad' should not be mapped onto equilibrium and disequilibrium concepts, even though we may be guided by political or value positions towards selecting the particular problems that we wish to analyse in terms of these concepts.

Three main lessons for data protection can be drawn from Machlup's points. First, if it is often fallacious to talk of equilibrium even where there are measurable quantities on both sides of the balance, with privacy we are, at best, in a mixed qualitative – quantitative world in which regulators cannot calculate the equivalence even of what can be observed. If 'balancing' is taken literally, it would mean that there is some way of ascertaining whether parity exists between the items being weighed. But there is no ready reckoner for this; it is a matter of judgment, but that judgment may well be open to dispute about the weights that were deemed to attach to the competing claims or about other considerations that were overlooked.[33]

Both the disputed weighting and arguments over the inclusion or exclusion of particular factors may reflect a 'mobilization of bias' in the system in which such decisions are made. Schattschneider's classic observation provides an apt analogy: 'All forms of political organization have a bias in favor of the exploitation of some kinds of conflict and the suppression of others because *organization is the mobilization of bias*. Some issues are organized into politics while others are organized out.'[34] There is no need to imagine conspiracies in order to entertain the possibility that the structures, processes, and preconceptions through which data protection balances are sought may ensure that some considerations and weightings may be 'organized in' while others may be 'organized out.' Or their treatment might reflect ad hoc and not structural factors, such as decision makers' personal predilections, the level of their understanding, time pressures, and the like.

The weight given to privacy's antagonist in the scale of politics or values is therefore important. As has been seen, the nature of this antagonist may vary as between another basic right and a specific management criterion. Most often, it is not another fundamental human right, but a convenient or desired policy or practice. Because the weight of any of these – like privacy itself – is socially, culturally, and politically constructed, privacy's counterweight may be more solidly formed than is privacy through what typically passes as evidence of worth in the worlds of public policy and politics. Costs expressed in terms of money, votes, jobs, time, crime rates, and patients' deaths can be calculated and expressed in the persuasive hardness of numbers, however spurious. So too can management objectives like economy and efficiency.

Against these, privacy may count, but is not counted and is perhaps not countable, even if surveys of public opinion often show that large majorities are concerned about its loss. Therefore the numbers will tend to fall mainly on one side of the line, unless valid privacy 'price tags' can somehow be constructed for estimating the dangers to be offset against the efficiency or profit gains from privacy invasions.[35] But, like truth or beauty, privacy often seems inexpressible in the currency of serious policy debate, in which some numbers are thought to be better than no numbers. Thus, the phenomenon of 'balancing' is structured by factors external to that process itself and may, thus, be biased; more colloquially, the playing field may not be level. Over time, too, the structure of the situation may shift: when catching criminals becomes an urgent matter of policing and politics surveillance increases, privacy claims are given less credence, and a different balance is struck than in less anxious times.

The second point is this. We can only claim to observe a balance or imbalance in any relationship between privacy and other values or interests, or in negotiated or adjudicated settlements of competing claims, if we ignore an array of actors and their transactions that are distilled into variables and relations in a theoretical model of information processes. In the world of privacy protection, the prevailing model that is based mainly upon relatively undifferentiated 'data transactions' (even if divided into 'sensitive' and 'non-sensitive'), relatively undifferentiated 'data users' (even if moderately disaggregated into sectors), and almost completely undifferentiated 'data subjects' (even if they inhabit different sectors) is not rich enough to translate into discernible patterns of equilibrium or disequilibrium in the real world. If we had a more finely grained model, we could more intelligently locate, and thus understand better, the contending forces and what is at stake in any attempt to balance their claims.

Third, even if we could describe a situation in equilibrium terms, we should question whether 'balance' as such is a sufficient aim for a data protection system without enquiring whether the degree of privacy protection that a certain balance achieves is satisfactory in terms of the moral and political values that underlie privacy policy. The term 'balance' has a misleadingly positive ring – else why should regulators seek it? – that may not be warranted if the situation it describes falls short of substantive goals, despite the application of procedural safeguards.

Putting it another way, a balance between privacy and some other political or social objective may be consistent with a wide range of privacy outcomes, from scant to maximal protection. Following the lines of Machlup's argument, whether or not a deficiency of privacy constitutes a balanced or an imbalanced settlement of privacy conflicts is beside the point. More to the point would be an appreciation of the possibilities for securing more privacy by disturbing the supposed balance and moving towards another one that incorporated a higher level of privacy. That might involve a creative combination of strategy and opportunism, akin to governing or steering. This will be considered later, but the nature of the process of governance that produces a balance needs first to be clarified in order to gain practical insights into the kinds of steering activity that might improve privacy protection.

The Process of Balance Production

This process includes a variety of participants, or 'stakeholders,' who play a part in shaping the data-protection outcome. Stakeholders include data subjects, data users (or controllers), regulatory officials and organizations (in most, but not all countries and jurisdictions), technology designers, pressure groups, and governments. Their roles enable them to bring not only different values and interests, but also different power positions, to bear on the avoidance, production, or resolution of conflict.

There are alternative modes of relationship and interaction among participants within the conceptual framework signified by 'balancing.' The purpose of indicating different modes is to illustrate a few ways of construing the balancing of privacy, in which the structures of decision making and the activities of participants will vary under different sets of assumptions about what ought to happen.[36] Three modes are sketched below as abstract 'ideal types' that may overlap or shade off into each other; all are subject to the earlier criticism about the ability to observe equilibria, yet they may tell us something about how far privacy is protected and about where power lies. They also frame the subsequent discussion of how steering can affect the balancing process.

Each mode is capable of producing some conclusion that could be construed as a balanced one. Each involves the exercise of different skills or attributes by participants, the enactment of different roles, and the formation or avoidance of particular kinds of relationships. Whereas in the first mode balancing is nobody's business, the second involves participants in independent balancing, and the third constitutes mutuality or collective decision making towards a balanced outcome. As emphasized in Machlup's argument, the result in each can be evaluated in accordance with substantive political and ethical values, indicating to stakeholders what further activity might be needed to change or maintain the status quo. A further issue concerns the designing or shaping of these modes through legislation and its implementation. In all this, it is the official regulator's role – where it exists – beyond mere balancing that may be crucial.

The first mode can be termed *uncompromised pluralism*, in which each participant seeks to maximize an objective: for example, the pursuit of profit or of privacy, the elimination of fraud, or the receipt of goods and services in exchange for one's personal details. The aggregate result of their independent activities – the 'balance' – constitutes a by-product of a market-like situation as described by an observer, rather than a negotiated or reasoned outcome. 'Balancing' is not anyone's goal, nor is it subject to decision; any outcome is deemed to be 'a balance,' one that is likely to reflect relative power positions. Data protectors, if they exist, are authorized to act as regulators and, to the extent that they consider themselves to be privacy advocates, they may seek to advance privacy claims. But in a given situation they may have little power to assert privacy goals in countervailance against other participants, although they may bring legal sanctions to bear if they are available.

Uncompromised pluralism resembles the predicament where there are conflicting objectives pursued by opposed maximizers in an administrative organization, without a mechanism which could order priorities among these, or which could optimize either by deciding centrally or by encouraging or inhibiting one of the interested parties. This situation is discussed by Dunsire, who points out that the system is self-controlling in the sense that 'the balance ... can be held at several different "levels" ... equilibrium has more than one possible value ... [and] as such is not a "desired state"; it is merely an outcome.'[37] However, decision-makers who have overall responsibility – in our case, data protection officials – may doubt the acceptability of the balances achieved in this way; we have already seen the British Columbia commissioner's complaint about the 'automatic' locus of the balance in government. Balancing, in this 'market' mode, is not a reliable outcome from the standpoint of privacy as perceived by data subjects, their supporters in regulatory offices, and other privacy advocates, given the preponderant weight of interest in the maximal use of personal data in business and government.

A second mode, *decentralized balancing*, is likewise dispersed but consists of many independent balancing processes undertaken by participants, even though they do not interact. Each participant weighs privacy considerations against other ones and thus internalizes a position which may differ from the initial one that, for example, might have been adopted in the maximizing mode. Thus, data users take privacy considerations into account in organizing their activities, while privacy advocates recognize the legitimacy and value of personal-data usage of business and government and modify their stance. Individual data subjects pragmatically weigh the cost to privacy of their desire for goods and services. Data protection regulators strike balances between privacy and other interests or values when declaring their position on an issue.

As in the first mode, the governance or control of the system is difficult to comprehend beyond the attitudes and actions of its component players. However, there is room for influence to be exerted over the personal trade-offs that are separately made, based on the disposition of participants to entertain compromises. This influence takes place through shaping the general culture and climate of attitudes and practices in which each participant weighs privacy against other values, and not through interacting at the point of making decisions in particular instances in which bargains might be struck. Where law and principles exist, they exert an influence over practices, attitudes, and decisions. In addition, privacy regulators try to educate, advise, and inculcate greater appreciation of privacy among data users, policy makers, and the public so that they may each balance more effectively.[38] They may encourage technologists to build privacy in, rather than to ignore it or bolt it on belatedly in particular applications. For their part, data users try to foster a better appreciation of the importance of using personal data. Thus, the degree of privacy protection in specific cases may reflect a convergence, or at least a narrowing of the differences among participants arrived at through independent means in which, however, influences have been at work. Whereas the balancing in the second mode is done by each participant separately, in the third mode, *negotiated balances*, it is done together. The balance is a bargained outcome of the interactions of these interests, including those of the data protector, but even if there is no such decision maker at the centre. In this third mode – one of compromised pluralism or 'partisan mutual adjustment'[39] – data protectors as well as other participants recognize discrepant interests but strike a compromised bargain that can be regarded, maybe only temporarily, as a balanced solution. In a sense, this mode can resemble the first in that the participants need not relinquish their core values, even though they find a way of giving and taking over issues. Their behaviour, not their convictions, is at issue. On other occasions, they each might still fight to win. But unlike the 'market' mode, their relationships in this mode are interactive and structured to involve deliberations over privacy and other values. Networks of relationships, informal cooperation, coalitions, and alliances may be involved, and these sociopolitical processes can be engineered. In another sense, the likelihood of successful negotiations might depend on how far the dispersed, internalized balancing of the second mode has narrowed the gap.

The result can be seen as reflecting at least some practical recognition, by each, of the adversary's position on particular issues, and an acknowledgment that pragmatism or flexibility pays dividends in the bargaining process in which they mutually participate. This process and its outcome may reflect the relative general power positions of the different interested parties, but in any particular instance it need not, because participants understand that the process extends over time and that they may concede over an issue today in the hope of gaining concessions over another issue tomorrow. Sometimes, of course, the sides that have to be balanced are not as opposed as they may appear to be. A balance might be struck by settling upon a level of regulation that minimizes the conflict between privacy and data processing and instead enables privacy protection to facilitate the activities of data users.

This might happen if, in the second mode but perhaps in negotiations as well, data users realize that public confidence could well be strengthened if people knew that their data were well protected, and if the procedures in which the data were put to use were transparently fair. In turn, administrative efficiency and effectiveness may benefit if the data that are held by organizations are not excessive, inaccurate, obsolete, or insecure. There are signs that direct-marketing and electronic-commerce interests, as well as governments seeking to intensify their use of personal data,[40] are moving in this direction. But we cannot say how much efficiency a little bit of protection should be worth. Nor is it clear, without a more precise assessment of privacy risks, how far the balance point could vary across the many private and public sectors in which data are used.

From Balancing to Steering

From the standpoint of public policy makers who are promoting privacy protection, and also from the standpoint of official privacy regulators who are implementing policy, there are several dangers in the balancing process. One is that interests and values might be irreconcilable, so that no bargains can be struck. Another, conversely, is that balances are all too easily struck at a certain level, so that privacy is traded off in concessions to managing surveillance, rather than restricting it. This could be because power positions are unequal, as mentioned earlier, with privacy as typically the lightweight interest. In this way, the result is too little privacy. A further danger is that solutions, even if negotiated at a strategic level, cannot be implemented or imposed. Clearly, balanced outcomes that significantly protect privacy depend on how participants play their roles in decision making and in action, whether in the third mode or in the others. Outcomes also depend on attitudes and dispositions. Moreover, they depend on the governability of highly complex, diverse, and dynamic situations,[41] involving rapid developments in information and communications technologies and on the economic and governmental systems in which they are used.

This is where the conventional balancing paradigm most loses credibility, for two reasons. First, while the regulators are supposed to be promoting privacy, they are also implementing legislation that already subsumes a balance between privacy and other objectives. The expectation that regulators should themselves also find or promote balances vests in them a function that is more legitimately, and perhaps better, performed at the higher level of governmental policy making itself, if this responsibility is to be fixed in one place at all. Second, the injunction to seek a balance does not adequately indicate what to do, or how to do it, especially when such solutions are not readily found. For regulators to move towards privacy protection requires a somewhat different conception, one that does not reject balancing as such but goes beyond it. A revised paradigm of governance would emphasize steering as the essential part of a decision-making process in which balancing is an instrument to be manipulated in the interests of privacy, rather than a desirable outcome at any level. The applicability of the steering concept cannot be fully elaborated in this chapter, but some indications can be given.

Steering is more easily understood if the discussion of the production of balance is related to other ideas of governance: in particular to systems that equilibrate through the selective inhibition, using leverage, of opposed maximizing forces in tension, thus upsetting the balance and resetting it in a different configuration of the forces. Dunsire's analogy for this 'managed equilibrium' form of control is as follows: 'There is a type of desk-lamp which is supported by two strong springs pulling in opposite directions, so that when ... you move it to the angle and position you desire, you are effectively inhibiting the actions of one of the springs and allowing the other to 'win,' temporarily. When you stop the movement the lamp stays in its new position ... It employs a kind of self-regulation, for the system retains equilibrium after being disturbed ... A position of "balance" ensues.'[42]

The 'steering' idiom of governance contrasts analytically with that of 'comptrol,' in which control is sought through 'self-conscious oversight, on the basis of authority, by defined individuals or offices endowed with formal rights or duties to conduct inquiries, to call for changes in behaviour where performance is unsatisfactory and perhaps also to punish miscreants.'[43] In this conception, improvements are typically considered in terms of traditional bureaucratic resources: more legal powers and personnel, oversight strategies, tightening up compliance standards, and the formal institutional position of the regulatory organization. These devices are clearly important in privacy protection, but they are not the only, or even the most available, ways of achieving results.

In contrast, steering, or 'interpolable balance,' rests on an elaborated cybernetic conception of movement in a particular direction, perhaps governed by a controller (for example, a privacy regulator) who 'balances' in the sense of throwing weight against built-in tendencies and moving towards a desired state of affairs. Explaining that this perspective identifies and builds on any system's self-policing mechanisms, Hood pointed to the redesigning of government in order to 'strengthen immanent control rather than taking the existing structure as given and seeking to strengthen formal oversight.'[44] Control need not come from some fixed institutional location, because it makes use of networks of complementary, overlapping devices for finding out what is going on and for taking action.

If we take the target to mean movement towards achieving privacy goals, then regulatory agencies – underpinned by governmental privacy policies – can be examined in terms of their ability to know and to steer;

other participants, in terms of their capacity to learn and change. The regulator, in the steering model, cannot authoritatively prescribe priorities among the contending forces, but can rig, tip, or alter the balance and thus move the equilibrium to a new state. This has the ring of truth in the case of data protection, in which prescriptive 'comptrol' is evidently a scarcer resource than is leverage. Such steering requires that there be a desired pattern, standard, or target to be attained, an understanding both of the boundaries within which a course must be steered and of what is actually occurring in the system, and ways of moving the latter closer to what is desired. Moreover, 'a control device is only as good as its weakest element.'[45] The elements in question are tools for establishing the direction or standard, for detecting the state of play 'out there,' and for reducing the gap between the first two by effecting some change.[46] Regulators, as well as their governments and other participants, play a part in designing or discovering the requisite detectors and effectors and in deploying them. A cardinal point about considering steering more than mere balancing, and more than the enforcement emphasis of 'comptrol,' is that it may lead regulators in particular to think somewhat differently, and more comprehensively, about the kind of tool kit they need, about how to get it, and about how to use it.

Intervention involves monitoring, supervising, and inhibiting some data practices in ways that are not very different from traditional control methods, using the law and the powers of a regulatory authority. However, it also includes leverage exerted through the policy-making process in government and business in order to incorporate privacy protection more effectively into the systems for delivering goods and services. This may alter the balances within government thinking about relations with citizens and their needs and wants. The technologies used in data processing are likewise susceptible to steering, in which designers are encouraged to apply better encryption standards, access protocols, and the like. Of considerable importance are interventions to help data subjects to become better maximizers, and stronger negotiators, by asserting their claims to privacy, by understanding more about how they leave a trail of personal data when they use the telephone or a credit card or log onto the Internet, by taking risk-reducing precautions to minimize the privacy consequences of their transactions with data users, and by knowing how to seek redress. Some of these interventions are, of course, already happening as regulatory agencies perceive the growing importance of shaping the world of policy and practice, not just reacting or pretending to dominate it. To that extent, they are already steering, although the extent to which they have developed philoso-phies, strategies, and infrastructures for this is not clear.

This leads immediately to the consideration that interventions may best steer towards privacy protection by bringing data users and other participants to a keener appreciation of the effects of their practices upon privacy, so that they may regulate or police themselves, as in the second mode of balancing. Self-regulation is finding increasing favour, related to a realization of the limits to which privacy protection can be enforced or imposed. This perception may be realistic, given the prolif-eration, decentralization, and global spread of computing facilities and of information industries that deal in personal data. National or even international official regulators cannot themselves effectively regulate these using conventional instruments of administration, legislation, and the courts. It is intriguing, therefore, that an important theoretical dimension or premise of the steering approach is, in fact, the recognition that what is steered by the overall regulators are the self-controlling mechanisms or subsystems that make up a system. In this conception, there are many points of (self-)control, and the overall regulator may develop, institutionalize, and work with them even though formal authoritative oversight is not abandoned.

The current vogue for privacy regulation through sectoral codes of practice seems squarely in keeping with this approach. The Nether-lands, New Zealand, and the United Kingdom are prominent examples, and the European Union Data Protection Directive provides further encouragement. This is especially relevant if standards can be estab-lished and, moreover, adherence to them ensured through better detect-ing and effecting by the self-policing code maintainers themselves, both at sectoral level and at the level of the individual organization. Self-regulating industries need to improve their own steering. In this per-spective, overlaps and redundancy among checking mechanisms at dif-ferent levels are not to be eschewed, for they may achieve objectives better than a single 'control room.'[47]

Publicity also plays a part in steering: the highlighting of cases of infringement of privacy laws and principles in privacy officials' annual reports, and in the media, sends signals to others to control themselves more effectively. Such licensed 'whistle blowing' may be part of the offi-cial regulator's steering role, but it might become legitimated at other levels where data protection officers, and even ordinary employees, received encouragement within their industry, firm, or agency to report on poor adherence to privacy standards. The celebration of those who have exposed corruption and waste in bureaucracies in recent times, when efficiency, economy, and probity have been watchwords, points a lesson for privacy, although the climate would need to be very different from the present. But if this is a risky and sometimes distasteful path, the improved ethos that greater transparency and openness in bureaucracies could bring about would obviate the need for such informing, as Hood argued.[48] In addition, the encouragement of public pressure groups as adjuncts to official regulators in the overall steering of data protection, and even to self-controllers who take privacy seriously, would be consistent with interpolable balancing.

However, it is certainly not perverse or outmoded to think that privacy protection and the pursuit of balances should continue to favour 'comptrol,' especially given the statutory basis of data protection and the institutional forms of its implementation. There is still a need for authoritative standards, and for sanctions and controls to be enforced. Debates within contemporary data protection circles are over how far the way forward lies in an increase in these authoritative powers and capabilities for privacy regulators, including a tighter stipulation of standards against which to find balances, and how far it lies in a greater appreciation of steering and interpolable balance, in which regulators make subtle but telling use of the tensions by, in effect, putting their thumb on the scale in situations where others are acting.

The contrast between these two strategies is sharper in theory than in practice, but it involves different emphases upon the importance of controls, sanctions, and oversight, on the one hand, and, on the other, upon network manipulation, creative structural redesign, and other novel approaches that search out and capitalize on the conflicts and in-built tendencies of existing processes. The steering conception of governance brings these into better focus, validates them, and makes them available for deliberate reform; the traditional balancing approach accords them little value and leaves them out of account despite some evidence that they are, in fact, already in use to a certain extent.

Self-regulation, or self-policing, has its limits as well if left to its own devices. Regulatory agencies and centrally devised public policy will still be necessary in order to produce an effective mix of incentives and penalties – 'carrots and sticks' – so that self-regulating data users will adopt rigorous codes of conduct and actually implement them in their organizations. Government procurement policies requiring technical standards of privacy protection to be incorporated when contracts are awarded can play an important part in shaping technological developments that are consistent with privacy protection. These are only some examples of 'thumb-on the-scale' action that is controlled from a central point, albeit not exclusively.

Conclusion

Molière's Monsieur Jourdain discovered that he had been speaking prose all the while. Rather like him, it is arguable that privacy regulators already steer and interpolate in many of these ways and through other devices for which space has not allowed discussion here. They may employ an array of steering mechanisms while couching them in a 'balancing' rhetoric that only serves to point up the limits to authoritative, formal intervention, rather than to embrace and to find coherent and legitimate grounding for more systematic ways of surpassing them. Officials' brief descriptions, cited earlier and in this volume,[49] testify to this, particularly regarding their attempt to apply leverage in the legislative process, influence data users' practices, and raise consciousness.[50] However, we need fuller accounts of how they do this, which would convey their perception of which instruments to wield, when, and why, in manipulating their ensemble of control levers. We lack analyses of how this ensemble itself is constructed in the first place, and later reconstructed, across a range of data protection systems in which formal powers differ, and in which political and other opportunities to steer also differ as well as change over time. We also need assessments of the efficacy of steering.

For the future, it is not a question of choosing one approach or the other. For one thing, we do not know enough about what in the control armoury already works in favour of privacy and what is likely to work in a future that is transformed technologically and in other ways. For another, we have barely begun systematically to understand steering innovations that might be developed into a reliable repertory, although there are many indications that opportunities for interpolation and steering can be, and have been, discovered in privacy commissioners' attempts to advise, educate, shape public policy and structure the networks of relationships. We need to know more about whether the expectation that privacy regulators should simply 'balance' serves to inhibit their efforts to steer towards privacy goals in an advocacy manner, and whether political prudence marks an upper boundary of what can be achieved through any approach.

Some combination of regulation and self-regulation, along with better public education and the availability of privacy-enhancing technologies may succeed in steering towards privacy protection. This is not to reject the idea of 'balance' as such, but to find more sophisticated conceptualizations of its role and to embody it in more subtle and creative ways that match the dynamic growth of the 'information age' with dynamic modes of privacy protection, leaving bureaucratic limits to intervention behind.

NOTES

1 In this chapter, the terms 'privacy protection' and 'data protection' are used interchangeably.
2 See James Rule, Douglas McAdam, Linda Stearns, and David Uglow, *The Politics of Privacy* (New York: Mentor Books, 1980), chs. 7 and 8, where they object to the notion of restoring a balance, as used in Alan F. Westin, *Privacy and Freedom* (New York: Atheneum, 1967) and in Arthur R. Miller, *The Assault on Privacy* (Ann Arbor: University of Michigan Press, 1971).
3 In this chapter, the term 'privacy regulator' denotes privacy commissioners and others in official positions who oversee privacy protection in a particular jurisdiction and are responsible for implementing specific privacy protection legislation.
4 I have briefly discussed some of this chapter's points in 'Is Gegevensbechirming een Kwestie van Evenwichtskunst?' ['Data Protection: A Balancing Act?'], *Zeno* 4, no. 5 (Oct. 1996), 24–7, and in 'The Governance of Data Protection,' in *Modern Governance*, Jan Kooiman, ed. (London: Sage, 1993), 89–103. Other aspects of the argument were presented to the Study Group on Informatization in Public Administration of the European Group of Public Administration, Budapest, 24–8 Aug. 1996, for whose critical comments I am grateful. I should also like to record my thanks to Bärbel Dorbeck-Jung, Andrew Dunsire, Dag Elgesem, and Jan Kooiman for helpful suggestions.
5 Council of Europe, *Explanatory Report on the Convention for the Protection of Individuals with Regard to Automatic Processing of Personal Data* (Strasbourg: Council of Europe, 1981), 8.
6 Ibid., 10–11.
7 *Directive 95/46/EC of the European Parliament and the Council of 24 October 1995 on the Protection of Individuals with Regard to the Processing of Personal Data and on the Free Movement of Such Data* (Brussels: Official Journal of the European Communities, no. L281/31, 23 Nov. 1995).
8 Ibid., Recital 7.
9 Article 9; these exemptions are allowed 'only if they are necessary to reconcile the right of privacy with the rules governing freedom of expression.'

10 Here is one illustration: 'Where potentially clashing public policies occur, the problem will be to achieve the appropriate balances between different public objectives, for example, efficiency and the privacy of individuals.' *Sixth Report of the Data Protection Registrar*, HC 472, Session 1989–90, 29.

11 Information and Privacy Commissioner/Ontario, *Annual Report 1990* (Toronto: Information and Privacy Commissioner/Ontario, 1991), 3.

12 David H. Flaherty, 'Controlling Surveillance: Can Privacy Protection Be Made Effective?' in *Visions for Privacy in the 21st Century: A Search for Solutions*, Conference Proceedings, Victoria, B.C., 9–11 May 1996), 204.

13 Ibid., 201.

14 Ibid., 203.

15 Anitha Bondestam, 'What Can Privacy Commissioners Do? The Limits of Bureaucratic Intervention,' in *Visions for Privacy in the 21st Century*, 182.

16 Joachim Jacob, ''What Can Privacy Commissioners Do? The Limits of Bureaucratic Intervention,' in ibid., 185.

17 *Report of the Privacy Commissioner for the Year Ended 30 June 1994* (Auckland, New Zealand, 1994), 6.

18 Kevin O'Connor, 'What Can Privacy Commissioners Do? The Limits of Bureaucratic Intervention,' in *Visions for Privacy in the 21st Century*, 193.

19 *Eleventh Report of the Data Protection Registrar*, HC 629, Session 1995–6, 4; emphasis added.

20 The relevance – and problems – of the jurist Roscoe Pound's discussion of interests, and their weighing or valuing, can only be noted here in passing. Pound emphasized the importance of balancing interests on the same plane, whether public, social, or individual. See Roscoe Pound, *Jurisprudence* (St Paul, MI: West Publishing, 1959), vol. 3, chs. 14 and 15, esp. 327–34.

21 For example, Equifax, Inc., *The 1996 Harris–Equifax Consumer Privacy Survey* (New York: Louis Harris and Associates, 1996).

22 See the discussions of the social value of privacy in Priscilla M. Regan, *Legislating Privacy* (Chapel Hill and London: University of North Carolina Press, 1995), ch. 8, and in Ferdinand D. Schoeman, *Privacy and Social Freedom* (Cambridge: Cambridge University Press, 1992), chs. 1, 6, 7, and 9.

23 In that case, the privacy standard should be stabilized and determined outside the exchange relationship itself, albeit with the agreement of stakeholders. The Canadian Standards Association Model Code is a relevant example; see Canadian Standards Association, *Model Code for the Protection of Personal Information*, CAN/CSA-Q830–96 (Rexdale, ON: CSA, 1996).

24 Ronald Dworkin, *Taking Rights Seriously* (London: Duckworth, 1977), 197–8.

25 Ibid., 198–9.

26 Ibid., 199.

27 Ibid., 269.

28 See, however, the argument that privacy is an important condition of democracy, in Charles D. Raab, 'Privacy, Democracy, Information,' in *The Governance of Cyberspace*, Brian D. Loader, ed. (London: Routledge, 1997), 155–74.

29 Elgesem took issue with the conventional distinction between data protection and privacy, in which interest-balancing pertains to the procedural data protection principles rather than to the privacy right, which confers ownership and control upon the individual. Arguing that a property claim also inheres in the principles in terms of the individual's consent to the transfer of information alongside the minimization of the cost of the transfer, Elgesem viewed both data protection and privacy as involving restrictions on the channels through which information flows, albeit in different ways. See Dag Elgesem, 'Remarks on the Right of Data Protection,' in *25 Years Anniversary Anthology in Computers and Law*, Jon Bing and Olav Torvund, eds. (Oslo: Tano, 1995), 83–104.

30 *The Shorter Oxford English Dictionary*, 3rd ed., gives the following definitions at 138–9: *Noun*: an apparatus for weighing, a beam poised so as to move freely on a central point, with a scale pan at each end; the balance of reason, justice, or opinion; the wavering balance of Fortune or chance; hesitation, doubt; risk; power to decide; equilibrium; equipoise of mind; sanity; the process of finding the difference, if any, between the debit and credit sides of an account; a comparative reckoning; to weigh. *Verb*: to weigh (a matter); to ponder; to weigh two things, considerations, etc. against each other; to bring to or keep in equilibrium; to equal in weight, to counterpoise; to neutralize the effect of; make up for; to waver, deliberate. A balancer is an acrobat; one who maintains the balance of power; something which helps to preserve the balance.

31 See, e.g., N.J. Demerath III and Richard A. Peterson, eds., *System, Change, and Conflict* (New York: Free Press, 1967); F.E. Emery, ed., *Systems Thinking* (Harmondsworth: Penguin, 1969).

32 Fritz Machlup, 'Equilibrium and Disequilibrium: Misplaced Concreteness and Disguised Politics,' *The Economic Journal* 68, no. 1 (1958), 1–24.

33 See the proposal for such weighting in Alan F. Westin, *Privacy and Freedom* (New York: Atheneum, 1967), ch. 14, and its criticism by James Rule et al., *The Politics of Privacy*, ch. 7.

34 Elmer E. Schattschneider, *The Semisovereign People* (New York: Holt, Rinehart and Winston, 1960), 71; emphasis in original.

35 This issue is discussed further in Charles D. Raab and Colin J. Bennett, 'The Distribution of Privacy Risks: Who Needs Protection?' *The Information Society*

14, no. 4 (1998). See also the discussion of risks in James Rule et. al., *The Politics of Privacy*, ch. 22.

36 Space does not permit a fuller elaboration of these dynamics, but useful guidelines for this analysis are found in Dunsire's cybernetic perspective on public sector management and in Hood's work on control in public bureaucracies. See Andrew Dunsire, *Control in a Bureaucracy* (Oxford: Martin Robertson, 1978; Dunsire, 'A Cybernetic View of Guidance, Control and Evaluation in the Public Sector,' in Franz-Xaver Kaufmann, Giandomenico Majone, and Vincent Ostrom, eds., *Guidance, Control, and Evaluation in the Public Sector* (Berlin: de Gruyter, 1986), 327–46; Dunsire, 'Modes of Governance,' in Kooiman, ed., *Modern Governance*, 21–34; Christopher Hood, 'Concepts of Control over Public Bureaucracies: "Comptrol" and "Interpolable Balance,"' in Kaufmann et al., eds., *Guidance, Control, and Evaluation*, 765–83. Although these works specifically concern what goes on inside public organizations, and especially as regards steering the balances among procedural rather than substantive objectives, many of their insights into problems and processes can be made relevant to other contexts of decision making and control and are adapted in the present discussion.

37 Dunsire, *Control in a Bureaucracy*, 201.

38 Charles D. Raab, 'Data Protection in Britain: Governance and Learning,' *Governance* 6, no. 1 (Jan. 1993), 43–66. See also Jacob, 'What Can Privacy Commissioners Do?,' 184–6; O'Connor, 'What Can Privacy Commissioners Do?' 192–4; Flaherty, 'Controlling Surveillance,' passim.

39 Charles E. Lindblom, *The Policy-Making Process* (Englewood Cliffs, NJ: Prentice-Hall, 1968); Charles E. Lindblom, *The Intelligence of Democracy* (New York: Free Press, 1965).

40 For example, the British government's prospectus for electronic service delivery, *government.direct*, Cm 3438, Nov. 1996.

41 Jan Kooiman, 'Governance and Governability: Using Complexity, Dynamics and Diversity,' in Kooiman, *Modern Governance*, ch. 4.

42 Dunsire, *Control in a Bureaucracy*, 207–8.

43 Hood, 'Concepts of Control,' 766.

44 Ibid., 772.

45 Dunsire, 'A Cybernetic View,' 334.

46 See Christopher C. Hood, *The Tools of Government* (London: Macmillan, 1983).

47 Hood, 'Concepts of Control,' 778–80.

48 Ibid., 780.

49 See also David H. Flaherty, *Protecting Privacy in Surveillance Societies* (Chapel Hill: University of North Carolina Press, 1989).

50 Strictly speaking, where there are maximizers, a steering controller 'need

never reinforce a maximiser, [but] simply remove obstacles,' although, by analogy with equilibrium processes in the body, distress calls may require intervention with, say, drugs; in which case 'the pharmacologist sits on the fulcrum of a see-saw and throws his weight on one side for a while.' See Dunsire, *Control in a Bureaucracy*, 201, 215.

PART II

TECHNOLOGICAL AND REGULATORY CHOICES

4

Privacy and Individual Empowerment
in the Interactive Age[1]

JANLORI GOLDMAN

This essay outlines the contours of the privacy landscape in the United States, addresses the difficulty of enacting enforceable rules even against the backdrop of heightened risks and concerns, and suggests that privacy advocates may be presented with some new opportunities for privacy by pressing for the development of policies and tools that empower individuals to make and enforce individual choices. The existing power imbalance often leaves individuals helpless against the rapacious information gathering of the state and the private sector. Technologies of privacy offer a potent strategy for turning that power imbalance upside down. A dual policy and technology approach is critical if we are to flourish as a vibrant, free society, with strong communities as well as autonomous individuals. These values are not exclusive of one another; they are necessary for each other. Without privacy, other societal goals such as free speech, association, dignity, and liberty, will be compromised. As Roberto Unger wrote, 'The most radical freedom is the freedom to be, to be a unique person in the world as it is.'[2]

The Landscape

The era we have come to characterize as the 'Information Age' is evolving into the 'Interactive Age.' The communications technologies that made possible the collection, storage, transmission, and linkage of enormous quantities of information are now expanding to engage the individual consumer in a variety of activities. More and more people are communicating by electronic mail; sites on the World Wide Web allow people to 'browse,' download information, and get linked to other sites;

electronic malls invite people to window shop, inquire further about particular products, and even make purchases; people are subscribing to newsgroups and participating in chatrooms to gather and share information on topics of interest to them.

The potential benefits to society from these new digital media are undisputed and well documented. Freedom of speech and the right to receive information may enjoy a nearly limitless opportunity to flourish. The commercial potential of the Internet is also vast. What is troubling, however, is that this same technology makes it possible to generate, capture, store, and reuse a tremendous amount of personal transactional information and communications from diverse media, over the course of a person's lifetime. The 'womb-to-tomb dossier' that Harvard Professor Arthur Miller warned of thirty years ago may now be real – not collected in a mainframe computer, but through a distributed and largely unregulated network.[3]

However, at this moment the impact of the Digital Age on individual privacy remains an open question. Will the Digital Age be a period in which individuals lose all control over personal information? Or does the Digital Age offer a renewed promise for privacy? Technologies that empower individuals to control the collection and use of personal information, and devices such as encryption, anonymous remailers, web browsers, and payment systems, are inspiring examples of the privacy-enhancing possibilities of interactive technology. However, a conscious and collective decision must be made that the architecture of the Internet will be designed to advance individual privacy by facilitating individual control over personal information.

The rise of technologies that empower Internet users affirmatively to express control over personal information can fundamentally shift the balance of power between the individual and those seeking personal information. This technological, economic, and social shift is both possible and necessary, if we hope to harness this opportunity to advance individual privacy.

Rather than responding to the very real privacy risks posed by new technology with the Luddite call of 'smash the machine,' this essay calls for a reversal of the technological status quo by demanding that technology be designed to empower individuals. We should seize the opportunity to vest individuals with the information and tools to express their desire for privacy in clear and effective ways and to have those desires acknowledged and adhered to by information users. Such a post-Luddite approach may revitalize individual privacy in this new era.

The Current State of Privacy in the United States

Although more focused attention is being paid to addressing the privacy issues that threaten to undermine the U.S. First Amendment potential of the Internet, few concrete solutions have been proposed. There seems to be general agreement that individual privacy must be preserved – and even enhanced – in cyberspace, but we are just beginning to explore the means to make privacy work in this new medium.[4] The recent deliberations, by both the U.S. government and the private sector, come at a time of increasing public concern with the loss of privacy. A 1995 survey by Louis Harris and Associates revealed that 82 per cent of Americans were very concerned about their privacy.[5] This proportion has increased steadily over the past twenty years. A finding of even greater importance in a survey the previous year is that the public's concern with privacy reaches new heights when computerization is a factor.[6]

Fear and confusion over the lack of privacy rules and standards act as a barrier to the public's willingness to use new media such as the Internet. As information about the current practices of collecting and using personal information trickles out in news stories and in online discussion groups, public concern escalates. The recent revelation that a marketer was gathering hundreds of thousands of individuals' E-mail addresses culled from use of the World Wide Web and Usenet discussion groups, created a furor over the use of this transaction data.[7] And, the swift and furious public outcry against Lexis-Nexis's P-Trak, an online search directory of personal information, led the company to scale back the availability of some of the personal information, such as social security numbers, and to give people the option of being removed from the directory altogether. A dialogue must occur among privacy and consumer advocates, and the private sector, before privacy policies and practices can be identified. Once identified, privacy policies and practices can guide and influence the development and deployment of new technologies to our collective benefit.

A consensus emerged in the mid-1990s among policy makers, businesses, and privacy advocates that personally identifiable transaction data deserves strong legal protection, akin to the protections we afford content.[8] Codified in the Communications Assistance and Law Enforcement Act (CALEA) of 1994,[9] the expanded protection centres on limiting law enforcement access to transaction data. However, CALEA fails to address the significant privacy issues posed by the private sector's use of identifiable personal data. Before people will fully and openly take advantage of the new communications technologies and applications, they must have trust and confidence that their expectations of privacy and security are not undermined. As John Markoff concluded in the *New York Times* in 1995, 'The recent rush to the Internet by companies seeking to exploit its commercial possibilities has obscured the fact that giving the system a new purpose has unearthed fundamental problems that could well put off true commercial viability for years.'[10] A 1996 poll conducted for CommerceNet found that even though Internet use was growing, 'a wide variety of businesses selling goods on the Internet have been disappointed so far, hindered by security issues and a cautious attitude about commerce on the Internet among consumers.'[11]

We must seize the opportunity to move beyond the current debate over the intrusive nature of technology. We must instead embrace the technology's capacity to give individuals meaningful choice over the disclosure and use of personal information. In the traditional information privacy realm, various interests have wrestled with awkward, mechanistic, and largely unsuccessful approaches to allowing people some say over how and whether their personal information should be used by others. We debate the merits of opt-in over opt-out and how to categorize sensitive information. We argue over who owns information and whether one is a privacy 'fundamentalist' or a privacy 'unconcerned' or a privacy 'pragmatist.'[12] Essentially, privacy and consumer advocates have been engaged in a tug of war with the communications and information industries for control over personal information.

This is not to say that these 'tugs' have not produced results that benefit privacy and free speech, as well as commerce.[13] However, interactivity provides us with the opportunity to fashion a truer privacy paradigm that promotes individual choice and empowerment, robust speech, more secure communications and transactions, and vigorous commerce. For instance, interactivity makes possible real-time notice and choice options that acknowledge a direct relationship between individuals and the companies with which they do business. Notice and choice options can be presented at varying levels of granularity, depending on the individual's desire at the time of a particular transaction. Interactions can once again be tailored by and for the individual.

As the 1995 Department of Commerce report *Privacy and the NII: Safeguarding Telecommunications-Related Personal Information* concluded: 'The promised interactivity of the NII may diminish the need to make a policy choice between opt-in and opt-out. Such interactivity would make it possible for service providers to obtain consent to use [transaction-related personal information] from subscribers electronically before any services were rendered.'[14] Today, the privacy potential of interactive technology remains largely hidden and untapped. Unique facets of this new medium can be bent to advance privacy and encourage full and open participation. A range of policy and technical options will be discussed in greater detail below.

Privacy, Democracy, and Individuality

The difficulty of defining privacy and its underlying principles has stymied and paralyzed policy makers and philosophers. One privacy scholar who has written on privacy issues for decades resorted to defining it in these visceral terms: 'You know it when you lose it.'[15] Yet defining privacy and its value to individuals and society is essential if we are to develop cohesive and rational information privacy policies. We must understand why preserving and enhancing privacy is an ultimate 'good' before we can expect policy makers, the private sector, and privacy and consumer advocates to reach some common ground on core privacy principles and their application. From a privacy perspective, people must be able to maintain some control over personal information in order fully to realize other core values, including autonomy, liberty, free expression, and civic participation. This facet of privacy is uniquely implicated as more and more of our society's critical activities take place within the interactive, digital realm.

Information privacy is defined here as incorporating two components, at times distinct and at times inextricable. The first component is the right to retreat from the world, from one's family, neighbours, community, and government. This component allows us to shield ourselves, physically and psychologically, from the prying eyes of others. We think of this privacy value as it was initially conceived by Justice Louis Brandeis over a century ago as 'the right to be let alone.'[16]

The second component of privacy is the right to control information about oneself, even after divulging it to others. This component acknowledges the critical value of being able to step forward and participate in society without having to relinquish all control over personal information. To maintain privacy in modern times, as Professor Alan Westin defined it, individuals need to 'determine for themselves when, how, and to what extent information about them is communicated to others.'[17]

Privacy, as defined here, allows individuals to choose when to withdraw and when to participate. People must be able to seek solitude and isolation from others to develop a sense of themselves apart from others. Developing one's unique identity is critical to a person's ability to form his or her own thoughts and opinions and to establish intimate connections with others. A society that preserves privacy for its people is one that acknowledges the individual's interest in maintaining control over his or her life. One aspect of this control is being able to determine the presentation of one's self, or various pieces of one's self, to others. A person who is unable to retreat feels constantly watched, dehumanized, and powerless to make fundamental decisions affecting his or her life.[18] Equally important to having the capacity to retreat from society is having the ability to step forward to participate in the affairs of society. It is axiomatic that an individual's willingness to engage in the activities of the community will be tempered by the degree to which he or she is able to maintain control over the development and presentation of one's self.[19] In the absence of control over the development of one's self, individual autonomy and self-determination are eroded.

An emblem of a vibrant, participatory democracy is the ability of people to develop as individuals, separate and distinct from one another, with the confidence to hold and express their own political opinions, beliefs, and preferences. A free society tolerates – even revels in – such individuality, recognizing it as the bedrock of an open society and as a necessary precursor to ensuring free speech and political participation.

Once divulged, bits of personal information can reveal what we think, believe, and feel. Personal information, disclosed over a period of time in a variety of circumstances, can be culled to create a 'womb-to-tomb dossier.' As people lose the ability to control how others see them, and judgments are made about them based on information gathered thirdhand, people grow to distrust information-gathering entities. They become reticent to communicate fully for fear the information will be used for unintended purposes, and they may ultimately lose confidence in their ability to participate in a range of traditional and emerging settings.[20] Buttressing these conclusions, a number of recent polls document people's growing concerns that their privacy is increasingly threatened as they lose control over personal information.[21]

In this context, privacy means controlling who can know what about us. It means that we, as individuals, can regulate the flow of personal information, whether we are alone, in social settings, engaged in business transactions, or, to a less absolute extent, dealing with the government. The following section is a brief review of the current state of privacy law and practice, which will serve as the foundation for a proposal for a new privacy paradigm for the interactive age.

The Traditional Privacy Paradigm

Neither prong of the privacy right – to be let alone or to control personal information – is fully developed in law or practice to preserve or advance individual privacy. In a paper-based, information-gathering society in which the individual lacks sufficient bargaining power, the notice and consent models have failed to provide people with the ability to make meaningful, uncoerced choices about how much personal information to divulge and how and whether their information can be used for purposes unrelated to those for which it was initially collected.

Over the past thirty years the United States' information privacy policy has been loosely and unevenly patched from a series of Supreme Court decisions, federal statutes, executive branch reports, and industry self-regulation. The *Code of Fair Information Practice Principles*, originally developed by the U.S. Department of Health, Education and Welfare in 1973, has served as the basis for much of the information privacy legislation and policy in place today.[22] The central principle is that information collected for one purpose shall not be used for a different purpose without the individual's consent. The principle is more extensively discussed than it is applied.

Even where the private sector has voluntarily adopted such a consent principle, it has fallen short of empowering people to make informed, uncoerced choices about secondary use information. Nevertheless, it is fair to say that in theory, a general consensus has developed among many privacy and consumer groups, the private sector, and even the government, that individuals should be informed of and able to make choices about the secondary use of personal information.[23] The challenge has always been how to craft workable and enforceable mechanisms to put the policy into practice.[24] With few exceptions, industry representatives argue vigorously that 'opt-out' must be the maximum privacy mechanism, which means that unless an individual specifically objects to a secondary use of information, the information gatherer is free to reuse and disclose personal information. As privacy advocates have long argued, the opt-out approach places the burden of restricting information use on the individual, and thereby creates a presumption that ancillary, unrelated uses of personal information are acceptable. Another criticism leveled at the opt-out mechanism is that it insufficiently reflects peoples' true privacy values. Only a small percentage of people actually exercise the option, a situation one can attribute to a lack of notice, fear of negative consequences, and a reluctance to engage in one more step beyond what is minimally necessary to complete a transaction.

Exacerbating the insufficiency of privacy law and practice is the weak state of constitutional jurisprudence in the area of information privacy, most notably the interpretation of the Fourth Amendment: the 'right of the people to be secure in their persons, houses, papers, and effects.'[25] The U.S. Supreme Court is the ultimate arbiter and interpreter of the meaning and scope of the Constitution. Unfortunately, the Court has both narrowly interpreted the Fourth Amendment's scope and crafted standards for applying the Amendment which have resulted in weak actual protections. In one of its seminal privacy cases, *U.S. v Katz*, the Supreme Court ruled that the Fourth Amendment protects 'people, not places' from unwarranted searches and seizures.[26] In *Katz* the Court found that what a person 'seeks to preserve as private, even in an area accessible to the public, may be constitutionally protected' provided the individual has a subjective actual expectation of privacy that the society will recognize as reasonable. The reasonable expectation is then weighed against the government's interest in access and the extent of the intrusion. Although hailed as a landmark privacy decision, the *Katz* test has been applied in later cases to undermine privacy interests.

In *Katz*'s progeny the court has applied the 'reasonable expectation' test as a relative standard informed by the technological and social realities of the day. As technology has advanced, and as societal demands for sensitive personal information have increased, the Court has increasingly circumscribed the 'zones' one may justifiably consider private. Thus, in *California v Ciraolo* the Court held that the use of a fixed-wing aircraft to observe marijuana on the defendant's property from 1,000 feet did not violate his protected 'zone of privacy' even though he had built a 10–foot fence around his backyard with the intent to shield it from passers-by.[27] The Court stated that the defendant's subjective expectation of privacy was not one 'that society is prepared to honor ... [in] an age where private and commercial flight in the public airways is routine.'

Similarly, in *California v Greenwood* the Court found that people have no reasonable expectation of privacy in garbage once it is removed from the home and placed on the curb for pick-up, even if a county ordinance requires the trash to be placed on the curb and does not allow for disposal in any other way.[28] The court reasoned that the defendants deposited their garbage 'in an area particularly suited for public inspection and .for the express purpose of having strangers take it' and could not expect Fourth Amendment protection for items they 'knowingly expose[d] to the public.'

The 'reasonable expectation' test has proven particularly troublesome in the information privacy context. The Court has continually held that individuals have no privacy interest in information divulged to the private sector, even though modern society leaves citizens no option but to disclose to others, where, for example, disclosure is a condition of participation in society.[29]

The distinction is blurring between the content of a communication and the transactional data generated in the course of a communication. In the nine years since the enactment of the Electronic Communications Privacy Act (ECPA), society's patterns of using communications technologies have changed dramatically. Millions of people have electronic mail addresses; large numbers of businesses and non-profit and political groups conduct their work over the Internet; and use of the World Wide Web to access and share information is exploding. Detailed information about a person's visits to Usenet and World Wide Web sites can be logged, and may be used, without a person's knowledge.[30]

Records of all of these activities – who sends a message to whom, where a given communications device is located, which political party one contacts for information, and which online discussion group or virtual community one associates with – are available both in real time and in stored form as part of the transactional information generated by advanced computer and communications networks. This transactional information reveals almost as much about our private lives as would be learned if someone literally followed us around on the street.

To varying degrees people expect that these transactional data are 'private.' There are contentlike characteristics to transactional data that require they be afforded a level of legal protection akin to content. Political consensus exists to support raising legal protections for such increasingly sensitive and unprotected transaction data.[31] However, so far, the legal limits on access apply only to the government.

Other factors have contributed to the weak state of individual privacy protection in the United States. Until fairly recently technology has been largely in the hands of the government and large corporations. Technology has been deployed to meet governmental needs – often the need to monitor, survey, and track individuals – using increasingly invasive techniques. Similarly, technology has been used by businesses to collect information on individuals without their knowledge or consent and, frequently, to use personal information collected for one purpose to make decisions about the individual in quite unrelated contexts.

Second, in addition to weak Supreme Court jurisprudence, other legal and policy protections for personal information are incomplete and scattered throughout case law,[32] federal and state statutes, and executive branch reports.[33] Despite the clear articulation of principles that would, if implemented, preserve individual privacy, individuals continue to experience an erosion of privacy. In particular, individuals in the United States report an escalating fear that individual privacy is in greater peril each day because of increased computerization of personal information.

The use of technology to meet the information needs of government and business has disempowered individuals. Technology has escalated the collection of detailed personal information and enabled massive data sharing between entities for unrelated purposes – all without the individual's consent. Today, privacy protection frequently takes the form of a many-paged disclaimer waiving any claim to privacy which the individual must sign prior to receiving a service or benefit, most notably in the health care and financial arenas. The perception of technology as an invasive tool of Big Brother and 'big government' has led civil libertarians and average citizens consistently to demand legal protection – be it judicial or legislative – from the incursions on privacy and liberty made possible by the uncontrolled use of technology.

Even where there has been an attempt to codify fair information practices through statute, regulation, or industry guidelines, the results have generally fallen far short of the desired goal – to control the collection, use, and disclosure of personal information. This is not to underestimate the importance of hard-fought battles to craft statutory privacy protections for personal information. Existing privacy laws in areas such as banking, cable, credit, educational, and video records set important limits on the use and disclosure of personal information. Ironically, no comprehensive federal law exists to protect the information many consider to be the most sensitive and private – medical information.

There is no statute on the books in the United States that gives the individual simple, meaningful, and up-front control over personal information. In sum, efforts to preserve information privacy can be characterized as a constant struggle to set limits on the invasions of privacy – the misuse, unauthorized collection, and unauthorized disclosure of personal information – made possible and practical through technology.

New Privacy Paradigm: Designing, Implementing, and Enforcing Individual Empowerment Technologies

New media present us with the opportunity to more fully realize constitutional principles of privacy, at the same time that they foster free speech and other democratic principles in the digital environment. To advance privacy more completely, a number of policy and technical approaches must be developed in concert. No single response can adequately address the individual's ability to control personal information in an electronic environment. Thus, we must develop enforceable rules concerning the capture and reuse of personal information that reflect fair information practices, while also developing the technical capacity for people to achieve anonymity and security.

This essay focuses on achieving a number of key privacy-empowering approaches. We must build into the technology and its applications the capacity to move beyond 'opt-in' and 'opt-out' to mechanisms of meaningful individual choice. Widespread availability of choice options will also reverse the use of the *Katz* standard to undermine privacy protections. For example, if technology can be a tool for people more easily to manifest their subjective expectations of privacy, then those expectations are more likely to be recognized by the society, and the courts, as objectively reasonable.

In the interactive sphere, technology may be designed to empower individuals to gain greater control over their lives by making decisions about the use of their personal information. Those decisions may vary from transaction to transaction, depending on the nature of the transaction, the recipient of the personal information, the offers proffered, and a host of other variables. For instance, some people consider their address to be sensitive information. Others may be unconcerned about disclosure of their phone number, age, salary, or even travel patterns. In the interactive realm, technology has the capacity to be the individual's ally, not the intrusive villain it is often perceived to be.

Both privacy prongs can be more fully addressed by interactive technologies that allow people to filter out unwanted communications that may come into their home, as well as to make choices about the use of the personal information they are divulging. The experience with caller identification is instructive here in that technology can be designed to give people greater control over the information they both divulge and receive. With caller-ID technology, it is possible for people to make a wide range of choices about whether to divulge the number they are calling from, whether to view the number of the receiving calls, and/or whether to block all of their calls from being disclosed to the receiver. In their use of telephones, people are both makers and receivers of calls; they desire varying levels of privacy protection in each role, depending on their preferences and circumstances.

Interactive technologies can be designed with features that empower individuals to control the flow of information. The initial point of contact is ideal for conveying information about the information practices and policies of an information user to the individual and providing him or her with the ability to make choices concerning use to which the information is to be put.

Traditional opt-out or opt-in mechanisms for obtaining consent usually involve an 'all or nothing' approach. The ease and economy of interactive communications offers an opportunity for more levels of choice. Information collectors and users can more easily ask specific questions, request more detailed information, and tailor their requests and responses. To some extent, exercising choice in the use of personal information may alleviate the fear of surveillance and abuse that makes many individuals reticent about using new technologies.

An individual must be given clear and conspicuous notice of information policies and practices in order to make informed choices about information uses. Transparency, a central principle of fair information practices, requires that individuals be told about the information that is being collected from them and how it will be used and disclosed. Software can be designed that allows individuals access to additional information about information practices and to actually see the amount of information they are revealing by engaging in a given activity.

Technology that allows individuals to exercise a number of options regarding information flow can be used to gather consent to information use and to record limits on information use. Software can be designed to require the individual to take an action prior to engaging in a specific activity.[34] Through such choice mechanisms, information gatherers can educate consumers about information flow, while empowering individuals to take a more active role in controlling their personal information.

Technology that empowers individuals to make choices about the use of personal information will benefit consumer privacy and ultimately commerce. Not only does a more informed, active citizenry breed a robust, participatory democracy, but voluntary, knowledgeable participation in the marketplace will lead to more confident consumers. The opportunity for entities to establish more direct relationships with the individual can lead to a more refined, detailed, useful awareness of the consumer. As people gain greater trust in the interactive environment, they will be less reticent to participate. As some segments of the private sector already recognize, allowing people to make decisions about the use of personal information is an essential business practice. Good privacy practices are both crucial to individuals and necessary to foster free speech and commerce.

Just as industry, researchers, and the public interest community have joined together to design technologies to empower people to filter out objectionable material on the Internet through the Platform for Internet Content Selection (PICS), so too can the PICS model be harnessed or expanded with a privacy focus.[35]

The Next Steps

Once divulged, bits of personal information can reveal what we think, believe, and feel. No other medium generates personal information as revealing as that produced by the Internet. Information is generated and captured each time an individual enters a web site, views a picture, downloads a file, or sends E-mail. Information is needed to complete each transaction; however, this information, disclosed over a period of time, in a variety of circumstances, can reveal details of the individual's habits, beliefs, and affiliations. The individual womb-to-tomb dossiers of personal information that Arthur Miller warned us of thirty years ago may be readily available – not stored in a central database, but culled from a variety of sources and pulled together instantaneously to create a detailed profile of nearly anyone on the Internet.[36]

Currently, few people seem to be aware of the vast quantity of information generated and captured – and potentially used and disclosed – during the use of interactive communications media. Unlike the traditional paper-based world where the individual is typically aware that she or he is providing an entity with information (by presenting a credit card or through a billing statement from the phone company) much of the information gathering on the Internet occurs during browsing or other relatively passive activities. Individuals visit web sites, read articles, and examine pictures under the illusion that their activities are anonymous or at least unobserved.

In an effort to increase public demand for privacy protection, the Center for Democracy and Technology (CDT) launched a privacy demonstration web site that greets each visitor with detailed personal information including their name, E-mail address, computer and browser type, and the universal resource locator (URL) indicating the web site from which they came. Initial visitors expressed alarm at the detailed personal information that is routinely recorded by web sites, Internet providers, and online commercial service providers.[37]

Another important initiative is the Internet Privacy Working Group (IPWG), formed shortly after the 1995 Federal Trade Commission Hearings on Commerce and Global Information Infrastructure.[38] Participants in the IPWG effort represent a broad cross-section of public interest organizations and private industry engaged in commerce and communications on the Internet. IPWG's mission is to provide a policy framework for addressing privacy concerns in the online environment. Towards this end, IPWG is developing a language for users to communicate privacy preferences and for web sites to communicate information practices. The work of IPWG will enable computer users to make choices about the flow of their personal information on the Internet. The mission is to implement the concepts of 'notice' and 'choice' by developing a platform that enables web sites to describe easily their privacy practices, enables users to set preferences about the collection, use, and disclosure of personal information, and facilitates the two to communicate and in some instances reach agreement when the two are at odds. However, the IPWG vocabulary, along with the World Wide Web Consortium's Platform for Privacy Preferences (P3) Project, only address a limited set of privacy issues. The project does not address many important privacy considerations, such as providing people access to their own personal information.[39]

Interactive media offer new challenges to privacy. There is growing public concern that the non-consensual, surreptitious collection of personal information is undermining individual privacy. The lack of transparency about information collection and use on the Internet builds on this concern. Without the knowledge that information is being collected and used, individuals are unable to make informed decisions to preserve their privacy. People are uncomfortable when they learn that software currently available allows web site operators and other content providers to record easily their online activities unbeknownst to them.[40]

As news stories expose the privacy risks of new services and applications such as Deja News[41] and cookies,[42] individuals may become more reticent in their use of the Internet. The lack of accurate information about the collection, use, and disclosure practices of entities on the Internet may chill speech and political activity. Individuals may hesitate and pull back from participating in desirable activities such as signing online petitions to Congress.[43] They may withdraw from participating in online discussions or visiting web sites that contain information on sensitive topics, such as sex and health.

Policy makers around the world are beginning to address the privacy concerns that threaten to undermine individuals' willingness to partake in First Amendment and commercial activities on the Internet. Although few concrete solutions have been proposed, the pivotal role of privacy in promoting speech and other democratic values has been recognized. Despite general agreement that individual privacy must be preserved – and even enhanced – in cyberspace, we are just beginning to explore the means to make privacy work.[44]

NOTES

1 I am grateful to my colleague, Deidre Mulligan, for her insights and assistance.
2 Roberto Unger, *Passion: An Essay on Personality* (New York: Free Press, 1984).
3 Arthur Miller, *The Assault on Privacy: Computers, Databanks and Dossiers* (Ann Arbor: University of Michigan Press, 1971).
4 The Federal Trade Commission has been examining privacy issues and the Global Information Infrastructure (GII), marked by the creation of its Privacy Initiative in 1995. See Christine Varney, 'Consumer Privacy in the Information Age: A View from the United States FTC,' *Privacy Laws and Business* 36 (1996), 2–7. See also CDT's statements to the FTC (at www.cdt.org). The National Information Infrastructure Advisory Council issued its 'Privacy and Security-Related Principles' early in 1997, followed by the inter-agency Information Infrastructure Task Force's Privacy Principles. See U.S. Information Infrastructure Task Force (IITF), *Privacy and the National Information Infrastructure: Principles for Providing and Using Personal Information*, Final Version, 6 June 1995 (Washington, DC: IITF, Information Policy Committee, Privacy Working Group). More recently, the U.S. Department of Commerce released its report on *Privacy and Telecommunications-Related Data* (Washington, DC: Department of Commerce, 1996), which concluded that the private sector must implement privacy standards or face a legislative mandate.
5 Louis Harris and Associates, *Mid-Decade Consumer Privacy Survey* (New York: Harris, 1995).

6 Louis Harris and Associates, *Interactive Services, Consumers, and Privacy*, (New York: Harris, 1994), 70.

7 See John Schwartz, 'When Direct Mail Meets E-mail, Privacy Issue Is Not Fully Addressed,' *Washington Post*, 9 Oct. 1995. Similarly, public reaction in Missouri was so intense to a new product called 'Caller Intellidata' that Southwestern Bell withdrew it the day after introduction. Caller Intellidata packaged Caller ID information, including date and time of call, from Southwestern Bell, with caller address and demographic information compiled by Equifax. In addition to individual profiles of callers, this service was to include a statistical profile of the businesses customers based on demographic information from census reports and Equifax. The Public Counsel for Missouri objected to the service calling it 'Big Brother' and stating that 'consumers should not be forced to become statistics in a marketing study merely by placing a telephone call.' See Jerry Stroud, *St Louis Dispatch*, 5–6 Oct. 1995.

8 See Section 207 of the U.S. Communications Assistance and Law Enforcement Act of 1994, providing heightened protections for transactional data. Pub L 103414, 108 Stat 4279 (1994).

9 Ibid.

10 See John Markoff, 'Discovery of Internet Flaws Is Setback for On-line Trade,' *New York Times*, 11 Oct. 1995; see also 'Internet's Reach in Society Grows,' *Washington Post*, 31 Oct. 1995, that describes peoples' fear of engaging in commerce on the Internet, 31 Oct. 1995.

11 CommerceNet poll, 1996.

12 The characterization of privacy fundamentalists, privacy pragmatists, and privacy unconcerned was originally made by Alan F. Westin. See Louis Harris and Alan F. Westin, *Equifax/Harris Consumer Privacy Survey* (Atlanta: Equifax, 1996), 13. In this report, 16 per cent of Americans were found to be 'unconcerned,' 24 per cent to be 'fundamentalists,' and 60 per cent 'pragmatists.'

13 See, e.g., the U.S. Electronic Communications Privacy Act of 1986, 18 USC s2510 et seq. (1995); the Cable Communications Act of 1984, Pub L 98–549, 98 Stat 2779 (1984; codified as amended in scattered sections of 47 USC); and the Video Privacy Protection Act of 1988, 18 USC s2710 (1995).

14 U.S. Department of Commerce, *Privacy and the NII*.

15 David Flaherty made this remark to me in a conversation about privacy, and it reminds me of Supreme Court Justice Potter Stewart's infamous attempt to define obscenity in a First Amendment case: 'I know it when I see it.'

16 Samual Warren and Louis Brandeis, 'The Right to Privacy,' *Harvard Law Review* 4 (1890), 193–220.

17 Alan Westin, *Privacy and Freedom* (New York: Atheneum, 1967), 3–9.

18 See, Erving Goffman, *The Presentation of the Self in Everyday Life* (New York:

Doubleday, 1958); Edward J. Bloustein, 'Privacy Is Dear at any Price: A Response to Professor Posner's Economic Theory,' *Georgia Law Review* 12 (1978), 429; and Julie C. Inness, *Privacy, Intimacy, and Isolation* (New York: Oxford University Press, 1992) for more discussion of the societal impact of inadequate privacy.

19 For a discussion of legal theories related to the development of 'personhood' and autonomy in society, see Margaret Radin, 'Property and Personhood,' *Stanford Law Forum* 34 (1982), 957; Margaret Radin, 'The Consequences of Conceptualism,' *University of Miami Law Review* 41 (1986), 239, and 'Market-Inalienability,' *Harvard Law Review* 100 (1987), 1849; Charles Reich, 'The New Property,' *Yale Law Journal* 73 (1964), 733, 'Beyond the New Property,' *Brooklyn Law Review* 56 (1990), 731, and 'The Liberty Impact of the New Property,' *William and Mary Law Review* 31 (1990), 295.

20 One need only look at the growth of a health information infrastructure without adequate privacy safeguards to understand the escalating public distrust of doctors' and payers' ability to maintain confidentiality.

21 See recent polls on the public's growing worries over the lack of information privacy by Louis Harris and Associates, Time/CNN, Mastercard, and the American Civil Liberties Union.

22 U.S., Department of Health, Education and Welfare, *Records, Computers and the Rights of Citizens* (Washington, DC: HEW, July 1973).

23 See U.S. Privacy Protection Study Commission, *Personal Privacy in an Information Society* (Washington, DC: Privacy Protection Study Commission, 1977); *Privacy and Related Security Principles for the NII*, Mega-Project III of the National Information Infrastructure Advisory Council (1995); *Principles for Providing and Using Personal Information*, Report of the Privacy Working Group of the Information Infrastructure Task Force (Oct. 1995); and corporate privacy policies, such as those of the of the Direct Marketing Association, American Express, Experian, and the Interactive Services Association.

24 See the discussions that preceded enactment of the U.S. Video Privacy Protection Act, and the Driver's Privacy Protection Act, as well as the current debate over how to craft strong legal privacy protections for peoples' medical records.

25 The Fourth Amendment to the U.S. Constitution reads in full: 'The right of the people to be secure in their persons, houses, papers, and effects, against unreasonable searches and seizures, shall not be violated, and no warrants shall issue, but upon probable cause, supported by oath and affirmation, and particularly describing the place to be searched, and the persons or things to be seized. '

26 389 U.S. 347 (1967). *Katz* reversed *U.S. v Olmstead*, which held that the Fourth

Amendment covered only physical places, and thus the warrant requirement did not apply to police wiretaps: 277 U.S. 438 (1928).

27 476 U.S. 207 (1986).

28 486 U.S. 35 (1988)

29 In *Smith* v *Maryland*, a case involving pen registers, the court held that people have no constitutionally protected interest in the numbers dialed from their homes, 442 U.S. 735 (1979); and in a case involving personal bank records, *U.S.* v *Miller*, the court found no reasonable expectation of privacy in personal information divulged to a third party, even though the individual had no choice but to divulge, 425 U.S. 345 (1976). Both *Smith* and *Miller* were later 'overturned' by Congress through enactment of the Electronic Communications Privacy Act and the Right to Financial Privacy Act, statutes that created legally enforceable expectations of privacy.

30 Numerous articles in 1996 and 1997 detail the privacy problems posed by online use: 'No Privacy on the Net, ' *PC World* (Feb. 1997), 223; 'Do I Have Privacy On-Line?' *Wall Street Journal*, 9 Dec. 1996, R12; 'Many Net Surfers Mislead to Protect Privacy,' *USA Today*, 9 Dec. 1996.

31 See note 6, above.

32 Although there is no definitive case finding a constitutional right of information privacy, the Supreme Court acknowledged that such a privacy right exists in *Whalen* v *Roe*, 429 U.S. 589 (1977) – upholding a state statute that required doctors to disclose information on individuals taking certain highly addictive prescription drugs for inclusion on a state database. 'This information is made available only to a small number of public health officials with a legitimate interest in the information. [Broad] dissemination by state officials of such information, however, would clearly implicate constitutionally protected privacy rights.' *Ibid.*, 606. However, the 'reasonable expectation' standard set out in *U.S.* v *Katz*, initially hailed as the landmark privacy decision, has consistently been used to permit the use of technology to undermine privacy interests. As technology has advanced, and as societal demands for sensitive personal information have increased, the court has increasingly circumscribed the 'zones' one may justifiably consider private. Subsequent decisions have consistently allowed the circumstances of modern existence to define the 'reasonable expectation of privacy.' If an intrusion is technically possible, one's expectation of privacy in certain activities is unreasonable.

33 The lack of strong constitutional privacy protection has placed added emphasis on federal and state statutory protections. Although statutory privacy protections for personal information have been crafted on a sector-by-sector basis, many are based on a common set of principles – the 'Code of Fair Information Principles,' developed by the Department of Health, Educa-

tion and Welfare in 1973, printed in the Report of the Secretary's Advisory Committee on Automated Personal Data Systems, and entitled *Records, Computers and the Rights of Citizens*.

34 Netscape currently uses a pop-up screen to warn individuals about the lack of security of the network prior to allowing them to send a credit card number or other information. The screen prohibits individuals from proceeding until they acknowledge the risk.

35 See www.cdt.org for materials on the 'Internet Online Summit' held in Washington, DC, 1–3 Dec. 1997, where PICS filters and free speech issues were widely discussed, particularly with reference to how to shield children from objectionable material online.

36 Deja News is an example of the profiling capacity made available to anyone on the Internet. Through the use of a search engine it is simple to compile all usenet postings of a single individual. Usenet is a public forum, and the capacity of Deja News to pull together at the stroke of a key an individual's words scattered between, say, 1979 and 1996 in potentially thousands of different Usenet groups provides a glimpse of the type of profiling that is made inexpensive and practical in this medium.

37 http://www.cdt.org/privacy/

38 See the CDT's testimony before the Federal Trade Commission (at www.cdt.org).

39 In addition to the IPWG and P3, TRUSTe is a complementary effort initiated by the Electronic Frontier Foundation to bring the private sector into a licensing structure to establish and adhere to privacy practices online (see www.truste.org).

40 See Margot Williams, 'Usenet Newsgroups Great for Research, but Watch What You Say,' *Washington Post*, 11 March 1996, and 'Public Cyberspace,' *Washington Post*, 14 March 1996, A26; Anne Eisenberg, 'Privacy and Data Collection on the Net,' *Scientific American*, March 1996, 120; Mark Powell, 'Orwellian Snooping,' *USA Today*, 2 April 1996, 13A.

41 Deja News is a service that organizes all Usenet postings into a searchable index by author's name.

42 Cookies is a Netscape feature that assists merchants in tracking users activities at web sites. See Joan E. Rigdon, 'Internet Users Say They'd Rather Not Share Their "Cookies,"' *Wall Street Journal*, 14 Feb. 1996, B6.

43 *McIntyre* v *The Ohio Elections Comm.*, 115 S. Ct 1511 (1995); *NAACP* v *Alabama ex rel. Patterson*, 357 U.S. 449, 463–5 (1958) – reversing a civil contempt judgment against NAACP for failure to turn over a membership list.

44 For example, Rep. Bob Franks (R–NJ) introduced in 1997 the Children's Privacy Protection and Parental Empowerment Act to protect children's privacy.

5

The Promise of Privacy-Enhancing Technologies: Applications in Health Information Networks

ANN CAVOUKIAN

This essay will explore medical privacy, the growth of health information networks, and the need for privacy-enhancing technologies. Increases in the automation of previously paper-based records, combined with the growth in networked communications, will lead to a decrease in the data subject's ability to control the uses of his or her personal information. Privacy-enhancing technologies that serve to anonymize and de-identify personal data will be advanced as one of the leading technological solutions to this problem. This essay begins with a brief review of the legal protections, or lack thereof, pertaining to medical records in Canada and the United States.

In North America, medical records are subject only to the weakest forms of protection. In the United States, video rental records are afforded greater protection through the U.S. Video Privacy Protection Act than medical records,[1] for which no comparable legislation exists. Both in Canada and the United States, a patchwork of provincial or state laws, policies, and procedures, generally lacking in uniformity, inspire little confidence that one's medical records are strongly protected. And yet, that is what most people seem to think – in a 1993 Louis Harris poll, 85 per cent of those sampled believed that protecting medical confidentiality was very important, and 67 per cent thought that strong confidentiality laws were in place.[2] They were wrong. Laws in this area are either non-existent or extremely weak.

Numerous observers from the U.S. Privacy Protection Study Commission in 1977, to the Canadian Krever Commission in 1980, and the U.S. Office of Technology Assessment in 1993 have commented on the lack of protection for privacy in the area of medical records. Both in the United States and in Canada, there are no federal laws for medical privacy, and the small number of state laws that protect medical records vary considerably in their scope and coverage. As Professor Paul Schwartz, a noted expert on privacy legislation, has pointed out: 'The present regulatory scheme in the United States consists of federal law that applies only to data in the control of the government or to certain, specific kinds of health data. The regulatory scheme also includes state measures that create a patchwork of insufficient protection.'[3]

Access to One's Medical Records

In the absence of consistent medical privacy legislation, there are no uniform means by which an individual can access his or her medical records, thereby leaving such decisions in the hands of hospital or health records administrators. Advocacy groups such as the Patients Rights Association report that while one hospital may permit access to your medical chart, another will not; while one department may grant you access, another department within the same facility, will not.[4] Inconsistency in such practices appears to be the norm, not the exception. This violates one of the most fundamental privacy principles in the OECD's *Guidelines Governing the Protection of Privacy and Transborder Flows of Personal Data* [5] (commonly referred to as the 'code of fair information practices'), namely, that the data subject must be given access to his or her personal data – in this case, personal medical records – and must have the ability to correct any inaccuracies. The right of access and correction form the bedrock of fair information practices, but it generally lacks any basis in legislation in the area of medical records.

The absence of consistent medical privacy laws raises a number of privacy-related concerns. Fair information practices require that personal information be collected directly from the data subject and be used only for the purpose identified at the time of the collection. Any secondary uses of that information are prohibited (with limited exceptions) without the consent of the data subject. However, secondary uses of medical information, often obtained from indirect sources, are widely reported: the subsequent disclosure of medical records to a variety of third parties such as insurance companies, health maintenance organizations (HMOs), laboratories, MIB Inc., pharmacies, clinics, and others is said to be quite common. This is the area that poses the most serious threat to medical privacy, and it is greatly exacerbated in the move from paper-based to electronic records and the speedy transmission of electronic records via networked communications, be they through private dedicated networks or public open systems such as the Internet.

Automation of Medical Records

With the automation of medical records and the ease of electronic access via computers and telecommunications networks, the growth in the secondary uses of medical data for purposes not intended at the time of the collection becomes even greater, as does the potential for abuse. The development of massive health information networks will permit the speedy transmission and exchange of medical records, X-rays, computerized axial tomography (CAT) scans, and magnetic resonance imaging (MRI) scans. The considerable benefits of such transmissions must, however, be balanced against the attendant costs. The importance of confidentiality to the quality of health care cannot be overstated. Dr James Todd, a member of the American Medical Association, cautioned that without confidentiality, proper treatment could become jeopardized: 'Without such assurances [of confidentiality], patients may not provide the information necessary to properly diagnose and treat. The evolution of electronic medical records, typified by interstate electronic transmissions and the aggregation of information into large databases that are used for non-treatment purposes, has intensified concerns about patients' confidentiality.'[6]

In commenting on one case involving the secondary use of medical information and unauthorized access to multiple patient records, the president of the Massachusetts chapter of the Coalition for Patient Rights, Dr Denise Nagel, cautioned: 'People are being assured privacy as their medical records are being computerized, and this is a sad example that there is no privacy once records are computerized. Unauthorized access to paper records was always feasible, but the computer takes a small problem and magnifies it enormously.'[7]

Not only do health networks create a greater potential for the secondary uses of medical information, often unbeknownst to the data subject, but with this comes another threat. The risk of transmitting incorrect or inaccurate information, or worse, the possibility of information about one individual being linked incorrectly with that of another, grows dramatically, leading potentially to fatal results. The stakes are much higher when medical records are involved. Therefore, the importance of adhering strictly to fair information practices that emphasize the need for security and place restrictions on the secondary uses of personal information grows ever stronger.

Health Information Networks

Fair information practices alone, however, will not be enough. Take, for example, a community health clinic that follows such practices closely: with the written consent of the patient, the clinic electronically transmits a batch of test results via the Internet to a surgeon at a remote hospital. The disclosure is quite proper, consent has been obtained, and the surgeon has been notified – she is expecting to receive the records and is awaiting their arrival. Once the surgeon has obtained the test results transmitted, she uses them only for the intended purpose, determining a suitable diagnosis. But unbeknownst to the sender or receiver, a 'computer activist,' commonly referred to as a hacker, has intercepted the records along the way. What is worse, he has altered them – making some minor but significant modifications which the surgeon at the receiving end has no means of detecting. Given the remote distance involved, perhaps no one will unearth the error until it is too late.

Without technological protections to complement fair information practices, such occurrences are not outside the realm of possibility. What level of security will be attached to new networks and electronic holdings of medical information? What policies and control mechanisms will be put into place to ensure that they are followed? What are the electronic audit trails to allow one to retrace the path of records gone astray? These safeguards are vital to the protection of medical records, and yet they are seldom addressed.

What is needed is a convergence of these principles with those found in systems design; what is needed are the *design correlates* to fair information practices. The systems design and architecture should translate the essence of these practices into the language of the technology involved. Privacy-enhancing technologies (PET) incorporate many of the protections contemplated by fair information practices. Historically, however, concern for privacy and levels of security have tended to be very weak, with little use made of PET such as encryption or anonymous identifiers.

Although technologies of privacy will not address all the problems associated with misuse of health data, they will go a long way. Even in cases of abuse involving insiders, as opposed to external hackers, technological solutions can be used to create additional barriers to deter both the curious and unscrupulous employee from accessing patient data. Take, for example, a new practice introduced by two hospitals in the United States. The University of Maryland Hospital requires that an additional access code be entered before access to 'VIP' patient data is granted.[8] Staff must answer whether they are directly involved in the care of the patient whose information they are seeking to access. When combined with an audit trail and a policy notifying employees that all attempts to access patient data will be recorded, a powerful deterrent has been created – one that should deter both idle browsers and bribed employees alike.

At the Beth Israel Hospital affiliated with Harvard Medical School, 'famous' patients are permitted to take on pseudonyms instead of having to use their real (identifiable) names. 'To identify patients within the system whose medical information has a higher-than-normal risk of being looked at, the hospital attaches a tag to the names of all public figures, hospital employees, relatives of employees, trustees, relatives of trustees, donors or VIPs.'[9] This hospital has extended the practice beyond VIPs to employees and their relatives, but why stop there? Why not extend the practice to cover the records of *all* patients?

The creation of additional access requirements, audit trails, and the use of pseudonyms or anonymous identifiers will all reduce the incidence of unauthorized access to health data. But even that may not be enough. Encryption is the ultimate defence against both *casual* insiders, who will not be in possession of the keys, and outsiders, who will try to decipher them. In addition, the creation of anonymous databases of sensitive information, linked only by encryption means to the personal identifiers associated with them, removes the need to routinely attach nominal identifiers to the actual records, thus addressing both privacy and security-related issues.

Privacy versus Confidentiality or Security

It may be useful to outline the difference in meaning between privacy and confidentiality or security. These terms are often used interchangeably, but they are not the same. Privacy may subsume what is implied by confidentiality, but it is a much broader concept involving the right to be free from intrusions, the right to remain anonymous, and the right to control the circulation of information about oneself.

Privacy involves the right to control one's personal information and the ability to determine whether and how that information should be obtained and used. The Germans have referred to this as 'a right to informational self-determination': in 1983 the German Constitutional Court ruled that all citizens possessed this right to determine the uses of their information. Most countries with privacy laws have this notion of self-control as one of the goals of their legislation. However, they do not usually have an explicit constitutional guarantee to privacy, as is the case of Germany.[10] It is in this sense that privacy is a much broader concept than confidentiality, because it entails restrictions on a wide range of activities relating to personal information: its collection, retention, use, and disclosure. Confidentiality, however, is only *one* means of protecting personal information, usually in the form of safeguarding the information from unauthorized disclosure to third parties.

Confidentiality only comes into play *after* the information in question has been obtained by a company, organization, or government (commonly referred to as 'data users'). Data users are expected to be responsible for the safekeeping of the personal information entrusted to them. In this sense, they have a custodial obligation to protect the information in their care. Thus, a relationship of trust exists between data subjects and data users, requiring a duty of care and an expectation of confidentiality. The latter involves containment of the personal information to only those permitted access to it and safeguarding it from disclosure to unauthorized third parties. The *means* by which this is achieved involves security.

The full spectrum of data security, computer and network security, physical security, and procedural controls must be deployed to protect personal information from a wide range of threats: inadvertent or unauthorized disclosure; intentional attempts at interception; data loss, destruction, or modification; and attempts to compromise data integrity and reliability. Measures that enhance security enhance privacy: the two are complementary, but not one and the same. Therefore, simply focusing on security is not enough. Security is an essential component of protecting privacy, but it is not sufficient in and of itself. For true privacy protection, fair information practices, complemented by technological solutions such as PET must be adopted.

Building In Privacy Protection

One of the most important principles in fair information practices is the 'use limitation' principle, referring to the limitations that should be placed on the uses of personal information. This requires drawing a clear distinction between the *primary* purpose of the collection and any subsequent or *secondary* uses, unrelated to the primary purpose. In other words, personal information collected for one purpose (paying taxes) should not be used for another purpose (compiling a mailing list of people with incomes over $100,000), without the consent of the individuals involved. Thus, the use of the information should be limited to the primary purpose (tax collection), which was the purpose specified to the data subject at the time of the data collection. This may sound fairly straightforward, but it is seldom put into practice without some mechanism (a privacy law or code of conduct) requiring that such principles be followed.

When systems are not built with privacy in mind, which is generally the norm, one may not be able easily to isolate the primary purpose of the collection (in order to restrict the uses of the information to that purpose alone). In addition, if different types of information have been gathered by the same organization for different purposes, then access should be restricted to those with a *need to know* a particular type of information – not the entire set. This requires the creation of segregated fields of data, with a clear demarcation of who should be permitted access to what fields. Far better, however, would be the anonymization of personally identifiable data through PET.

New and emerging information technologies have led to a massive growth in the quantity of personal information accumulated by organizations. In identifiable form, this trend increasingly jeopardizes the privacy of those whose information is being collected. Minimizing or entirely eliminating identifying data, however, through technologies of privacy, will go a long way to restoring the balance. To the extent that new systems can be designed with anonymity in mind, privacy interests will be advanced enormously.

Why must it be the case that every time you engage in a wide range of activities – using a credit or debit card, making a telephone call, subscribing to a magazine, joining a club, ordering goods from a mail order catalogue, or buying something at a grocery or department store, an identifiable record of each transaction is created and recorded in a database somewhere? To obtain a service or make a purchase (other than with cash or a cash card), organizations require that you identify yourself. This practice is so widespread that it is treated as a given. The time has come to challenge this view. It is now possible for transactions to be conducted anonymously, yet securely, with proper authentication. Emerging technologies of privacy not only make this quite possible, but quite feasible.

Consumer polls repeatedly show that individuals value their privacy and are concerned with potential losses in this area when so much of their personal information is routinely stored in computers, over which they have no control.[11] Anonymity is a key component of maintaining privacy. Protecting one's identity is synonymous with preserving one's ability to remain anonymous. Technologies that provide authentication without divulging identity not only address privacy concerns, but also provide much-needed assurances to organizations regarding the authenticity of the individuals with whom they are doing business.

Privacy-Enhancing Technologies

Two examples of a privacy-enhancing (anonymizing) technology are provided below, each of which relies upon the 'blinding' of identity through the use of encryption – in the first case, through an extension of *public key encryption*, and in the second case, through the use of an *encrypted biometric*.

Blind Signatures

The *blind signature*, created by David Chaum of *Digicash*, is an extension of the digital signature – the electronic equivalent of a handwritten signature.[12] Just as a signature on a document is proof of its authenticity, a digital signature provides the same authentication for electronic transactions. It provides a high level of assurance that only the individual who created the signature could have done so and permits others to verify its authenticity.

Digital signatures are an extension of an *asymmetric cryptosystem* – public key encryption. In a public key system, two different keys are created for each person: one private, one public. The private key is known only to the individual, whereas the public key is made widely available. When an individual encrypts a document with his or her private key, this is the digital equivalent of signing it by hand because the private key is unique to that individual. The intended third party can decrypt the message using the individual's public key, which corresponds to his or her private key. The successful decryption of the information provides the necessary assurance that it could only have been transmitted by that individual, because otherwise it would not have been possible to decode the information using the corresponding public key.

A digital signature provides proof of authenticity that a transaction originated from a particular sender. It also reveals the identity of the individual in the process. The blind signature is an extension of the digital signature but with one additional feature: it ensures the anonymity of the sender. Digital signatures are intended to be identifiable to serve as proof that a particular individual signed a particular document. Blind signatures provide the same authentication but do so in a non-identifiable or 'blind' manner. The recipient is assured of the fact that a transmission is authentic and reliable, without knowing who actually sent it.

One application of blind signatures involves the use of 'E-cash' which can be used as an electronic form of payment that can be transmitted via networks such as the Internet. Just as cash is anonymous, E-cash is also anonymous in that it cannot be traced to a particular individual. Chaum called it 'unconditionally untraceable.' The service provider, however, is assured of its authenticity; the only thing missing is the ability to link the transaction to a particular person. Chaum emphasized that his system also provides much-needed protections against fraud and abuse, but it is predicated on the use of non-identifier-based technology: 'A supermarket checkout scanner capable of recognizing a person's thumb print and debiting the cost of groceries from their savings account is Orwellian at best. In contrast, a smart card that knows its owner's touch and doles out electronic bank notes is both anonymous and safer than cash.'[13]

Encrypted Biometrics

Biometric measures provide irrefutable evidence of one's identity because they offer biological proof that can only be linked to one individual. Biometrics are unique biological characteristics that distinguish one person from another. They include fingerprints, finger scans, voice verification, retinal scans, and hand geometry but the most common biometric measure is the fingerprint. Fingerprints have historically raised concerns over loss of dignity and privacy, through their association with criminality. The central retention of fingerprints and multiple access to them by different arms of government invokes images of Big Brother surveillance.

The introduction of an identifiable fingerprint can act as a powerful unique identifier that can bring together disparate pieces of personal information about an individual. If used as a unique identifier, a fingerprint enables individuals to be pinpointed and tracked. It also creates the potential for personal information from different sources to be linked together to form a detailed personal profile or 'dossier' about an individual, unbeknownst to that individual. Apart from the surveillance this represents, it raises additional concerns that the information may be used out of context to the detriment of the individual and that unjust decisions about the individual may be made simply on the basis of their 'profile.'

It is this accumulation of disparate pieces of information, and the compilation of a fairly detailed picture of a person's life, that contribute to the public's concern that 'someone out there knows something about me.' However, the concerns noted above relate to the use of an *identifiable* fingerprint being used as an instrument of surveillance. The threat to privacy comes not from the positive identification that biometrics provides best, but the ability of others to access this information in identifiable form, linking it to other information. This is achieved through the use of identifiable biometrics. With the application of encryption to biometrics, biometric technology has now evolved to the point where systems can be configured to put the power of the biometric into the hands of the individual as opposed to the government or the police.

Encrypted biometrics, with proper safeguards (as outlined below), can serve to enhance privacy instead of diminish it. But viewing it in this new light will require a paradigm shift of massive proportions. It will require that one take an entirely different perspective – looking at encrypted biometrics as serving the needs of the individual instead of the state. Consider the following new lens through which to view this: Encrypted finger scans (not prints) are being contemplated for use by government administrators (not the police) to make it easier for people eligible for social assistance to receive their benefits quickly (in contrast to the status quo) and to protect their privacy in the process. The use of suitable encryption technology can protect privacy because the encrypted finger scan is not intended to function as a unique identifier. It is only to be used for the purpose of authenticating eligibility for services or benefits. However, only the most privacy-protective encrypted biometric, containing, but not restricted to the following procedural and technical safeguards, will be acceptable.

In the context of encrypted finger scans, these safeguards include:

- Restricting the use of the biometric information to authentification of eligibility only, thereby ensuring that it is not used as an instrument of social control or surveillance.
- Ensuring that a fingerprint cannot be reconstructed from the encrypted finger scan stored in the database.

- Ensuring that a latent fingerprint (that is, picked up from a crime scene) cannot be matched to an encrypted finger scan stored in a database
- Ensuring that an encrypted finger scan cannot itself be used as a unique identifier
- Ensuring that strict controls are in place as to who may access the information and what it is used for
- Requiring the production of a warrant or court order prior to permitting access by external agencies such as the police or other government departments
- Ensuring that benefits data (personal information, for example, history of payments made) is stored separately from personal identifiers such as name or date of birth, etc.[14]

Even more remarkable is the use of a biometric as a tool for encryption: using a finger scan, for example, as the instrument by which information is encrypted. The use of one's finger to encrypt information is called *biometric encryption*. With this technology, one's finger functions as one's private key with which to lock or unlock information. The information encoded by one's finger bears no resemblance to the user's actual fingerprint. No record, template, or copy of the fingerprint is retained on file. Nor can the coded information be converted back to the corresponding print from which it is originated. Designed to confirm user eligibility without divulging identity, its strength lies in using it for comparative purposes. Because this technology precludes the need for a unique identifier, individuals can carry out their business in a 'blind manner.'

Take the example of someone receiving health benefits. The government needs to ensure that only those eligible to receive such benefits actually receive them, thereby minimizing fraud. People who are eligible for health benefits, however, should get what they are entitled to. So what is needed is confirmation of the fact that person A (who we have already determined is eligible for assistance) is in fact person A and not someone impersonating him. Biometric encryption can do that anonymously, without revealing the fact that person A is John Larking. So if A uses his benefits to obtain treatment for a sensitive medical condition, he should be able to do so privately, once his eligibility has been confirmed. No one needs to know that A is your neighbour John Larking who sought treatment for impotence on 23 July. But the insurer does need to be assured that A is eligible to receive the benefits in question and, equally important, that someone *else* cannot impersonate A and claim the same benefits.[15]

Herein lies the paradox of biometrics: a threat to privacy in identifiable form, a protector of privacy in properly encrypted form; a technology of surveillance in identifiable form, a technology of privacy in encrypted form. As noted earlier, reliable forms of encryption can anonymize data and prevent unauthorized third parties from intercepting confidential information. In the case of biometrics, they permit authentication without identification of the user.

Conclusion

In an age of electronic records and networked communications, a coordinated effort will be needed from all sectors to preserve the privacy of medical information. The process of building privacy into information systems and software applications begins by recognizing the distinction between privacy and security. Introducing fair information practices into the process will, of necessity, broaden the scope of data protection, expanding it to cover both privacy and security concerns. The greatest protection, however, will come from *de-identifying* or anonymizing personal information, especially in the context of health information networks.

Both blind signatures and biometric encryption provide for maximum privacy through advanced systems of encryption. Privacy-enhancing technologies such as these should receive the full support of those interested in protecting privacy *and* those interested in eliminating fraud. They achieve the goal of fraud reduction without giving away the individual's identity – or privacy – in the process.

The use of anonymizing, privacy-enhancing technologies such as those described above, which minimize or eliminate personally identifiable information, are ideal in that they serve the needs of *both* individuals and organizations: personal privacy is maintained through the anonymity afforded by such systems, while organizations are assured of the authenticity of the individuals they conduct business with, in their ongoing attempts to combat fraud. Both needs are met, resulting in a true win/win scenario.

NOTES

1 This is a point originally made by Sheri Alpert in 'Smart Cards, Smarter Policy: Medical Records, Privacy and Health Care Reform,' *Hastings Center*

Report 23, no. 6 (1993), 13–23. See also Robert Gellman's essay herein on the attempts to pass medical privacy legislation in the United States.

2 Louis Harris and Alan F. Westin, *Health Information Privacy Survey* (Atlanta: Equifax Inc., 1993).

3 Testimony of Paul Schwartz to the Government Information, Justice and Agriculture Subcommittee of the House Committee on Government Operations, House of Representatives, 103rd Congress, 4 May 1994.

4 Mary Margaret Steckle, Patients Rights Association, *Access to Records Project* (Toronto: Ontario Patients Rights Association, 1994).

5 Organization for Economic Cooperation and Development (OECD), *Guidelines on the Protection of Privacy and Transborder Flows of Personal Data* (Paris: OECD, 1981). The principles of the Guidelines are as follows: collection limitation, data quality, purpose specification, use limitation, security safeguards, openness, individual participation, and accountability.

6 Dr James Todd, as quoted in *Privacy Times* 16/5 (29 Feb. 1996), 5.

7 Evan Hendricks, 'Hospital Records Misused by Massachusetts Obscene Phone-Caller,' *Privacy Times* 15, no. 15, (2 Aug. 1995), 4.

8 Robert Ellis Smith, 'Some Are More Equal than Others,' *Privacy Journal* 22, no. 1, (Nov. 1995).

9 C. Safran, D. Rind, M. Citroen, A.R. Bakker and W.V. Slack, 'Protection of Confidentiality in the Computer-Based Patient Record,' *M.D. Computing* 12, no. 3, (May/June 1995). 187–92.

10 See David H. Flaherty, *Protecting Privacy in Surveillance Societies* (Chapel Hill: University of North Carolina Press, 1989), 46–7.

11 Ann Cavoukian and Don Tapscott, *Who Knows: Safeguarding Your Privacy in a Networked World* (Toronto: Random House, 1996), esp. ch. 7.

12 Warwick Ford and Brian O'Higgins, 'Public-Key Cryptography and Open Systems Interconnection,' *IEEE Communications* (July 1992), 31.

13 David Chaum, 'Achieving Electronic Privacy,' *Scientific American* (Aug. 1992), 101.

14 These issues were considered in the development of a biometric in the Client Identification and Benefits System in the municipality of Metropolitan Toronto. However, it is important to note that the use of encrypted finger scans in this context (Metro Toronto) was for a very defined, narrow purpose (combatting 'double-dipping' fraud) and does not necessarily justify its need in other applications.

15 See the discussion in Cavoukian and Tapscott, *Who Knows*, ch. 10.

6

Personal, Legislative, and Technical Privacy Choices: The Case of Health Privacy Reform in the United States

ROBERT GELLMAN

What kind of mechanisms are appropriate and effective for protecting the privacy of personal information? This is a question that bedevils legislators, policy makers, record keepers, and privacy advocates around the world. While fair information practices provide a widely accepted[1] policy direction, no simple, obvious, or universal answer to privacy concerns is available. For each type of record and record keeper, a different implementation of fair information practices may be possible and suitable.

A key threshold issue, and one that is not always recognized, is who makes which choices. Some decisions appropriately belong to the subject of the record. Other decisions must be made by the record keeper, and some may be imposed by the legislature. Some options are defined or limited by available rapidly changing technology, a reality that makes policy making even harder. Real-world choices must always be made in a context and not abstractly, and the result may not always be what was anticipated.

One familiar example of how choices are framed for record keepers and for consumers comes from direct marketing. It is common to find that record keepers employ a default rule governing secondary use of marketing information. The terminology used is *opt-in* and *opt-out*. *Opt-in* requires the affirmative consent of the record subject before secondary use of personal information. *Opt-out* means that information can be reused unless the record subject has taken action to object. A third alternative that may work best in an online environment is direct consumer choice. Consumers can be required to select between two or more alternatives as a condition of accessing a computer service so that default options no longer need to be defined.[2] Another alternative, used too often today, is no choice. Some marketers use consumer information as they see fit and provide no options at all to consumers. Default rules determine who makes the choice about secondary use of data and what happens without an express selection by the decision maker. The rule employed makes a tremendous difference to the outcome. It is widely believed, in most if not all circumstances, that consumers will accept the default. With an opt-out policy, marketers know that they will be able to use consumer information more freely than with opt-in.

Outside the marketing context, the terminology of default choices arises only occasionally. Yet the same issues may be present with other records and other record keepers. Default choices about information use and disclosure are important because basic principles of fair information practices can usually be implemented in several ways. Ultimately, attention must be paid to who makes the decisions about how choices will be configured and which options will be offered to which participants. This essay explores selected aspects of privacy choices for health records, beginning with the rules governing disclosure.

Personal Choices: Informed Consent and Health Records

One basic option for regulating use and disclosure of a personal record is to require the consent of the record subject. After all, if the individual agrees to the use or disclosure of his or her data, who can object? Yet this option is not as simple as it appears. It is not necessarily clear that the individual will make choices knowledgeably or even in his or her best interest. How an individual is asked for consent, and what he or she is asked to consent to, can make a major difference to the result. The shortcomings of consent can be illustrated using health records in the United States as an example.

In many respects, health records are not representative of all third-party records. Health information is generally acknowledged to be more sensitive than most other personal information maintained by third-party record keepers. The structure of the U.S. health care system differs significantly from other industrialized countries, with many separate institutions playing a major role in the United States. Legal protections for the confidentiality of health records in the United States are sporadic, incomplete, and out of date.[3] Federal laws only cover narrow categories of records (that is, alcohol and drug abuse records[4]) or records maintained by or for federal agencies.[5] For most health records, legal protections can only be found in state laws, and these laws vary considerably in scope, quality, and recency. Partly because of this sensitivity, administrative complexity, and legal uncertainty, informed consent has been generally accepted as a core principle for regulating the disclosure of health records. The medical establishment and others rely on the notion of informed consent, irrespective of the reality or practicality of the choice presented to the individual. Although health records may offer something of a 'worst case' example, they most clearly illustrate the limitations and consequences of informed consent.

In the United States many independent institutions participate in health care treatment and payment, including providers, insurers, and claims processors. Employers provide coverage for many Americans and play a significant financial and administrative role in health care. The analysis becomes even more complex as a result of the merging of once separate functions. For example, health maintenance organizations (HMO) combine the role of provider and insurer in a single entity with a single record-keeping system. Similarly, self-insured employers may be directly responsible for payment and claims processing.

Federal, state, and local agencies serve as providers, insurers, and processors as well, and they also engage in health care oversight activities. Health researchers, public health investigators, cost containers, law enforcement agencies, credit card companies, and others also use identifiable health information in directly or indirectly supporting or overseeing health care functions and institutions. Tertiary users of health information, including the courts, employers, police, and media, only add to demands for disclosure of health information.

One consequence of having so many separate institutions performing separate but related functions is that information about individuals must flow between the institutions to direct and support the different functions.[6] Typically, a physician creates a treatment record and shares it with the patient's designated insurance company for payment. A claims processor is usually the intermediary between the treatment and insurance entities. The same record may be accessed from multiple locations and used in different ways by health researchers, cost containers, and public health authorities. Health database organizations allow different organizations to access centralized, computerized health information.[7] The amount of sharing of identifiable patient information is enormous and largely unregulated.

Few state or federal laws apply to health information maintained by insurers, researchers, public health authorities, auditors, and others in the health care establishment beyond physicians or hospitals.[8] In any event, because health care treatment and payment are largely interstate activities today, state laws cannot provide comprehensive or uniform rules that apply beyond the borders of the state.

Given this welter of institutions and laws, how is the disclosure of individually identifiable health information controlled? The traditional model for the disclosure of patient information is informed consent. At a 1993 House of Representatives hearing on confidentiality of health records, witnesses representing important segments of the health care industry and consumers identified informed consent as the basic device controlling the disclosure of individually identifiable health information.[9] Yet when approached privately, most witnesses acknowledged that informed consent is more of a fiction than a realistic model for control over health records.

For the disclosure of health information, informed consent is rarely either informed or consensual. Most patients have little, if any, ability to refuse to consent to the disclosure of health information to an insurance company paying for their treatment. For most Americans, a third party pays most personal health bills.[10] Few have the financial ability to pay a significant hospital or medical bill without insurance. Nothing is terrible or unreasonable about requiring individuals to agree to disclosure when someone else is paying the bill. This does not mean, however, that agreement to disclosure as a condition of payment is voluntary.

Signing an insurance form with a disclosure authorization is a standard part of a visit to a doctor or hospital. Typically, patients receive consent forms from a clerk or receptionist when they present themselves for treatment. Most patients sign consent forms permitting disclosure of 'any and all' information to their insurance companies. The forms do not limit how insurance companies may use the information nor do the forms identify downstream users or limit the use of information by those users.

Consent forms offer a Hobson's choice, which is to say, no choice at all. The opportunity to refuse or to negotiate changes really does not exist. Most patients do not read the forms or understand what they are signing. Even those who know better routinely sign standard consent forms. I have heard from lawyers, physicians, and ethicists that when their child needs care, they will sign anything. Dr Don Detmer, Professor of Health Policy and Surgery, University of Virginia, observed that a person's view of privacy may differ greatly depending on whether that person is horizontal (ill) or vertical (well).

Under current law and practice, little about the information consent process can be fairly characterized as 'informed.' Patients are rarely told how their information will be used or to whom it will be disclosed. Federal legislative proposals[11] would address this shortcoming by requiring that patients be provided with a notice of information practices. It is not clear, however, how effective these notices might be in actually informing patients or giving them the ability to negotiate the terms of informed consent disclosures. The complex health care information system may be beyond the ability of the average patient – and perhaps even the average lawyer – to control by drafting or revising a consent form.

Another problem with the consent model is the need for many exceptions. Many who use health information obtain access without patient notice or consent. This includes a wide range of health care and other institutions not directly engaged in treatment, such as public health agencies, health researchers, accreditation authorities, auditors, licensing authorities, peer reviewers, cost containers, law enforcement agencies, and others. When a patient is asked to consent – principally for payment – there is little real choice. For many other uses, a patient has no say at all. Many non-consensual disclosures are mandated by law, regulation, or contract. For the most part, therefore, patient consent is little more than a convenient illusion.

Different conclusions can be drawn from this analysis. One is that patients do not care about the privacy of their medical information. Yet public opinion polls show a high level of public concern about privacy for health records. A 1993 public opinion survey conducted by Louis Harris found that significant majorities favoured a legal right of access to their health records; disapproved of use of health records for direct mail, research, or fund-raising; and supported federal legislation to protect the privacy of health records.[12] An alternate conclusion is that patients are acting in their best interest under the current system because it is essential to agree to disclosure to obtain and pay for health care. That may be a higher priority for patients than privacy. Still another conclusion is that the health system has grown too complex for most patients to make effective choices about how health information is used. Whether patients sign consent forms is not a measure of concern about privacy.

The paradox of informed consent is that giving the patient more of a say in the disclosure of health records for payment can result in the patient having less actual control. The current informed consent process protects the interests of everyone except the patient. Consent forms are often written by insurance companies and typically allow broad disclosure and unrestricted use by recipients. Some health or automobile insurance policies make consent to disclosure a condition of coverage. This type of consent is obtained without any effective notice to patients because the requirement appears in the unread fine print of an insurance policy. When consent is obtained concurrently with a visit to a health care provider, the provider who collects the signature also has an interest in broad use and disclosure. The provider wants to be sure that it can make disclosures necessary for payment and other purposes as well, including management, teaching, and research. No one looks out for the interest of patients, and patients cannot protect their own interests effectively.

Even if informed consent were supplemented with legislatively imposed protections, the routine signing of consent forms might still result in the waiver of those protections. For example, assume that legislation restricts non-consensual secondary uses by insurance companies. If a consent form provided by an insurance company waives this restriction, then the intended statutory protections will be unavailable. Of course, legislation can limit the ability of an insurance company to obtain waivers of rights granted under a health records bill. But it may not be possible to foresee and close all loopholes. In any event, if legislation restricts the ability of a patient to vary the terms of a 'consensual' disclosure, the result may be much the same had a non-consensual disclosure policy been in effect. Regulating disclosure and use of health records is a challenging task, whether or not patient consent is routine.

Most current federal or professional health record legislative proposals in the United States continue to rely on informed consent as the central concept.[13] Records are not disclosed without consent, except under specified conditions. Basic disclosures for treatment and payment usually require patient consent.[14] The 1994 House bill introduced by Rep. Gary Condit (D–CA) offered a different approach.[15] The legislation proposed a default rule that disclosures for treatment and payment are non-consensual and defined the terms and conditions for these disclosures in the statute. Those who obtain patient information under the statutory scheme would be fully subject to the statutory rules for maintenance, use, and disclosure of the information.

Patients with specific, additional concerns about payment or treatment disclosures would still be allowed under the Condit bill to arrange with health care providers for more restrictive disclosure practices. The burden of seeking a different restriction on disclosure for payment or treatment would fall on the patient. For example, if a patient did not want an insurance company or employer to know about a particular treatment, then the patient could agree with the physician on a form of payment that would not require disclosure to the insurer or employer. Under the Condit bill, this agreement would be binding on the physician and enforceable by the patient. Similarly, if a patient objected to sharing of information with a particular consulting physician, that objection would also be binding and enforceable.

The goal of the Condit bill was to make the signing of consent forms an unusual event instead of a routine one. The current system asks everyone to sign a consent form when only a small percentage are likely to object. The Condit bill proposed to do away with routine consent forms and require those with special concerns to come forward on their own. In exchange, the bill would have granted stronger protections for all patients than are routinely available today, and the statutory protections could not be waived by the patient. Neither providers nor insurers would have an incentive to obtain consent because patients could not waive the basic legal protections.

If patients learn that the granting of consent is an unusual event, they will learn to be more wary when asked for consent. The current consent system offers patients no cues that agreeing to a disclosure requires careful review. Whether most patients could effectively protect their own interests in health information is an open question. Informed consent for payment is an extension of current practices that offers patients little hope of fair treatment for their health information. Legislation can provide patients better protection than they can negotiate through one-sided, misnamed informed consent agreements.

The 1994 Condit proposal represented a significant break from the traditional approach to informed consent. The notion was well received by many who worked on the bill. Perhaps surprisingly, it did not become a controversial issue during congressional debates in 1994. However, other bills introduced in the following Congress abandoned the Condit approach and returned to the traditional informed consent model. As of this writing, health privacy legislation remains on the congressional agenda, but the timing and substance of the legislation is uncertain. The Health Insurance Portability and Accountability Act of 1996[16] (Kennedy–Kassebaum) establishes a three-year timetable for congressional action on health privacy.

The structuring of default choices for information disclosure is important in other contexts as well. For some records, individuals can and should be allowed a full range of choice for the disclosure of personal information. Yet where a given system of disclosure control fails as a matter of fact to protect the interests that individuals believe to be important, alternatives should be explored. Providing individuals with better information about the consequences of their choices can be an important element of the process. It may not always be sufficient, however, to inform individuals and allow them readily to accept the default choice made by others with different interests. Patients may not be capable of absorbing the information provided and exercising effective judgments. When this is the case – and when the stakes are sufficiently important to warrant it – defaults should be adjusted to recognize shortcomings of individual decision making. Technology may offer more options than have been previously considered. Even if most patients may not be interested in or able to make disclosure choices, some will be vitally interested and fully competent. In the past, uniform and default rules were important because a largely paper-driven system was not readily capable of satisfying individual desires. Treating each patient differently would have been too complex and too expensive. In the future, this may change as computers take over more health care record functions. If properly programmed, computers can record and implement patient disclosure choices with little additional cost or trouble. Records passed from one computer to another can include patient-selected disclosure restrictions that would be impossible to comply with in a paper-based system. It will be a long time until health industry computers are able to provide this degree of personalized control, but it is something that may be worth including as new systems are designed.

Legislative Choices: The Question of an Identification Number

The paradox of informed consent shows the difficulty of regulating disclosures and uses of health information through individual choice and action. A strong case can be made that direct rules in legislation may produce more equitable results in almost all cases than decisions by individuals. This may be less clear for other choices, records, and record keepers. In some areas, however, legislators must make decisions that relate to privacy protections because common technological standards are essential to support the planning and investment necessary to make the standards successful. Of course, technology can be used either to enhance or to undermine privacy interests.

One of the many unresolved health privacy issues in the United States is the identification number to be used for the health system.[17] This is an issue that is fundamental to any health data system, and a choice must bc made legislatively. An increasingly interconnected and computerized health care system will not function efficiently if record subjects and record keepers cannot rely upon a uniform standard for identification.

The leading candidates are the Social Security Number (SSN), a variant of the SSN, and a newly created, but otherwise undefined, health identification number. Many in the health care establishment prefer SSNs, or variants, because the numbers are already in widespread use and because the cost would be lower. Many privacy advocates object to expanding use of SSNs because of the ease of linking health records with other SSN-based records. Public opinion appears to support the industry position. A 1993 public opinion poll found that 67 per cent supported use of the SSN as a health identification number, and 30 per cent wanted a new number.[18]

The 104th Congress (1995–96) did not pass a focused health privacy bill. The broader Health Insurance Portability and Accountability Act of 1996[19] (Kennedy–Kassebaum), which did become law in 1996, addressed the identifier issue but in a curious, unclear, and unsatisfying way. The law requires the Secretary of Health and Human Services to adopt standards for a unique health identifier for each individual.[20] The law provides no specific direction, but it does say that the standards shall specify the purposes for which a unique health identifier may be used.

In this legislation Congress neither directed nor prohibited the use of SSNs. Further, it is not clear from the text of the law whether the term 'unique health identifier' means simply a number that is unique to each individual or a number that is unique to the health care system. Another section of the bill provides a hint, however. Congress included a criminal penalty for a person who knowingly and in violation uses or causes to be used a unique health identifier. Because the SSN is in widespread use throughout the government and the private sector, it is not clear how the secretary could limit use of SSNs for health purposes through standards. It is not impossible, however, and until the secretary makes a decision, the result will not be known. Congress could easily have prohibited the use of the SSN in this legislation, but it did not. Congress may have ducked the choice for many reasons, including the cost of assigning new numbers to individuals and the expense of adjusting existing computer systems.

The choice of an identification number is not an easy one. There are three fundamental realities here. First, many major institutions in the United States play a role in providing, paying for, and overseeing health care. All would routinely have each patient's new health identification number. This includes physicians, hospitals, pharmacies, dentists, labs, claims processors, employers, insurers, public health authorities, nursing homes, government health agencies, and schools. Others likely to acquire or use the number include researchers, health database organizations, credit bureaus, the Internal Revenue Service, and social welfare agencies. In short, a newly issued, modern identification number for health would be widely available to many major government, commercial, and health care institutions. Worse, because many of these institutions currently use SSNs for identification, a service that linked a new health identifier with the SSN would almost certainly be needed.

The second reality is that a high-quality, unique identifier would also be of great value for other activities unrelated to health care. There would be enormous pressure to allow use of the identifier for welfare programs, motor vehicle licensing, debt collection, child support enforcement, immigration control, and other uses. Legislation could, in theory, deny use of a health identifier for these purposes. In practice, however, it is unlikely that the Congress would refuse use of the new number for other politically popular purposes, especially if expanded use of a new identifier would produce cost savings through better identification.

History shows clearly that expanded use of an identification number is likely, if not certain. Originally, the SSN was to be used only for social security purposes and not for identification. In the Privacy Act of 1974, Congress expressly restricted the collection of SSNs by federal, state, and local agencies.[21] Over the years, however, subsequent legislation specifically authorized the use of SSNs for tax, military, welfare, motor vehicle, draft registration, and other purposes.[22] There is every reason to believe that any legislative attempt to restrict maintenance of a health number would fail, either initially or over time. The most recent example is from 1996, when Congress included in an immigration reform bill a requirement that the states collect and display SSNs on drivers' licences.[23]

The argument offered here does not deny any of the concerns raised by privacy advocates over the increased use of SSNs. Many of their concerns are valid. Nevertheless, the cure of a new identifier might be worse than the current disease. A new, unique health identifier would likely become a universal identification number within a few years, supplanting the SSN entirely.

Third, the identifier issue is something of a red herring. An identification number typically reveals little or nothing about an individual. Its importance is that it can be used to link disparate records or records maintained by unrelated record keepers. If linking can be accomplished without a number, then the number loses its significance altogether. Modern computers and database programming offer the prospect of linking records without the need for identification numbers. To be sure, the linking function is simpler with a number. But if the use of numbers were prohibited, it would not take long for record keepers to manage linking with a high degree of accuracy using other identifying information, including non-unique identifiers.[24] The real issue is the linking itself. The debate over the identification number has become a proxy for linking, but it has also grown to be a separate issue with a highly emotional component. This is unfortunate. It accomplishes little to protect an identification number if the linking of records continues in other ways.

Selecting a health identification number is hard because there are no good choices. Each option discussed here has major drawbacks, and new identification technology – such as public key infrastructure, biometric identifiers, or digital signatures – will become widely available in the next few years that will offer even more choices. Resolution of the identification number issue may not matter, however. Debate and discussion should focus less on the number and more on the rules that govern access and use of records. By addressing this harder and more important question, the emotional concerns that attach to the SSN or to another number might be mitigated. If the identification number issue is resolved as part of a comprehensive legislative scheme for health record privacy, the choice of the identification technology ultimately selected may be less important from a privacy perspective. If legislation effectively restricts use, disclosure, and linking of health records, concerns about additional linkage using an identification number may be minimized.

Technical Choices: Encryption and Privacy-Enhancing Technologies

In the search for better ways to protect privacy, expanded use of encryption is sometimes proposed. Encryption clearly has a place, but it is not apparent that it offers a broad or complete response to privacy concerns. Its most obvious application is for protection against eavesdropping, but encryption is also useful for authentication and validation.[25] When personally identifiable data of any type are transmitted through computer and telecommunications facilities, encryption prevents an unauthorized interceptor from using or understanding the data. This is clearly important as more records are computerized and shared over networks. Reports suggest that some health care institutions transmit unencrypted health care information over the Internet, with obvious threats to confidentiality.

However, with health data as with other personal information, misuse is much more likely to come from insiders than from hackers.[26] This has been the case with credit records, criminal history information, telephone toll data, and other personal records.[27] Insiders who are willing to abuse health records will likely have access to the unencrypted data. At best, encryption is responsive to some concerns about misuse of personal information, but not all.

A second shortcoming is that encryption is not directly responsive to data linkage. Encryption can offer the capability of linking data without making identifiers available to the recipient, but this is not an essential element. Encrypted data can still be linked with other data. Encryption does not now offer a complete solution to meeting both the confidentiality interests of patients and the legitimate needs of data linkers. Future developments are likely to increase the value of encryption, however.

The linkage imperative is one of the most important dynamics in the use of health records. Linkage is frequently an element in record keeping about individuals. Health records retain their vitality longer than most personal records. The simplest example of data linkage comes from the treatment process. Over the course of a lifetime, an individual can easily have dozens of providers in multiple locations around the country or the world. Today, those records are linked haphazardly, if at all, and treatment may be less effective or more expensive as a result. As more fully computerized records become routine, one advantage will be the ability to maintain complete, lifetime treatment records for individuals. At the same time, any computer system that can link treatment records will pose threats to privacy in much the same way that a centralized data bank would.

Medical advances are complicating the linkage problem. Health information can remain relevant not only during the lifetime of a patient, but also during the lifetime of the patient's offspring. The increasing body of knowledge about genetics and disease may extend the utility of health records indefinitely. Demands for linkage of records among related individuals and across generations are certain to increase.

Beyond the treatment process, many others use identifiable health records and benefit from the linking of data from multiple sources and over many years.[28] Some health activities expressly create sets of patient data, often designed to be linked for research or evaluation purposes.[29] Many health research projects, cost containment activities, fraud controls, public health functions, and other health endeavours require the linking of identifiable records. Consider, for example, a research project seeking the most effective treatment for a particular disease by looking at patient records. Any patient who sought treatment might have visited a number of physicians. To evaluate fully the alternative treatments provided, all records must be found and linked. The analysis may not require maintenance of identifiers once records have been linked, but this may depend on the nature and time frame of the research.

Similarly, an insurer needs to link payment records over time to make sure that it does not pay for several appendectomies for the same patient. Another example comes from the current movement to increase vaccinations among children. This too is an exercise in data linkage as records from multiple physicians and locations must be available to make sure that each child receives one and only one of each required vaccination.

For research that does not require absolute precision, it may be possible to link records without the use of standard identifiers like the SSN. Some large-scale research results are unaffected even if disparate records cannot be linked with certainty. The New York Statewide Planning and Research Cooperative System (SPARCS) collects information on patient encounters using an identification number composed of non-unique elements.[30] Accuracy is more than 99 per cent but less than 100 per cent. This is adequate for the purposes of the program.

Any technique that permits socially valuable use of health records without identifying individuals to third parties is welcome. Technologically based solutions like encryption can be helpful when available. The federal legislative proposals have been uniformly weak in considering privacy-enhancing technologies. In part, this is understandable because legislation is not especially suitable for mandating specific technological applications of this sort.[31] Record keepers do not need legislation to implement technological protections.

This does not mean, however, that legislation is irrelevant. One 104th Congress health privacy bill (S.1360) envisioned the establishment of a Health Information Service that would be a repository of health data that can be used by others only in a non-identifiable form. This is a step in the direction of meeting the needs for linked health data without providing users with identifiers. However, the privacy implications of a central repository or pointer system are significant, and a central data service can be a threat to privacy as well as a convenient target for activists. In any event, the proposal did not establish such a service. It only authorized record keepers to disclose identifiable data to a qualified repository. This is obviously an area that requires considerably more thought and discussion. Interest in a health data repository waned during the 104th Congress.

Some responses to conflicts between privacy and the need for linked health records may come through privacy-enhancing technologies. Legislation may help to pave the way by supporting research, through direct funding for the technology or by the creation of incentives for record keepers to use privacy-enhancing technologies. However, legislation changes slowly, and technology changes much more quickly. Neither patients nor legislators should play a direct role in detailed decisions about use of encryption in health care. Decisions about using privacy-enhancing technologies to protect health records are best left to those responsible for the records, with statutory standards limited to requiring that reasonable levels of protection – as defined by technologies actually available in the marketplace at a cost-effective price – be maintained.

Conclusion

The widely accepted principles of fair information practices offer basic solutions and approaches to many privacy policy concerns. The code of fair information practices is, however, much too general to expect to find a detailed blueprint for all types of personal records. The code merely offers a list of the issues that must be addressed and suggests a clear but general set of answers. Much more work is required to transform the principles into operating rules for record keepers.

This essay has attempted to focus attention not so much on the substance of a privacy policy but on the identity of the decision makers. For health records in the United States, different decisions are made by different players. Physicians ask patients to make basic decisions about the disclosure of health records, but this may not be a realistic or effective way of protecting patient interests. Other choices, such as selection of a health care identification number, must be made at a much higher level. Selection and application of privacy-enhancing technologies are decisions most likely to be made by record keepers.

In the development and implementation of privacy policies for health and other records, attention should be paid to the manner in which choices are structured and to the level at which these choices are exercised. In at least some instances, these procedural determinations will have a great significance and will make a major difference to the protection of personal privacy interests.

NOTES

1 Colin J. Bennett, *Regulating Privacy: Data Protection and Public Policy in Europe and the United States* (Ithaca, NY: Cornell University Press, 1992).
2 Robert Gellman, 'In Cyberspace, Having a Choice Favors Marketers,' *DM News* 12 (22 Jan. 1996); Center for Democracy and Technology, *Testimony before the Federal Trade Commission Workshop on Consumer Privacy on the Global Information Infrastructure* (4–5 June 1996; available at www.cdt.org/publications/FTC_June96_test.html).
3 See Office of Technology Assessment, *Protecting Privacy in Computerized Medical Information* (Washington, DC: OTA, 1993), 12–13.
4 42 USC ss.290dd-3; 38 USC s.7332 (1994).
5 Privacy Act of 1974, 5 USC s.552a (1994).
6 For a descriptions of the purposes and value of information sharing, see generally Institute of Medicine, *Health Data in the Information Age: Use, Disclosure, and Privacy* (Washington, DC: National Academy Press, 1994).
7 The Health Insurance Portability and Accountability Act of 1996 (Kennedy–Kassebaum) will accelerate electronic sharing by establishing standards for the sharing of health data.
8 See Institute of Medicine, *Health Data in the Information Age*, 136–213.
9 *Health Reform, Health Records, Computers and Confidentiality*, Hearing before the Information, Justice, Transportation, and Agriculture Subcommittee of the House Committee on Government Operations, 103rd Cong., 1st Sess. (1993).
10 The proportion of the population under the age of 65 not covered by private health insurance or by Medicaid was 17.3 per cent in 1993. U.S. Department of Health and Human Services, *Health United States 1994* (Washington, DC: Department of HHS, 1995), 240.
11 In the 105th Congress, two leading bills were HR 52 and HR 1815. In September 1997 the Secretary of Health and Human Services presented legislative recommendations to the Congress as well. See *Confidentiality of Individually-Identifiable Health Information* (available at http://aspe.os.dhhs.gov/admnsimp/pvcrec0.htm).
12 Louis Harris and Associates, *Health Information Privacy Survey* (New York: Louis Harris, 1993).

13 Several model health privacy codes are reprinted in OTA, *Protecting Privacy in Computerized Medical Information*, Appendix B.

14 But see California Confidentiality of Medical Information Act, Cal. Civ. Code s.56 et seq. (1982 & Supp 1996). The California law permits non-consensual disclosures for payment and treatment.

15 The House bill began as HR 4077, 103rd Cong., 1st Sess. (1994). When reported by the House Committee on Government Operations, the bill became part of the Health Security Act, HR 3600, 103rd Cong., 2d Sess. (1994). See House Committee on Government Operations, HR Rep. 103-601 Part 5, 103rd Cong., 2d Sess. (1994) (report to accompany HR 3600). The Condit bill was reintroduced in subsequent sessions of Congress as HR 435 (104th Congress) and HR 52 (105th Congress).

16 Public Law 104-191, 21 Aug. 1996.

17 See OTA, *Protecting Privacy in Computerized Medical Information*, 64–6; Institute of Medicine, *Health Data in the Information Age*, 168–70.

18 Louis Harris, *Health Information Privacy Survey*, 96.

19 Public Law 104-191, 21 Aug. 1996.

20 42 USC 1173(b).

21 5 USC s.552a note (1994). The SSN language was section 7 of Public Law 93–579, but it was not codified.

22 See, e.g., 42 USC s.405(c)(2)(C)(i) (1994).

23 Public Law 104-208, 30 Sept. 1996.

24 National Bureau of Standards, *Accessing Individual Records from Personal Data Files Using Non-Unique Identifiers* (Washington, DC: Department of Commerce, 1977; Special Publication 500-2). See Latanya Sweeney, *Maintaining Patient Confidentiality when Sharing Medical Data Requires a Symbiotic Relationship between Technology and Policy* (May 1997; MIT Artificial Intelligence Laboratory, AI Working Paper AIWP-WP344b).

25 For an example of an application of encryption to health record security, see the discussion of smart cards in OTA, *Protecting Privacy in Computerized Medical Information*, 55–7.

26 See National Research Council, *For the Record: Protecting Electronic Health Information*, 61–2 (Washington, DC: National Academy Press, 1997). For a brief discussion of the documented history of abuse of health records, see House Committee on Government Operations, HR Rep. 103-601 Part 5, 103rd Cong., 2d Sess. (1994), 74–8 (report to accompany HR 3600). For a spectacular and detailed account of abuses of health records in Ontario, Canada, see *Report of the Commission of Inquiry into the Confidentiality of Health Information*, 3 vols. (Toronto: J.C. Thatcher, 1980) (Krever Commission).

27 House Committee on Government Operations, HR Rep. 103-601 Part 5, 103rd
    Cong., 2d Sess. 107 (1994; report to accompany HR 3600).
28 For a discussion of data linkage in the context of health database organiza-
    tions, see generally Institute of Medicine, *Health Data in the Information Age*.
29 See National Committee on Vital and Health Statistics, *Core Health Data Ele-*
    ments (Washington, DC: Department of Health and Human Services, 1996).
    The National Research Council identified twenty-three categories of infor-
    mation collected routinely by state health departments. See NRC, *For the*
    Record, 75–6.
30 The identification number consists of birthday (YYYYMMDD), last four
    digits of the SSN, first two characters of the last name, last two characters of
    the last name, first two characters of the first name, and sex (M/F). Anyone
    with access to a database of names, birth date, and SSNs could easily match
    these identification numbers with individuals.
31 See House Committee on Government Operations, HR Rep. 103-601 Part 5,
    103rd Cong., 2d Sess. 106 (1994; report to accompany HR 3600): 'It is not
    appropriate to specify appropriate security methods in legislation because
    technology is too varied and too dynamic.'

PART III

MARKET CHOICES

7

Managing Privacy Concerns Strategically: The Implications of Fair Information Practices for Marketing in the Twenty-first Century

MARY J. CULNAN AND ROBERT J. BIES

Civilization is the progress toward a society of privacy.

Ayn Rand, *The Fountainhead*

Marketers today are challenged by two converging trends, one competitive and the other technological. First, marketing is undergoing a paradigm shift, fuelled by advances in technology. To survive in the increasingly competitive global economy, companies depend on vast quantities of personal information to create switching costs for current customers and to attract new customers. Mass production and mass merchandising are being replaced by one-to-one marketing and personalized service such as loyalty programs including frequent flier or shopper programs, co-branded credit cards, and advertising messages on customer billing statements which are customized based on the customer's buying patterns.

Second, information technology (IT) continues to increase in capability and to decline in cost, allowing information to be used in ways that were previously impossible or economically unfeasible. As a by-product of each marketing transaction, consumers leave more and more electronic footprints. Companies are able to record the details of any customer transaction at the point-of-sale, to store vast quantities of data in their data warehouses, and to use these data to execute sophisticated marketing programs with a business partner or alone. The richness of the data varies depending on the technology employed at the point-of-sale, ranging from a scanner where customers may not identify themselves and only the date, time, location, and items purchased are recorded, to loyalty programs or credit card purchases where both the customer and the items purchased are identified, to cyberspace where all of the customer's 'mouse tracks' are recorded.[1]

Advances in telecommunications and database technology mean that all these transaction data should be accessible to everyone in the firm with a need for the data. For example, data collected about product returns in Europe can be used by marketers in the United States or by the plant manager in Canada to address changes in customer preferences or potential problems in product design as soon as enough products are returned, and the aggregated data about these returns make the organization aware that a problem may exist. Transaction data signal increased sales or the success of an advertising campaign for a target market segment. Even an absence of sales data where sales were expected serves a signalling function to the firm. Because these individual transactions are in reality 'messages' from customers to the firm that should be distributed as appropriate to functions across the value chain, information systems that process these transactions are in fact organizational information systems.[2] Organizations can gain competitive advantage by collecting and using transaction data effectively.

It is also technology that makes it possible for firms to deal with customers as individuals. Instantaneous access to the customer's history by a customer service representative allows standardized, impersonal encounters with anyone who answers the 800-number to assume the appearance of a personal relationship.[3] Because consumers increasingly demand value and service, the marketing strategies of successful firms are inextricably linked to the use of vast quantities of detailed customer data.

This essay addresses the tensions that arise in today's increasingly electronic world between the collection and use of personal information that people routinely disclose in the course of most consumer transactions and data protection or privacy. Firms have the right to record and use customer transaction data for legitimate business purposes. However, customers are increasingly interested in exercising control over the collection and use of their personal information. The challenge facing marketers, then, is to make consumers comfortable, even enthusiastic, about disclosing large quantities of personal information over the course of their relationship with the firm. This essay will first argue that treating customers' personal information according to a set of fairness principles can balance the competing forces of privacy with the power of information. Second, we will discuss some of the new challenges that the Internet and other electronic environments present to marketers. In concluding, we will discuss our vision of privacy for marketing in the twenty-first century.

Beyond Technology: Emerging Privacy Concerns

Over the past decade privacy concerns have become a focus of a public debate which has at its centre conflict between a firm's need to know and the individual's desire not to be known. Consider the following examples:

- Citicorp POS Information Services abandoned a plan to create a massive database of purchase behaviour for twenty-five to forty million households. Privacy concerns were cited as one reason for the program's failure, as consumers were unwilling to supply demographic information about themselves.[4]
- The Lotus MarketPlace: Households product was expected to revolutionize the mailing list industry by making names, addresses, and demographic data for 120 million U.S. consumers available on CD-ROM. The names and addresses originated in consumer credit reports. Most of the remaining information was inferred or from public records. Public opposition to the product began building after the product's announcement. Prior to its release, Lotus Development Corporation and Equifax, Inc., announced they were canceling the project, citing the 'substantial, unexpected additional costs to address consumer privacy concerns'[5] as a reason.
- American Express announced an agreement with the New York State Attorney General's office, whereby it agreed to inform its customers that it tracked their buying habits and used these data to compile mailing lists that it shared with other companies. Since 1974 American Express has had a long-standing policy of notifying its customers of their right to remove their names from any mailing lists.[6]
- In June 1996 Lexis-Nexis released P-TRAK, an online product for attorneys and other Lexis-Nexis subscribers to use to locate individuals. The file was based on header information from consumer credit reports. When news about P-TRAK spread on the Internet, Lexis-Nexis was flooded with phone calls from concerned individuals asking to have their names removed from the database.[7]

All of these examples share a common theme. That is, they illustrate public concerns about how personal information is used and reflect the fundamental tensions between personal privacy and legitimate business interests.[8]

The use of marketing data as an organizational resource can create either positive or negative outcomes to a company, based on how the information is used. In positive terms, the use of marketing data to yield higher quality products, personalized customer service, and new products that reflect consumer preferences yields benefits for both consumers and the firm. There is also a potential downside to the collection and use of greater amounts of increasingly detailed personal information. Ironically, the same practices that provide value to marketers and their firms' customers also raise privacy concerns. Privacy is the ability of the individual to control the terms under which her or his personal information is acquired and used.[9] Personal information is information identifiable to an individual.

Today's customers leave many electronic footprints detailing their behaviour and preferences; their buying habits are easily profiled and can be readily shared with strangers. Privacy concerns may lead to an unwillingness by customers to disclose personal information, customer defections, bad word of mouth, and difficulty attracting new customers. The growth of the Internet and other online communication systems makes it possible for people to engage in 'electronic retaliation' if they object to a company's practices, by 'flaming' the company directly by electronic mail,[10] or by posting negative public comments to a computer discussion group. As the texts of Internet discussion groups are archived and can be easily searched by keywords, such as product or company name, these negative comments live on long after they are posted.

The failure of firms to use personal information in accordance with social norms for acceptable use may raise two kinds of information privacy concerns if individuals perceive they have lost control over the personal information they have disclosed. First, an individual's privacy may be invaded if unauthorized access is gained to personal information as a result of a security breach or an absence of appropriate internal controls. Second, because computerized information may be readily duplicated and shared, there is the risk of secondary use, that is, information provided for one purpose is reused for an unrelated purpose without the individual's knowledge or consent. Secondary use includes sharing personal information with others who were not a party to the original transaction or the merging of transaction and demographic or psychographic data to create a computerized profile of an individual by the organization that originally collected the information.[11]

Research suggests that, in general, individuals are less likely to perceive information practices as privacy invasive when (a) the information is collected in the context of an existing relationship, (b) they perceive that they have the ability to control future use of the information, (c) the information collected or used is relevant to the transaction, and (d) they believe the information will be used to draw reliable and valid inferences about them.[12]

In their dealings with organizations, individuals may first question an organization's motives when they are asked to provide personal information, particularly when the information is perceived as irrelevant to the transaction at hand. The 1990 Equifax survey reported that 90 per cent of those surveyed felt that being asked to provide excessively personal information was a problem. Forty-two per cent refused to provide information to a company because they thought that the information was not needed or was too personal, and 30 per cent had decided not to apply for something because they did not want to provide certain kinds of personal information.[13]

Even if the principle of minimization – collecting only necessary information – applies when individuals are asked to provide information, other problems can emerge during the processing, storage, and use of personal information. These can include both deliberate or accidental errors, unauthorized or improper use, or secondary use – reuse without the individuals' knowledge or consent,[14] which are also illustrated by some of the examples provided earlier in this chapter. The 1990 Equifax survey found that 93 per cent of those surveyed believe inaccuracy and mistakes were problems for consumers, and 82 per cent believed the sharing of information by companies in the same industry was a problem.[15]

Managing Privacy through Procedural Fairness

Privacy exists when an individual can make autonomous decisions without outside interference and/or can control the release and subsequent circulation of personal information.[16] People often perceive a loss of privacy when their autonomy or control appear to be lost or reduced[17] or when their actions are unknowingly structured.[18] Underlying any definition of privacy is an implicit understanding that the individual's interests are balanced with those of society at large.

Prior research on privacy found that individuals are willing to disclose personal information in exchange for some economic or social benefit subject to the 'privacy calculus,' an assessment that their personal information will subsequently be used fairly.[19] The self-disclosure literature has focused on interpersonal relationships rather than customer relationships between individuals and firms; nevertheless, its findings are consistent regarding a balancing test. People disclose personal information to gain the benefits of a close relationship; the benefits of disclosure are balanced with an assessment of the risks of disclosure.[20]

Creating a willingness in individuals to disclose personal information, then, requires that the marketers also view the provision of personal information as a 'social contract' with their firm, where the customer makes non-monetary exchanges of personal information in return for intangible benefits.[21] Customers will continue to participate in this social contract as long as the perceived benefits exceed the risks. The literature on customer service has not specifically addressed privacy. It has, however, established a link between being treated fairly and customer satisfaction.[22] Berry found that consumers see fairness and service quality as 'inseparable issues' – because customer perceptions drive service quality, a service that is perceived as being unfair will also be perceived as being lower in quality.[23] Conversely, the perception of fair treatment of consumers has been shown to be positively related to higher levels of satisfaction in services.[24] Fairness is inherent in the consumer's basic need for justice. A violation of this need, such as violating a psychological contract, will result in angry and disloyal consumers. Heskett, Sasser, and Hart noted that 'many differences attached to the value of a service by customers are explained by the level of risk perceived by the customer ... and the degree to which such risks can be minimized by the service provider.'[25]

How Fairness Promotes Disclosure and Trust

Trust is central to the success of all interpersonal and organizational relationships, ranging from interpersonal relationships[26] to global trading relationships.[27] Trust has been the focus of researchers from a wide range of disciplines such as political science, psychology, sociology, economics, and organizational behaviour. In an organizational context, including marketing relationships, trust is built through social exchanges and reciprocity and is shaped by the relational context.[28]

Trust reflects a willingness by the consumer to assume the risks of disclosure.[29] Developing information practices that address this perceived risk results in positive experiences with a firm over time, increasing the customer's perceptions that the firm can be trusted. Trust creates switching costs, increasing the likelihood that the consumer will continue in the relationship with the firm.[30]

The literature on justice found that procedural fairness is important to individuals in assessing actual and potential outcomes. Procedural fairness refers to the perception by the individual that a particular activity in which he or she is a participant is conducted fairly. Factors that contribute to perceptions of procedural fairness include providing the consumer with a voice in how his or her personal information will be used and control over actual outcomes.[31]

For privacy, fair information practices operationalize procedural fairness. Similar to the cases with fair trade and labour, fair information practices define procedural guarantees that allow individuals to balance their privacy interests with the organization's need to gather personal information to support its marketing programs.[32] Fair information practices provide individuals with control over the disclosure and subsequent use of their personal information. They are global standards for the ethical use of personal information and are at the heart of U.S. privacy laws, the privacy directive adopted by the European Union in July 1995, and the Clinton Administration' guidelines, which were adopted in June 1995, for use of personal information by all National Information Infrastructure participants.

At the core of fair information practices are two concepts: knowledge and consent. These two concepts are reflected in the following principles. When they provide personal information, people have the right to know (a) why the information is being collected, (b) its expected uses, (c) the steps that will be taken to protect confidentiality, integrity, and quality of the information, (d) the consequences of providing or withholding the information, and (e) any means of redress available to the individual who is the subject of the information. People also have the right to control how their personal information will subsequently be used. They have the right to object to uses of their personal information when information will be collected for one purpose and used for other purposes. Fair information practices also state that personal information should not be used in ways that are incompatible with the individual's understanding of how it will be used unless there is a compelling public interest for such use.[33]

Fair information practices send a signal to the customer that the firm can be trusted with the personal information disclosed by the customer.[34] This signalling function is particularly important in consumer marketing relationships which are typically characterized by social distance; customers must depend on strangers to represent their interests.[35]

Fair information practices, therefore, mediate the privacy concerns raised by disclosure and subsequent use of personal information by empowering the individual with control and voice, *even if people do not choose to invoke the procedures,* as well as an assurance that the firm will adhere to a set of principles that most customers find acceptable.[36] For example, even if outcomes are not favourable to an individual, individuals are less likely to be dissatisfied with unfavourable outcomes if they believe that the procedures used to derive those outcomes are fair.[37] Fair information practices, then, make the 'deal' with the consumer fair.

In marketing, for example, a central element of fair information practices is the ability of individuals to remove their names from mailing lists. The 1990 Equifax survey found the majority of its respondents believed it is acceptable for direct marketers to use names and address on a mailing list if people who do not want to receive mail offers are able to withhold or remove their names from the mailing list. Culnan found that people who were aware of name removal procedures had a lower concern for privacy than those who were not aware of these procedures, suggesting that awareness of fairness procedures can address the privacy concerns associated with disclosure and use of personal information.[38]

Fairness of procedures and fairness of outcomes interact. There are certainly practices that cross the line in terms of acceptable use. However, when consumers are informed about subsequent uses of their personal information and provided an opportunity to exercise control over these uses, firms gain additional degrees of freedom for the reuse of customer information internally as well as making the information available for prospecting by third parties. For example, Culnan and Armstrong found that when fair information practices were observed, privacy concerns no longer distinguished individuals who were willing versus those who were *not* willing to have personal information gathered from their use of an online service used for profiling.[39]

Procedural fairness also influences the degree of trust in exchange relationships.[40] Trust is the willingness of one party, here a customer, to be vulnerable to the actions of another party, here a firm, based on an expectation that the firm will perform a particular action of importance to the customer, independent of the customer's ability to monitor or control the firm.[41] Procedural fairness communicates information about the firm's integrity and motivation to act in a trustworthy fashion. Positive or fair outcomes enhance the customer's perceptions of the firm's trustworthiness.

Figure 7.1 illustrates the organizational view of information use and fairness and how procedural fairness and trust interact over the life of a customer relationship. Prior to disclosing personal information, the customer assesses whether the benefits of disclosure exceed the risks. If the customer proceeds in the relationship, the firm collects, stores, and uses the information the customer has disclosed. Subsequently, the customer assesses these uses based on outcomes he or she experienced and decides whether or not to continue in the relationship based on these outcomes. If individuals continue in the relationship, each positive interaction with the firm builds trust and increases the likelihood that the consumer will continue in the relationship. Procedural fairness is shown as a 'privacy leverage point' that provides an intervention opportunity for the firm to build trust with its customers by sending a signal about its practices and to therefore make customers willing to disclose personal information by minimizing the risks of disclosure to the individual, particularly at the beginning of the relationship.

Fairness in Prospecting

The discussion to this point has focused primarily on customer relationships. For firms to grow they not only need to retain their current customers, but they also need to attract new customers through prospecting. Typically, one firm's prospects are another firm's customers, and prospecting is enabled by the sharing of customer names and addresses. Consumers' names are typically acquired because these individuals have already identified themselves in the course of a marketing transaction, say, by making a purchase, requesting information by mail or phone, or in filling out a survey.

Fair information practices make prospecting for new customers fair if individuals are aware that their names and addresses will be shared with other organizations, that these lists may be segmented based on other information individuals have disclosed, and that individuals can easily remove their names from these lists before they are transferred. These principles work well in the current world where prospective customers are typically recruited by mail or by phone. The norms that currently balance the power of information with privacy for mail and telemarketing may be crudely summarized from the firm's perspective as, 'If you don't opt out, we will come to you.' Fair information practices

FIGURE 7.1　An organizational perspective on fairness and privacy.

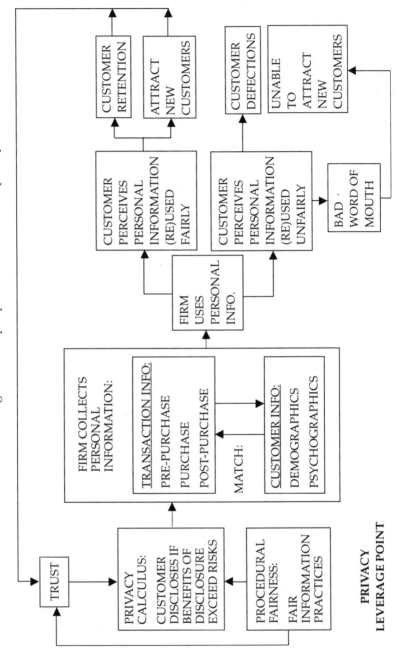

balance the competing interests of firms and consumers who do not wish to receive unsolicited commercial offers because responsible firms disclose how they will reuse personal information and invite the consumer to opt out of the mailing list before it is transferred. However, as will be shown in a later section of this essay, new norms will be needed to maintain these competing interests as marketing moves into cyberspace.

Implementing Fair Procedures: Creating a Culture of Privacy

As the discussion so far has shown, fairness can address consumer privacy concerns and reinforce perceptions that the firm is trustworthy, thereby making customers willing to disclose personal information to the firm. To gain the benefits that access to personal information provide to the firm, the firm needs to operationalize the fairness concepts – fair information practices – already described. Technology potentially makes customer data highly accessible throughout the organization and enables decentralized decision making. If fair information practices are not embedded in the work practices of all employees, there is a risk that a customer service or marketing representative may allow personal information to be used in a way that is at odds with the customers' norms for acceptable use, resulting in a customer, media, or regulatory backlash. For example, an employee of a large database company allowed a television reporter using a personal credit card and posing under the name of a well-known pedophile to acquire a list of children living in a California suburb. The transaction violated company policies; nonetheless, it resulted in negative publicity for the firm.

Creating a 'culture of privacy' within the organization involves more than creating a privacy policy: A senior manager needs to champion privacy. Employees need to be trained and retrained. Periodic audits should be conducted to ensure that practices conform to policy: Privacy should be made part of the business case for all new uses of personal information. In the course of evaluating the business case, decision makers need to ensure that the proposed application is consistent with what customers have been told about how their personal information will be used, that the individuals will not be harmed by any new use, and that customers have had a legitimate opportunity to 'opt out' if their information is to be shared with other organizations.

There is some evidence that not all U.S. marketers have assimilated this message.[42] The Equifax surveys consistently found that the majority of consumers believe they have lost all control over how their personal information is used by business. The 1990 Equifax survey found that a minority of corporations want to pioneer in adopting corporate policies that provide new privacy protections.[43] Smith studied how seven different organizations in four industries responded to growing public concerns about privacy.[44] He observed a three-phase cycle of response: drift, external threat, and reaction. Rather than address privacy issues proactively, these firms delegated responsibility for privacy to lower-level managers. New policies were developed only in response to an external threat or crisis.

There are a number of reasons that might explain why business does not appear to see that managing privacy concerns strategically is good for business and can also avoid such unwanted consequences as negative media coverage or new regulation or legislation. Privacy has yet to affect the bottom line: customers continue to participate in marketing programs without suffering any negative consequences, and there has not been a widely publicized privacy 'market failure' that has required the government to intervene. Osterhus argued that influencing consumer purchasing strategies through the use of 'pro-social consumer influence strategies' (such as the use of environmental or privacy claims) is a highly complex matter. Consumer decisions are affected by a number of factors such as norms of responsibility, economic preferences, and the extent to which the consumer trusts the firm.[45]

Marketing in Cyberspace

As marketing moves onto the Internet or other online services, it creates enhanced opportunities to gather personal information to support marketing programs and new challenges to firms to make the information-gathering process fair. Marketing in cyberspace differs from more traditional forms of marketing in terms of the quantity of information that can be gathered from consumers. In traditional marketing, the firm begins to collect information when consumers choose to 'raise their hands' by initiating a transaction with the firm as shown in Figure 7.1. These transactions could include purchases where the customers identify themselves, as well as interactions with the firm before the sale such as requesting a catalogue or other product information, or after the sale if the customer returns or exchanges a product, complains, or seeks additional information. Any browsing that precedes consumers initiating an interaction with the firm remains private, and a firm that sends mail to a prospective customer has no way of knowing whether its promotional materials are read by the consumer.

In cyberspace browsing becomes a point-of-sale transaction. Not only is the firm able to record traditional interactions with their customers, but because online systems provide the capability to record consumers' 'mouse tracks,' marketers are also able to record how consumers move through their web sites and to build profiles based on what formerly was a passive, private activity. This practice of tracking the browsing behaviour of individuals as they 'surf' the pages of various web sites without disclosing to the consumer how their information will be used and offering the individual a chance to decline the invitation to hear from the firm in the future is considered controversial by many because it does not reflect fair information practices. For example, the 1996 Equifax/Harris privacy survey found that less than one-third of the respondents believed that the providers of online services should be able to track the places users go on the Internet in order to send these users targeted marketing offers.[46] Nearly half of the respondents (48 per cent) felt they should be able to use the Internet without disclosing their identity.[47] Because young children are also online users, there is particular concern about the reuse of personal information disclosed by children about themselves and their families without parental approval.[48]

A second practice that has been labelled as controversial is harvesting E-mail addresses from public spaces on the Internet and generating lists for sending individuals unsolicited E-mail without first gaining the consent of these individuals. However, a new marketing paradigm is emerging on the Internet which says, 'We the customer come to you unless we have given you permission to contact us,' meaning firms should seek explicit consent from individuals, even their customers, before sending them unsolicited communications. Online technology makes it cost-effective for firms to seek this consent.

Recent survey data suggest that marketers wishing to take full advantage of the information-gathering capabilities of cyberspace need to establish a fair social contract with consumers. For example, a recent Georgia Tech Internet Survey found that of some 15,000 respondents only a small minority always register with a web site when asked. The most widely cited reason for not registering was that the terms and conditions of how the collected information was to be used was not clearly specified (70.15 per cent). Lack of trust in the collecting site was cited by 62 per cent of the respondents as a reason for not registering.[49] These results suggest that procedural fairness will be critical to building the trust needed to sustain successful marketing programs in cyberspace.

Because the Internet has no geographic boundaries, Internet market-ers face the additional challenge that consumer perceptions of accept-able behaviour are likely to vary across cultures.[50] In many parts of the world national privacy laws reflect fair information practices. The Euro-pean Community Directive is based on fair information practices. New norms of acceptable practice for marketing globally will need to evolve. Fairness and trust should continue to serve as the basis for this new gen-eration of new marketing relationships.

Conclusion: A Privacy Vision of Marketing for the Twenty-first Century

A marketer's vision of privacy is that consumers will be enthusiastic about disclosing all of their personal information to the marketer. As this essay has demonstrated, however, marketers will realize their vision only if they earn the trust of consumers. Marketers can earn con-sumer trust through procedural fairness: by saying what they do and by doing what they say. Marketers need to send a signal that they can be trusted by disclosing the rules that govern their practices when consum-ers first become their customers and then ensuring that their practices remain consistent with these rules over the life of each customer's rela-tionship with the firm. Therefore, it is in the bottom-line interest of mar-keters to observe fair information practices because fairness can help firms both attract and retain customers.[51]

Our vision of privacy for the next century is that all firms will begin to compete on their privacy practices and that market-based privacy solu-tions will become the norm: This means that marketers will see the com-petitive benefits of incorporating procedural fairness in their marketing strategies. As the Equifax surveys have shown, people vary in terms of their sensitivity to privacy. This means that privacy can serve as a seg-mentation variable; marketers can develop practices to attract the more privacy-sensitive consumers away from their competitors. For example, the Center for Democracy and Technology's web site has a table com-paring the privacy policies of the four largest online service providers (America Online, Compuserve, Prodigy, and Microsoft Network).[52] Consumers can assess the privacy policies of each service and choose the one that best reflects their privacy preferences.

Technology has the potential to address some of the new privacy challenges in cyberspace. For example, one proposal will give consumers control over the disclosure of their personal profiles to web sites; another technical solution negotiates privacy preferences between the consumer's web browser and the web site. For the latter case, the consumer sets his or her preferences for the use of personal information. Any attempt to visit a web site with lower privacy standards results in a warning message. The clear trend for Internet privacy is the need for greater individual responsibility.[53] Nonetheless, technology is no substitute for the basics of clear notice and meaningful opportunities for consumers to exercise control over the subsequent use of their personal information.

Lacking in the current environment of self-regulation is accountability. The Georgia Tech survey described previously found that consumers do not trust the majority of web sites and that this lack of trust is a barrier to disclosure. European countries have incorporated fair information practices for marketing into their national laws as well as into the EC directive. Canada has adopted a privacy standard that firms can adopt voluntarily and be certified as adhering to its principles.[54] In the United States there currently appears to be limited enthusiasm on the part of industry for either new laws or standards, nor are consumers yet voting for privacy with their wallets.[55] Yet, against the backdrop of little or no accountability, consumers expect their privacy to be protected.[56] It is an expectation as simple and fundamental as that. This expectation of privacy is also consistent with the norms of society.[57]

The opposing forces surrounding the privacy issue highlight the broader political and social implications. Privacy issues are political in the sense that there is the question of what is the proper balance of individual and business interests in the gathering and disclosure of consumers' personal information. Determining what is the proper balance of interests is not a straightforward rational process; for the balancing of interests is not only shaped by the push and pull of negotiation by managers internal to the organization, but also by court cases and legislative mandates in the larger political–legal environment. In the end, it may be the Internet that brings the vision of privacy to marketing in the United States. Because the Internet knows no national boundaries, marketers who want to do business globally on the Internet will need to respect the data protection laws of other countries and the privacy preferences of the consumers it wishes to serve.

Finally, and in a more fundamental social sense, the concern for privacy follows from the assumption that the individual has an 'inviolate personality ... [and] the individual's independence, dignity and integrity' is violated when his or her privacy is invaded.[58] Human dignity represents a radical criterion to judge the strategic processes and outcomes of organizations. However, for those of us theorists and researchers who adopt human dignity as a core assumption of management theory, our role is that of a social critic: on the margin, not in the mainstream, motivated by what Beaney called a 'never-ending quest to increase the respect of all ... for the essential values of human life.'[59]

NOTES

1 Mary J. Culnan and Pamela K. Armstrong, 'Information Privacy Concerns, Procedural Fairness and Impersonal Trust: An Empirical Investigation,' *Organization Science* (in press).
2 Mary J. Culnan, 'Processing Unstructured Organizational Transactions: Mail Handling in the U.S. Senate,' *Organization Science* 3, no. 1 (1992), 117–37.
3 Barbara A. Gutek, *The Dynamics of Service* (San Francisco: Jossey-Bass, 1995).
4 L. Jafee, 'Citicorp POS Inc. Phasing Out Supermarket Scanner Database,' *DM News*, 26 Oct. 1992, 61.
5 Mary J. Culnan and H. Jeff Smith, 'Lotus MarketPlace: Households – Managing Information Privacy Concerns,' in *Computers and Social Values*, D.C. Johnson and H. Nissenbaum, eds. (Englewood Cliffs, NJ: Prentice-Hall, 1995), 269–78.
6 A.B. Crenshaw, 'Credit Card Holders to Be Warned of Lists,' *Washington Post*, 14 May 1992, D11.
7 Elizabeth Corcoran and John Schwartz, 'On-Line Databases Draw Privacy Protests,' *Washington Post*, 20 Sept. 1996, A1.
8 Mary J. Culnan, H.J. Smith, and Robert J. Bies, 'Law, Privacy and Organizations: The Corporate Obsession to Know Versus the Individual Right Not to Be Known,' in *The Legalistic Organization*, S.B. Sitkin and R.J. Bies, eds. Thousand Oaks: Sage, 1994), 190–211.
9 Alan F. Westin, *Privacy and Freedom* (New York: Atheneum, 1967).
10 Robert J. Bies and Thomas M. Tripp, 'Beyond Distrust: "Getting Even" and the Need for Revenge,' in *Trust in Organizations: Frontiers of Theory and Research*, R.M. Kramer and T.R. Tyler, eds. (Thousand Oaks, CA: Sage, 1996), 246–60.
11 Mary J. Culnan, '"How Did They Get My Name?": An Exploratory Investigation of Consumer Attitudes toward Secondary Information Use,' *MIS Quarterly* 17, no. 3 (1993), 341–64; Cathy Godwin, 'Privacy: Recognition of a Consumer Right,' *Journal of Public Policy and Marketing* 10, no. 1 (Spring 1991), 149–66; Ellen R. Foxman and P. Kilcoyne, 'Information Technology, Market-

ing Practice, and Consumer Privacy,' *Journal of Public Policy and Marketing* 10, no. 1 (Spring 1993), 106–19; H. Jeff Smith, Sandra J. Milberg, and Sandra J. Burke, 'Information Privacy: Measuring Individuals' Concerns about Organizational Practices,' *MIS Quarterly* 20, no. 2 (June 1996), 167–96.

12 Robert J. Bies, 'Privacy and Procedural Justice in Organizations,' *Social Justice Research* 6, no 1 (1993), 69–86; Bies, 'Beyond the Hidden Self: Psychological and Ethical Aspects of Privacy in Organizations,' in *Codes of Conduct: Behavioral Research and Business Ethics*, D.M. Messick and A.G. Tenbrunsel, eds. (New York: Russell Sage Foundation, 1996), 104–16; Culnan, 'How Did They Get My Name?' Eugene F. Stone and Dianna L. Stone, 'Privacy in Organizations: Theoretical Issues, Research Findings, and Protection Mechanisms,' in K.M. Rowland and G.R. Ferris, eds. *Research in Personnel and Human Resources Management*, vol. 8 (Greenwich, CT: JAI Press, 1990), 249–411.

13 Louis Harris and Associates, *Equifax Survey on Consumer Privacy* (Atlanta: Equifax Inc., 1990).

14 Mary J. Culnan and Priscilla M. Regan, 'Privacy Issues and the Creation of Campaign Mailing Lists,' *The Information Society* 11, no 2 (1995), 85–100.

15 Harris, *Equifax Survey on Consumer Privacy.*

16 Colin J. Bennett, *Regulating Privacy: Data Protection and Public Policy in Europe and the United States* (Ithaca, NY: Cornell University Press, 1992); Stone and Stone, 'Privacy in Organizations'; Westin, *Privacy and Freedom.*

17 R.S. Laufer and M. Wolfe, 'Privacy as a Concept and a Social Issue: A Multidimensional Developmental Theory,' *Journal of Social Issues* 33, no. 3 (1977), 22–42.

18 Spiros Simitis, 'Reviewing Privacy in an Information Society,' *University of Pennsylvania Law Review* 135 (1987), 707–46.

19 Laufer and Wolfe, 'Privacy as a Concept and a Social Issue'; George R. Milne and Mary Ellen Gordon, 'Direct Mail Privacy-Efficiency Trade-offs within an Implied Social Contract Framework,' *Journal of Public Policy and Marketing* 12, no 2 (Fall 1993), 206–15; Stone and Stone, 'Privacy in Organizations.'

20 Valerian J. Derlega, Sandra Metts, Sandra Petronio, and Stephen T. Margulis, *Self-Disclosure* (Newbury Park, CA: Sage, 1993).

21 Milne and Gordon, 'Direct Mail Privacy-Efficiency Trade-offs.'

22 Benjamin Schneider and David E. Bowen, *Winning the Service Game* (Boston: Harvard Business School Press, 1995).

23 Leonard L. Berry, *On Great Service: A Framework for Action* (New York: Free Press, 1995).

24 Schneider and Bowen, *Winning the Service Game.*

25 J.L. Heskett, W.E. Sasser, and C.W.L Hart, *Service Breakthroughs: Changing the Rules of the Game* (New York: Free Press, 1990).

26 Derlega et al., *Self-Disclosure*.

27 Francis Fukuyama, *Trust* (New York: Free Press, 1995).

28 See Roy J. Lewicki and Barbara Benedict Bunker, 'Developing and Maintaining Trust in Work Relationships,' in Kramer and Tyler, *Trust in Organizations*, 114–39; Daniel J. McAllister, 'Affect- and Cognition-Based Trust as Foundations for Interpersonal Cooperation in Organizations,' *Academy of Management Journal* 38 (1995), 24–59.

29 Roger C. Mayer, James H. Davis, and F. David Schoorman, 'An Integrative Model of Organizational Trust,' *Academy of Management Review* 20, no. 3 (1995), 709–34.

30 Gregory T. Gundlach and Patrick E. Murphy, 'Ethical and Legal Foundations of Relational Marketing Exchanges,' *Journal of Marketing* 57 (Oct. 1993), 35–46.

31 Robert Folger and Jerald Greenberg, 'Procedural Justice: An Interpretive Analysis of Personnel Systems,' in Kendrith M. Rowland and Gerald R. Ferris, *Research in Personnel and Human Resources Management*, vol. 3 (Greenwich, CT: JAI Press, 1985), 141–83; E. Allan Lind and Tom R. Tyler, *The Social Psychology of Procedural Justice* (New York: Plenum, 1988).

32 Bennett, *Regulating Privacy*.

33 U.S. Information Infrastructure Task Force (IITF), *Privacy and the National Information Infrastructure: Principles for Providing and Using Personal Information* (Washington, DC: Department of Commerce, 1995).

34 A. Michael Spence, *Market Signaling: Informational Transfer in Hiring and Related Screening Processes* (Cambridge: Harvard University Press, 1974).

35 Culnan and Armstrong, 'Information Privacy Concerns.'

36 Robert Folger and Robert J. Bies, 'Managerial Responsibilities and Procedural Justice,' *Employee Responsibilities and Rights Journal* 2, no. 2 (1989), 79–90; Folger and Greenberg, 'Procedural Justice'; Stone and Stone, 'Privacy in Organizations'; 249–411; Jerald Greenberg, 'A Taxonomy of Organizational Justice Theories,' *Academy of Management Review* 12, no. 1 (1987), 9–22; Lind and Tyler, *Social Psychology of Procedural Justice*; Mayer et al., 'Integrative Model of Organizational Trust.'

37 Lind and Tyler, *Social Psychology of Procedural Justice*; Greenberg, 'Taxonomy of Organizational Justice Theories'; Folger and Bies, 'Managerial Responsibilities and Procedural Justice.'

38 Mary J. Culnan, 'Consumer Awareness of Name Removal Procedures: Implications for Direct Marketing,' *Journal of Direct Marketing* 9, no. 2 (1995), 10–19.

39 Culnan and Armstrong, 'Information Privacy Concerns.'

40 Joel Brockner and Phyllis Siegel, 'Understanding the Interaction between Procedural and Distributive Justice: The Role of Trust,' in Kramer and Tyler, *Trust in Organizations*, 390–413.

41 Mayer et al., 'An Integrative Model of Organizational Trust.'
42 Paul M. Schwartz and Joel R. Reidenberg, *Data Privacy Law* (Charlottesville: Michie, 1996).
43 Harris, *Equifax Survey on Consumer Privacy.*
44 H. Jeff Smith, *Managing Privacy: Information Technology and Corporate America* (Chapel Hill: University of North Carolina Press, 1994).
45 Thomas L. Osterhus, 'Pro-Social Consumer Influence Strategies: When and How Do They Work?' *Journal of Marketing* 61, no. 4 (1997), 16–29.
46 Harris, *Equifax Survey on Consumer Privacy.*
47 Ibid, 1996.
48 U.S. Federal Trade Commission (FTC), *Staff Report: Public Workshop on Consumer Privacy on the Global Information Infrastructure* (Washington, DC: Federal Trade Commission Bureau of Consumer Protection, 1996).
49 Georgia Tech Research Corporation, *Sixth WWW User Survey* (URL: http://www.cc.gatech.edu/gvu/user_surveys).
50 S.J. Milberg, S.J. Burke, H.J. Smith, and E.A. Kallman, 'Values, Personal Information Privacy, and Regulatory Approaches,' *Communications of the ACM*, 38, no. 12 (1996), 65–74.
51 Culnan and Armstrong, 'Information Privacy Concerns.'
52 Center for Democracy and Technology (URL: http://www.cdt.org).
53 Mary J. Culnan, 'What Is Plain to See ... There Are Ways to Protect Personal Data on the "Net,"' *Washington Post Outlook*, 13 July 1997, 3.
54 Colin J. Bennett, 'Adequate Data Protection by the Year 2000: The Prospects for Privacy in Canada,' *International Review of Law, Computers and Technology* 11, no. 1 (1997), 79–92.
55 Priscilla M. Regan, *Legislating Privacy.* (Chapel Hill: University of North Carolina Press, 1995); and see Regan's essay in this book.
56 Culnan et al., 'Law, Privacy and Organizations.'
57 Bies, 'Beyond the Hidden Self.'
58 Edward J. Bloustein, 'Privacy as an Aspect of Human Dignity: An Answer to Dean Prosser,' *New York University Law Review* (1964), 962–1007; Culnan and Regan, 'Privacy Issues and the Creation of Campaign Mailing Lists.'
59 W.M. Beaney, 'The Right to Privacy and American Law,' *Law and Contemporary Problems* 31 (1966), 253–71.

8

Towards Property Rights in Personal Data

JAMES RULE AND LAWRENCE HUNTER

Roughly a generation has passed since the original acknowledgment of privacy protection as a legitimate issue for public concern. This interval offers a good vantage for reflection. We privacy advocates might fruitfully ask ourselves, are the essential values of privacy better protected now than they were then?

Many privacy watchers would no doubt want to give a positive response to this question. They would point to the array of legal and policy safeguards enacted in the past decades for treatment of personal data – and to the many institutions that have been created to make these strictures work. Throughout the Western democracies, misuse of personal data has come to be officially defined – at least for public consumption – as a wrong. Various forms of recourse are provided to those suffering such wrongs, ranging from litigation, as favoured in the United States, to the sorts of direct intervention by privacy protection officials afforded in other countries. Surely, it would be held, the evolution of these protections gives assurance that the privacy abuses of yesteryear are now under check.

Other commentators, ourselves included, take a less sanguine view. By almost any standard, the sheer scope of appropriation and use of personal data has grown vastly over the past generation. Some forms of such appropriation, it is true, are now subject to a measure of control by the individual. But against such cases, one has to reckon the enormous growth in uncontrolled commercialization of personal data, that is, the sale and trade of personal information as a tool for shaping commercial dealings with the persons concerned. These dealings include direct marketing, allocation of consumer credit, selling and administration of medical insurance, and reporting on applicants for jobs and housing. In the

Unitcd States, at least, there is very little the individual can do to resist appropriation of personal data for such purposes. Information generated in dealings with retailers – or one's bank, one's physician, or pharmacist, or in any number of other settings – is apt to be transformed into a commodity for sale by information industries.

Thus, a generation's perspective yields an ironic juxtaposition: More formal legislation and policy aimed at protecting privacy, yet at the same time, apparently, more unchecked appropriation of personal data. How are we to explain why, in so many contexts, privacy interests have steadily been losing ground over the past thirty or so years? Perhaps one explanation is the difficulty that privacy advocates have in propounding simple, yet forceful principles to implement their views. Privacy is, after all, one of those 'essentially contested' values – bound always to remain in tension with other legitimate social interests. In their efforts to give all considerations their due, many commentators have been reduced to bland pronouncements about 'balancing' privacy interests with other concerns, without much in the way of a formula for assessing the relative 'weight' of the values to be 'balanced' in this way. As this on-the-one-hand-and-on-the-other-hand discussion continues, the unrestricted appropriation of personal data grows apace.

A New Right

In the face of such ambiguity, serious privacy advocates might well yearn for an unambiguous, universal principle for privacy protection – something that everyone could grasp, like the notion of habeas corpus. About the closest one comes to such principles in the real world are sweeping declarations of general 'rights of privacy,' as in Article 1 of the California State Constitution: 'All people are by nature free and independent and have inalienable rights. Among these are enjoying and defending life and liberty, acquiring, possessing, and protecting property, and pursuing and obtaining safety, happiness and privacy.'

It is of course salutary that the state of California officially ascribes to privacy an importance comparable to that accorded to the other fundamental rights noted here. But it would be a mistake to imagine that this 'inalienable right' necessarily prevails in situations where it is contested. There are simply too many contexts where, from almost anyone's viewpoint, interests in personal information other than those of the individual data subject deserve recognition. If governments are expected to tax income or commerce, for example, citizens can hardly expect absolute control over information about their personal finances. If physicians, lawyers, or accountants expect to be licensed or otherwise certified to the public trust, they must expect to yield to scrutiny over their records of competence and ethical conduct. If children are to be protected from those who would prey on them, institutions charged with their care must be able to make inquiries into the backgrounds of those they hire. In countless settings like these, almost no one would claim that individuals' privacy interests are the only values that require consideration. Thus, it is difficult to frame any categorical 'right to privacy.'

Yet we believe that creation of one such delimited right has great promise as a tool – just one legal tool, we stress, among many – for protecting personal data. *We propose creating a property right over commercial exploitation of personal information.* This right would pertain to the sale or trade of personal data for use in selling products or services or in setting the terms of commercial dealings with the people described in the data. Under the right we envisage, every citizen would own the rights over such forms of commercial exploitation of information about himself or herself. These rights could be exercised or ignored by the data subject; they could also be retained or sold, much like mineral rights, development rights, or air rights. In envisaging such a right, we join Kenneth Laudon and other privacy specialists who have sought to apply property concepts to the protection of personal data.[1]

The essential principle would be simplicity itself: No information could legally be sold or traded from any personal data file, for any commercial purpose, without express permission from the person concerned. Subject to this stricture would be the release of personal data from credit card companies, medical care providers, periodical subscription lists, mail order houses and other retail establishments, and any other source. All these forms of release – rampant today in the United States, and incipient elsewhere – would be illegal without evidence of permission from the data subject.

Such a right would constitute no obstacle to any organization's maintenance of any records of personal data collected from clients and customers. From American Express to the corner drug store, organizations would remain free to request and compile data from the persons they deal with. What the new right would constrain, however, is release of such information. Such release, for any commercial purpose, could only occur with the express permission of the data subject. The organization holding the data would have legal responsibility for determining that any release accorded with the instructions given by the data subject.

We have little doubt that most North Americans, and for that matter citizens of other consumer societies, would welcome the options afforded by such a right. Some, we imagine, might withhold permission for any and all commercial uses of their data; others would be happy to grant blanket permission for its appropriation, thus effectively regularizing the situation prevailing in the United States today. But a majority, we suspect, would want to permit release, but only for certain purposes and under certain conditions. And most of these people, we imagine, would want to insist on sharing in the considerable revenues generated in the commercialization of these data, that is, they would want to insist on something akin to royalties in exchange for release. The option of imposing such a condition is implicit in the right we propose.

Some readers may consider it a utopian scheme to envisage according individuals any meaningful control over the countless instances where data about themselves are commercialized. The notion of charging royalties on sale or trade of personal data – to mass marketers, credit or insurance reporting firms, retailers, or the like – may appear even more so. How could the vast welter of transactions, each worth perhaps only a small amount, possibly be charted, controlled, or compensated? In fact, the same technological and organizational innovations that have fostered mass commercialization of personal data provide ready mechanisms for implementing this right.

Establishment of the new rights and prerogatives envisaged here, we are convinced, would trigger far-reaching changes in the economics of personal information. Qualitatively new institutions would be brought into existence, as forums for the assertion of the new rights. Various authors have speculated about what forms such institutions might take. Kenneth Laudon, for example, has envisaged creation of what he calls a National Information Market, which would be 'the only legal avenue for the transfer of information about individuals being used for secondary purposes'; such a market would be self-supporting, he wrote whereby; 'a transfer tax ... [would be] charged and the revenue used to support the market's infrastructure, enforcement of rules, and monitoring activities.'[2]

Similarly, Hagel and Rayport have contemplated the rise of informational intermediaries between private citizens and would-be users of their data. These 'informediaries' would themselves be private-sector companies that would specialize in channelling the flow of personal information between the parties. They would connect 'information supply with information demand ... by helping both parties involved determine the value of that information, informediaries would be building a new kind of information supply chain.'[3]

To us, the form that seems most promising for such mediating institutions is that of what we would call data rights agencies. This new kind of enterprise would seek to enroll large numbers of clients, on the promise of collecting royalties for commercial use of their data. Much as the American Society of Composers, Authors and Publishers (ASCAP) and Broadcast Music, Inc. (BMI) represent writers of music, collecting royalties for its public performance, data rights agencies would raise revenues by collecting royalties for each approved release of personal data for commercial purposes. They would also be responsible for recording and implementing data subjects' wishes as to the purposes for which data could be released.

Could such organizations possibly cope with the vast traffic in such transactions? Could they really expect to determine whether all their clients' wishes as to the disposition of their data were being respected? How could instructions as to the desires of the data subjects realistically be communicated to those wishing to release personal data?

Here a simple principle would apply: In the absence of clearly expressed wishes, the 'default condition' would be *no release*. Lacking explicit instructions to the contrary, no person or organization – from the largest credit reporting agency to the local doctor's office – could legally sell or trade anyone else's data for commercial purposes. Note that the very existence of such a principle would by itself block all sorts of privacy abuses. Where permission for release were granted, it could take many forms. These could range from a signed statement on record with the organization holding the data, to blanket instructions held on file by a data rights agency. For most people who intended to permit release in significant numbers of cases, the latter would probably be the more appealing option. But again, how would the organization holding personal information learn the instructions of the data subject?

Perhaps the simplest convention for such determinations would involve a unique number that could be provided by any private individual who wishes to authorize release under any circumstances. This number would identify the individual and the agency authorized to represent him or her. The same number could also contain coded instructions on the forms or purposes of release authorized by the data subject and the fee required by the individual for release.

The organization holding the data would be strictly responsible for releasing data only in accordance with the data subject's instructions, however those might be expressed. Note that any royalties involved would be payable by the organization releasing the information, but presumably borne by the organization acquiring it. In other words, no holding organization would release any such data, unless the fees paid to it covered the required royalties. The fact that such releases normally take place en masse, and that agencies would normally represent large numbers of clients, would make the economics of implementing the new property rights quite attractive.

Consider, for example, releases for purposes of direct mail solicitation – just one form of commercialization that would be governed by this right. According to Direct Marketing Association figures, about thirty-eight billion pieces of direct mail were sent to consumers in 1996, which is an average of about 376 pieces of junk mail per year per household.[4] Of course, this is a highly aggregated figure, and many households are likely to receive substantially more or less mail. Each one of these mailings represents the effect of at least one release of personal data files from an organization.

Suppose that the consumer imposed a royalty of ten cents on all these releases. Assuming total expenditures would remain about the same, one could reasonably estimate a reduction of about 20 per cent in direct mail volume, leaving the average consumer with about 300 pieces of junk mail per year, and a royalty of $30 (of which the data rights agency might take $3). Since according to the DMA, total spending on telemarketing is roughly similar to that on direct mail, we can make a similar estimate for information releases for telemarketing purposes, doubling the total estimated annual payment for an average consumer to about $54. These estimates suggest that the potential commissions to all data rights agencies would total about $600 million per year.[5]

The agencies, that is, the organizations representing the interests of individual data subjects, would find it attractive to monitor all sorts of releases of personal data to make sure that no disclosure occurred that was not consistent with individuals' instructions. They would be attuned to the state of markets for data rights and would be quick to advise their clients when it appeared that the market would bear higher royalty fees. They would presumably, in their own enlightened interests, become entrenched advocates of privacy protection. Agencies would compete with one another to attract clients, both in terms of commissions charged to clients and services offered them. Economies of scale would be vast, such that entry into the industry would probably require a client base of at least fifty thousand. But the size of the total market would encourage considerable specialization among agencies.

Thus, we can readily imagine the data rights marketplace evolving so that some agencies serve more affluent clients and others the less prosperous. From all indications, commercial demand for personal data is greater, the more affluent the people whose lives are documented; accordingly, agencies representing more prosperous clients would normally seek higher royalties for them. In other cases, some clients might wish to trade off the royalties they demand against finer control over the release of data. People might stipulate that their data could be released for compensation, but only to non-profit organizations, or only to organizations meeting certain standards of social or ecological responsibility, or never to organizations that engage in telephone soliciting. Agencies willing to enforce such exacting discriminations presumably would charge higher commissions for doing so.

The Benefits of the Right

We believe that establishing a right of this kind would enhance the classic interests of privacy protection in a variety of direct and indirect ways. The first, and most basic gain would be in the realm of civic culture. Instatement of the principle proposed here would immediately make it plain to every citizen how much he or she shared an interest in the protection of personal information. Most people, we think, would greatly value the right to control commercialization of such information. Do we all not find something intuitively compelling about the notion that, having yielded our data for one purpose, we should not expect those data to be reused without our knowledge or permission? At least one American public opinion study has shown wide public assent for the idea that companies ought to pay for the commercial use of private citizens' data.[6] Securing a right of this kind would constitute a significant political victory for the privacy protection movement in the eyes of the general public. Our movement could use such victories.

If a right like this were established, it should then be far easier for anyone to determine when and where information about himself or herself were circulating. Indeed, we would favour making disclosure on these matters mandatory for anyone using personal data for commercial purposes. Those responsible for any mass mailing, any unsolicited phone call, indeed, any commercial use of personal information whose release is envisaged here ought to be responsible for stating the origin of such information and the circumstances under which the right to use it was obtained. Because no commercial release would be legal without direct or indirect permission, no one engaged in the commercial use of personal data should have any difficulty in offering such an account. In this way, the plaintive complaint, 'Where did you get my name?,' heard so frequently from ordinary American citizens, would be voiced more assertively.

In terms of power relationships between data-using institutions and ordinary citizens, the effect of instituting such a right would be extremely salutary. Organizations that now routinely release personal information without permission or compensation for commercial purposes, ranging from hospitals and pharmacies to charitable organizations, direct mail firms, and socially conscious publications, would have to change their ways. Either they would have to make their treatment of personal data acceptable to the persons concerned, or the permission necessary for such release would not be forthcoming.

One way of making such release acceptable, we have posited, would be by offering royalties. The immediate result of charging such royalties would be a decrease in the quantity of unsolicited appeals and an increase in their quality. If those selling their goods and services to targeted audiences faced higher costs for their activities, they would surely be more selective in going about them. To be sure, not all commercial release of personal data is aimed at advertising. Much personal information is sold or traded to enable organizations to discriminate in their dealings with the people it describes. This is the purpose of collecting medical data for use by prospective insurers, or the compiling of data on consumers' past credit accounts for resale to prospective future creditors. The point of the exercise in cases like these is to enable some organization, normally the buyer of a credit or insurance report, to avoid doing business with unprofitable customers and to set profitable terms for those whose business is sought.

Here, too, the right we propose would help generate a new balance of power, fostering tensions of an entirely desirable sort between individuals and credit and insurance reporting companies. Both sides in these relationships would have to consider carefully the value that they attribute to the transmission of the data involved. In some cases, we believe, ordinary citizens would make entirely rational decisions to stop the flow entirely. Imagine, for example, a consumer put off by a credit bureau's collection of information on her retail accounts or unable to resolve a dispute with the credit bureau over her records. Under the right that we propose, she could choose simply to veto the release of further data to credit bureaus or to stop the current bureau from selling further reports. The bureau might then have the right to report that the record was sealed at the consumer's request, but no more.

Of course, consumers would have to weigh the consequences of their decisions. Foregoing the benefits of having a credit record would mean accepting that some creditors would either decline to do business with an applicant or would insist on higher fees or interest rates for doing so. Providers of credit would obviously have to draw their own conclusions about the absence of an available credit report and weigh the terms that they offered customers accordingly. But we note that credit transactions do take place on such bases. It is common, for example, for mortgages to be offered on a 'no credit check' basis – at higher interest rates than those offered applicants willing to be investigated. Here, as elsewhere, we think that securing the right of data subjects to 'just say no' to release of their data would create incentives for the organizations concerned to make their activities as acceptable as possible.

We have no illusions that establishing the principle we have in mind would automatically create a 'level playing field' in every relationship between ordinary citizens and data-consuming commercial organizations. In some cases, individuals are in no position to refuse any demand for their data, so long as the existence and whereabouts of those data are known. This would be the case, for example, where someone applies for a mortgage and is asked to authorize release of personal data from accounts with public utilities, for example, for electrical or telephone service. Because nearly everyone has accounts of this kind, claims that such data are unavailable would be prima facie suspect. Faced with the possibility of losing the opportunity for a mortgage or a credit card, many consumers would feel that they had little alternative but to authorize release of any data whose existence could be identified. But where would-be consumers of personal data could not know in advance of the existence of data, the right we propose would make it easy to ensure that data were never released.

In this connection, we would think it reasonable to establish legal safeguards against certain categories of overweening demands that people renounce control over their data. We think it would be reasonable to mandate, for example, that no one be refused medical care, simply because he or she refuses to permit the eventual transfer of information emanating from that care for commercial purposes. Thus, a clinic doing HIV testing would have no right to insist on releasing the results of tests, or even on acknowledging the fact that a test had taken place, as a condition for carrying out such tests.

Some Potential Objections

Most privacy advocates, we find, are intrigued by the notion of a right like this. At the same time, some are concerned about any innovation that might appear to facilitate or condone commercialization of personal data. In its extreme form, this attitude pictures establishment of property rights of the kind proposed here as tantamount to an invitation to auction privacy interests to the highest bidder.

These reactions reflect a superficial take on what we propose. The first thing to note about the right envisaged here is that its establishment would leave no American worse off with respect to appropriation of his or her data than is the case today. It is not our intention to extend the possibility of commercial appropriation of personal information to any setting where it does not now exist. Instead, we aim to create a simple, forceful principle to check the endless erosion of control over such data to commercial interests where no such checks are now in place. It is undoubtedly true that some forms of personal data should never be commercially marketed – data on children, for example. This proposal leaves the matter open as to what those data should be; our purpose here is simply to fashion tools for protecting those forms of data that are deemed legal for commercial use.

In strictly political terms, we see no gain for privacy advocates from opposing uses of personal information that are in fact welcomed by the people concerned. Indeed, the idea of legal strictures categorically forbidding the release of personal data for mass marketing strikes us as politically disastrous, given that some citizens apparently actually enjoy the unsolicited communications that result. The privacy protection movement will do best if it can develop policies that both enable citizens to release personal data when it lies in their interest to do so, and to block such release when they prefer. We need measures to grant meaningful control over one's personal data, enhancing rather than removing individual discretion in this respect.

For some privacy activists, such insistences may not suffice. 'Privacy is a fundamental human right,' one critic noted, 'and is not subject to sale.'[7] The person quoted here went on to point out that not all forms of personal contracts are legal in the Western legal and political tradition. One may not legally sell one's self into slavery, for example, or exchange sex for money.

But the analogy of these cases to privacy protection does not withstand examination. Preserving the right of freedom of expression, or the right to not testify against one's self, does not require that everyone speak out on public issues or that no accused person ever take the stand on his or her own behalf. These important rights, like so many others, serve to preserve for individuals the option to make meaningful choices – the option to express one's opinion or no opinion, or to decide to testify on one's own behalf, or not to do so. So, too, with the treatment of personal information. Privacy advocates, and civil libertarians more generally, ought to seek principles and arrangements aimed at providing every citizen maximum meaningful discretion over his or her data. This means the right to disclose, as well as the right to withhold.

One further objection to our proposal could perhaps only be seriously put forward in the United States. It emanates most predictably from the vast industries – from direct marketing to credit and insurance reporting – that now appropriate personal data, their main 'raw material,' for nothing. Spokespersons for these industries have typically insisted that unfettered release of personal data represents a form of freedom of expression and hence that it is protected under the U.S. Bill of Rights.

It may be difficult for those from other national traditions to follow this quaint chain of reasoning. What, after all, has the right of private citizens to express themselves on public issues in common with the right of corporations to appropriate personal data on such citizens without their knowledge or consent? We are happy to note that the U.S. courts have been sceptical of this argument. Rights to commercial expression – in advertising, for example – have generally received less protection than freedom of expression in its classic sense.[8]

Some Qualifications

Nevertheless, any right like the one proposed here needs to be carefully circumscribed, so that it does not vitiate certain uses of personal data that deserve protection. Thus, we stress that our proposal here applies only to sale or trade of personal information for commercial purposes. Such a right would have no bearing, for example, on release of personal information for purposes of public debate or deliberation. It would not block journalists' practices of paying for 'tips' on the private conduct of public figures, for example. Property in personal data would apply only to its use as a tool for commercial dealings.

Even within the category of commercialized data, some distinctions need to be made. We think it reasonable, for example, that the holder of a debt be able to sell that debt to a third party, which could be a collection agency. What the logic of our plan would proscribe is the unauthorized sale or trade of information on accounts, without sale of the debt itself.

There are other cases that would require special qualification, as well. In certain situations we can see little justification in making it possible for individuals to censor specific items of information, as against categories of data. If consumers could review their credit records and withdraw permission selectively and retrospectively for release of all negative information, after all, the remaining data could obviously be rendered largely meaningless. But we see no reason why consumers should not enjoy the option of vetoing disclosure of broad categories of information in credit reporting, for example, all retail account information or all information on marital history. Users of such reports might then have the right to know that such an option has been exercised; they would naturally draw their own conclusions about the reasons for the missing data and guide their dealings with the subject of the report accordingly.

Beyond these distinctions, critics raise various other issues that need to be taken seriously. What if the sale of data on one person generates, by implication, identifiable personal information on someone else? If a HIV-positive patient releases information on his status, does this release not in fact amount to a disclosure of risk to the patient's spouse or other known sexual partners? Should the partner then have the right to veto the disclosure? We would say not. As we conceive it, the right outlined here would apply only to release of data linked by name or other individual identifier (like a social security number) to a single person. That person alone should have the unique right to approve or decline disclosure.

Another key practical issue, for example, is that of how long permission for release of personal data, once given, should remain in force. Obviously, people ought to be able to change their minds about the disposition of their data, for example, if they come to judge that access to a specific record has become a source of dissatisfaction. But where data rights agencies act on behalf of the individuals, such agencies could find it difficult to modify instantly the instructions on which they act. Perhaps there should be a standard contractual period, say, six months, in which one set of instructions for the release of particular forms of information ought to apply. Once such a period had lapsed, the default condition – no release permitted for any commercial purpose – would prevail, until the data subject entered new instructions.

This is not the place to take up all such legitimate practical questions. Let us simply say that we regard such issues as important and soluble. Certainly there will be borderline cases, for example, as to what constitutes a commercial purpose for release. But in comparison with other conflicts of legal principle involving individual rights – freedom of expression versus libel or slander, for example – we think the right proposed here is relatively amenable to specification.

Conclusion

Privacy advocates cannot expect their efforts to be blessed by the propounding of an equivalent of habeas corpus. Privacy values will always, quite properly, be qualified in practice by a host of other claims on personal information. But this fact should not stop us from seeking the most broadly applicable and, most politically appealing and defensible measures available to protect privacy interests.

We feel that we have identified an opening for one such measure. Creation of the property right we propose would work broadly to protect a principle held essential by nearly every privacy advocate – that the individual ought not to lose control over his or her data, once having confided it to a specific party for a specific purpose. This goal has been elusive, to say the least, in the more than a generation since the first privacy controversies.

Let us stress that the measure we propose here could never represent a panacea for legal and policy dilemmas associated with privacy protection. Many important questions are simply beyond the purview of our proposal; for example, the crucial matter of what forms of personal data ought to be subject to collection by state and private organizations in the first place. But where data are provided, for any purpose, the question remains of what can be done to protect them from subsequent misuse. The idea that people ought to 'own' their own data, for commercial purposes, is one tool that offers great promise in addressing such dilemmas.

NOTES

1 Kenneth Laudon, 'Markets and Privacy,' *Communications of the ACM* 39, no. 9 (Sept. 1996), 92–104.
2 Ibid., 100.
3 John Hagel III and Jeffrey F. Rayport, 'The Coming Battle for Customer Information,' *Harvard Business Review* 75, no. 1 (Jan.–Feb. 1997), 60.

4 Direct Marketing Association, *Statistical Fact Book* (Washington, DC: DMA, 1996), 313.
5 Direct Marketing Association, 'Economic Impact: Direct Marketing Today' (Washington, DC: DMA, 1997; available at http://www.the-dma.org/home pages/observatory/hgome-obsimpact.html).
6 A Time/CNN poll carried out 23 Oct. 1991 asked a representative sample of Americans, 'Do you think companies that sell such information to others should be required by law to ask permission from individual citizens before making that information available? Some 93 per cent of those polled responded affirmatively.
7 Robert Gellman, personal communication, 11 Nov. 1996; in the statement given here, Gellman was quoting an unnamed European privacy specialist.
8 See Scott Shorr, 'Personal Information Contracts: How to Protect Privacy without Violating the First Amendment,' *Cornell Law Review* 80 (1995), 1795–1811.

9

The 'Quebec Model' of Data Protection: A Compromise between *Laissez-faire* and Public Control in a Technological Era

RENÉ LAPERRIÈRE

Privacy protection in Quebec is the object of general statements of principles applicable to all persons, physical or corporate, in the Charter of Rights and Freedoms of the Person and the Civil Code. The legislature adopted in 1982 a piece of legislation applying to the public sector both favouring access to information and protection of privacy. In 1993 an Act Respecting the Protection of Personal Information in the Private Sector was also unanimously adopted. Because of its originality in North America, it is worth giving here a few indications on its content and implementation.

The private sector legislation applies to all private persons, corporations, and associations. It sets rules on the collection and disclosure of personal data, which must be carried out with the knowledge and consent of the data subject or by authorization of the law. On these counts, general principles are enunciated, but they are weakened by a vague terminology and plagued by multiple exceptions in favour of public and private police and inspectors, debt collection agencies, and general permission given to update or verify information. Commercial or charitable marketing and mailing lists fall under a special 'opting out' regime, and the law establishes liability of firms for personal data exported by way of transborder data flows. Credit bureaus are regulated by a distinct section of the act: essentially they must register with the Commission d'accès à l'information (CAI), update their information, and facilitate access by publishing codes of fair practices.

Data subjects are given general rights of access to their files and correction of errors: these rights are also the object of lesser exceptions. The regime is monitored and administered by an autonomous specialized body, the CAI, the same as for the public sector, which can decide quasi-judicially on requests for access or correction and which may hold investigations and issue orders of compliance with the law: there lies an appeal of its decisions to the Quebec Court on questions of law. The legislation is generally considered viable by the CAI and the private firms, even by those who protested it most energetically before its adoption. But the evaluation of its specific contribution to the protection of privacy and the containment of a surveillance society is highly debatable.

In June 1993 the Quebec National Assembly unanimously approved the Act Respecting the Protection of Personal Information in the Private Sector.[1] In so doing it added a significant block to the building of privacy protection in Quebec. The act was the culmination of seven years of scholarly studies, administrative reports, parliamentary commissions, private lobbying, and public pressure to take the benefits of the legal principles until then applying only to the public sector and extend them to the private sector. The subject of privacy had, in fact, been the object of nearly twenty years of legal activity, from the affirmation of a right to privacy in the Quebec Charter of Human Rights and Freedoms[2] to its explicit codification in the new Civil Code of Quebec.[3]

The Act Respecting Access to Documents Held by Public Bodies and the Protection of Personal Information[4] was adopted in 1982 to protect personal data held by public bodies from the general rule of access to public information stated in the same act. Both access and privacy would be overseen by the same agency, the Commission d'accès à l'information (CAI). A significant loophole of this law, and all existing laws in North America, was that it did not cover the private sector. The Quebec government ordered a survey to evaluate the extent of personal data possessed by and circulating in the private sector and the legal rules applying to such data. The report of the Groupe de Recherche Informatique et Droit (GRID), published in 1986 under the title *L'Identité Piratée*, demonstrated that the private sector still held and exchanged more data on Quebec citizens than did the public sector. This was especially true of financial data. Furthermore, protection fell far short of international standards as defined by OECD and the European convention on the subject.[5] It would take seven more years of administrative pondering and parliamentary discussion before a bill was finally adopted, probably influenced by the argument that Quebec would find an advantage in aligning itself on the new European Union directive – then in its final stage of discussion in Brussels.

Every five years since 1982 the CAI has proposed an assessment of its actions and an analysis of the relevance of the act as applied to the public sector. The first evaluation on the implementation of the private sector act was published in 1997. The secretary general of the CAI, André Ouimet, synthesized the Quebec model of privacy legislation at the Visions for Privacy Conference in Victoria,[6] and its president, Paul-André Comeau, offered his thoughts on the impacts on privacy of new technological developments and gadgets, recommending a commonsensical approach in preventing abuse and monitoring compliance.[7]

Keeping in mind the general themes of this book, this essay first analyses a new phenomenon, that of surveillance by design, and examines how it reflects technological imperatives. It then asks how the Quebec model answers the specific problems arising from these surveillance practices and considers the validity of legislative models in challenging the development and operation of surveillance technologies. In concluding, I propose my own vision for more global reflections and tentative solutions in the larger perspective of ensuring privacy in the coming century.

Surveillance by Design?

Much has been said and written about 'surveillance,' 'technology,' and 'privacy,' and the essays in this volume by Gary Marx, John Westwood, and Simon Davies give striking examples of the reach new technologies gains on the private lives of everyone.[8] But the originality of recent developments, as compared with old direct surveillance tools, is that they are becoming ever more discrete, that they draw on apparently neutral or inoffensive data for secondary uses, and that they now affect individuals through the collective modelling or profiling of behaviour.

Consequently, it becomes increasingly difficult to discover and monitor all surveillance techniques: the multiple derivations of legitimate information gathering are still largely unknown to the public, and their consequences on privacy are more diffuse and difficult to assess. Moreover, there is a paradoxical attitude of denouncing threats to individual privacy and isolated abuses, while accepting the routine use of visible tracking and identification systems and ignoring the build-up of integrated and designed surveillance megasystems.[9]

How can one relate a personal data bank to a surveillance system? There must be somewhere an intent to spy on or to control masses of people or some individuals, an available source of information, and a technical design to put the data to use for surveillance purposes. In a technological setting the word 'design' refers to the structure of an artefact or a program and the way things are set to function properly and give the desired results.[10] Of course, some systems are specifically meant for surveillance: police data banks, for example, store information on alleged criminals (or more extensively on whole populations) to watch, react to, and sometimes prevent crime or sedition. Private investigators, whether detectives or insurance adjusters, do much of the same sort of straightforward surveillance.

But the multifunctionality of new information and communication technologies brings novel surveillance possibilities. Many systems can be used for surveillance, even though that was not their original purpose. For example, to track down the terrorist authors of the Munich Olympic Games massacre, the German police browsed through the billing database of the electricity service provider. The same kind of database search was performed in Alberta in the Plant case.[11] There the Supreme Court of Canada decided that such a search was not contrary to the Canadian Charter of Rights and Freedoms,[12] because a citizen suspected of growing marihuana in his basement and paying high electricity bills could have no reasonable expectation of privacy over such information. In the same vein of ignoring the far-reaching and long-term social consequences of trite surveillance tools such as video cameras in convenience stores, consider the Supreme Court of Canada decision in Nikolovski.[13] In that case, the court accepted a videotape as a conclusive piece of evidence for the purpose of identifying an alleged criminal.

It used to be that people had to directly perform surveillance activities with the aid of technical devices such as cameras, microphones, telephone interception equipment, and the like.[14] Today information can be drawn from the growing personal databases that collect, sort, and analyse all types of information on citizens. Most of this information is seemingly innocuous and manifestly represents no legal danger to the protection of privacy. Yet although these databases were not designed for surveillance, they may be so used. Surveillance has become a creeping and potential function of all personal databases.

Other computing activities can generate transactional data with networked surveillance potential. We all know the reach of police and other administrative agencies in performing their inquisitorial tasks. A novel development of the right to a full defence vindicated by the Canadian Charter of Rights and Freedoms led the Supreme Court of Canada in the O'Connor case[15] to authorize the accused to require that plaintiffs produce, in court, information about those plaintiffs held by third parties such as therapists of victims of sexual abuse. The curiosity of courts seemingly has no limits, irrespective of privacy concerns. Surely, a woman, on entering therapy, would never imagine that the confidential relationship established with her psychologist could be exposed to the public and, even worse, revealed to her aggressor, by a court of law searching for 'the truth.' In this case, the therapist unwillingly became a cog in the surveillance machine.

Let us not forget that the new technologies combine and increase the amount of available information about each of us.[16] Furthermore, search software makes it possible to scan vast quantities of data and extract just the relevant information needed to identify, track down, intercept, or control the searched individual. Surveillance by design may also happen when no precaution is taken against its use as a surveillance tool. For instance, creating an operating system that requires users to identify themselves before performing transactions or storing information, instead of using procedures to ensure anonymity, leaves the door open for surveillance by default. The same can be said of systems allowing for searches from the inside or access from the outside by police, controllers, competitors, and the like.[17] Privacy-enhancing technologies may provide an antidote to surveillance by design systems, as Ann Cavoukian argues in this volume. But can we fight invasive techniques using protective techniques embedded in the system's design?

Technological Imperatives?

From a theoretical point of view, it has been widely demonstrated that technology is neither deterministic nor inevitable: the development of science and techniques historically result from human decisions in economic, political, and social arenas.[18] What seems a technological imperative is often a self-interested choice imposed on others. But these choices are socially crucial because, once made, they largely determine our future. Once new techniques are implemented, there may be no way back to the prior state of affairs. Enhanced systems capabilities or capacities may also drive the desire to upgrade an installation, independent of the real needs. Finally, technologies that mediate people and their activities aggravate dependence on those technologies, leading to greater vulnerability in case of accidental or voluntary breakdown of the systems and creating an urge for security.[19] The search for privacy can be considered as one particular response to this need for security against technological mishaps.

One regularly hears speeches on the need to introduce technologies to be more efficient, to rationalize the production of goods and services, or to save on production costs. We now live with the imperatives of computerization and globalization. Behind these claims, the push for techniques is essentially a sales pitch. We are surrounded by new technologies in search of uses or content. The purported need for surveillance techniques arises from the pressures of the manufacturers and the information business in general. These are aided by the fact that computers convey an image of power and that information processing promises enhanced control.

Many factors converge here. The availability of new technologies, such as the smart card or the Internet, is in itself an incentive to buy or subscribe, regardless of real needs or potential content. Rich information deposits, sitting in public and private sector files, feed new marketing and information industries. The use of technologies to save labour is ever-present, especially in the context of international competition. Add the need to help one country's export industries by providing an internal market in which to sell products and the desire to create a national information-processing industry.

This process must be seen in the context of the evolution of the world market economy: the technological push corresponds to a trend in the global division of labour and distribution of wealth. Countries with labour-intensive economies can only use cheap labour to compete with richer economies based on capital investments and technological developments. Occidental and northern economies (more precisely their owners and elites) are bound to live increasingly on incomes derived from capital and intellectual property. No wonder that technologies are rapidly replacing human labour and that polluting manufacturers and cheap repetitive tasks are moving abroad: we are witnessing a general change in our industrial and economic structure designed to implement adjustments to the new world economic order.

These changes seriously affect the balance between the public and private sectors. In the 1980s big government was seen as the principal threat to privacy, and so North American laws were first adopted to control the public sector. Today technological 'power trips' may still defeat the forecasts of planners and the calculations of accountants, when governments are driven to 'take the technological curve'[20] and throw millions of dollars into new systems, like national identity cards or information superhighways.[21] However, governments are also planning to divest management of public data banks to the private sector, selling some of their most efficient and profitable operations in order to reduce budget deficits.[22]

Paradoxically, the costs of acquiring and maintaining computer and telecommunications installations are not always well scrutinized, but security or privacy-enhancing devices are often considered unaffordable. This does, in fact, become true, if such devices were not initially planned in the conceptual phase of the system and must be added after installation. In such circumstances, technological imperatives are a poor excuse for lack of foresight. Shortsighted considerations of costs may also omit all social costs of technological decisions, in terms of dependence on foreign investments, loss or disqualification of jobs, the institution of harsher controls, and increased vulnerability.

The Quebec Model: A Legal Control of Surveillance Activities?

Instead of asking where one set the boundaries of privacy, as if it were an absolute right subject to reasonable limits, I would ask: what is left of privacy in a context of surveillance by design and of technological imperatives? As have other jurisdictions, Quebec adopted a defensive legal model to react to these overwhelming forces. There has been a general confidence that legal constraints would provide adequate protection of privacy. As a result, Quebec based its law on broad and generous principles that would define boundaries within which an individual would control information flows about himself or herself. Although this model may offer relief to individuals, it falls short of curtailing the development of generalized surveillance, especially in the private sector.

Let us examine briefly how one can slip through the law's loopholes to do business as usual in the commerce of personal information. First, the law still protects personal information to different degrees depending on whether it is in the custody of a public body, a private enterprise, or an individual. Yet data can and do move instantly between these organizations, be it for collection purposes, government subcontracting for services, or privatization of activities. The private sector law condones this situation by allowing free exchange of data between public and private investigators and between debt collectors and marketers (with a weak opting-out procedure).[23] Personal data can be collected or exchanged for verification purposes, which can mean almost anything,[24] without any quality control[25] and without any set time limit for destruction.[26] Firms are under no obligation to identify themselves when collecting data, to inform data subjects of their rights, or to appoint a person in charge of implementation and complaints. As long as the company can show 'legitimate' purposes (nowhere defined), it can go on accumulating and exchanging data on citizens with few limitations.

Second, the new responsibilities given to the CAI were not followed by proportionate budget increases. Thus, the commission has faced an increased workload to the detriment of other very important functions. Neglected functions include audit and investigation, on-site visits, and surveys, all of which enable the commission to probe the systems, assess their compliance to the law, and explore future developments.

But, third, and most important, the Quebec statute failed to institutionalize the participation of interested parties in determining privacy norms in their sectors. The law enunciates general norms of conduct, using such expressions as 'legitimate objects,' 'uses,' or 'serious interest.' However, it does not specify types of sensitive data whose collection or use should be curtailed or forbidden in particular circumstances to prevent discrimination. The law does follow the general rule that an informed consent is sufficient to allow anything to happen, without considering the data subject's economic situation or urgent need to obtain essential services. Nothing in the law tries to control more closely such practices as computer matching or profiling, which are developing in specific information industries.

This highlights the necessity of moving from a 'first' to a 'second generation' law, one that would allow for more precise norms by sectoral regulations. Such laws would indicate which data could legitimately be collected, processed, exchanged, and used in a variety of operations clearly defined. As basic technical and practical information is retained by private enterprises, it is essential that the businesses participate in formulating codes to render such norms realistic and applicable. This would come close to the objective of 'self-regulation' proposed in the international instruments of data protection. Yet it would still fall short of giving to the citizens real recourse against abuses, and it would neglect to empower a public body with authority to audit systems and prevent damage.

Thus, in 1986 GRID advocated a novel concept, that of 'sectoral autoregulation.' Under such a system, representatives of industry, consumers, and governments would meet together and develop norms and procedures to protect privacy in each information-intensive business sector.[27] Such a non-authoritarian process would define for each sector what information should or should not be collected, processed, retrieved, exchanged, used, and destroyed, in what circumstances, for what precise purposes, and with what type of guarantees. It would also set up procedures for audits and complaints. Then the public powers would step in and give legal effect to these norms and procedures by transforming them into public regulation and ensuring their implementation through an oversight scheme.

Without such a precise mode of regulation, the Quebec model cannot fully deliver on its promise. It is clearly desirable to have law that ensures at least a minimal protection of privacy, in both the public and private sectors. But one should not forget that the law offers only a limited type of redress for individual complaints. It does establish a public watchdog who can focus public attention on privacy problems and try to limit damage. However, most public sector initiatives must be publicly approved as a matter of principle. By contrast, the private sector develops its information superstructure without much legal guidance or constraints and with no obligation whatsoever to reveal its initiatives to the public. The occasional hearing of individual complaints and the awarding of redress cannot define the public policies needed to oppose creeping and often open surveillance using increasingly invasive technologies and techniques.

The Inadequacy of Law to Challenge Surveillance Technology

In this brave new world of global information law may seem to be a solution of the past. Privacy legislation does not contribute significantly to reducing the collection and flow of personal data, practices that undermine what is left of our informational privacy. Law is essentially reactive or curative, or it claims to be such. It is designed to punish abuse, not to restrain initiatives. We have seen that, to cut surveillance appetites, we must intervene before the meal is served: at the stage of conception of the systems and well before their implementation. GRID's inquiries into both public and private sectors revealed a uniform tendency of administrators not to favour any public discussion prior to their decisions concerning the creation or the design of data banks. The administrators considered such decisions to be investment decisions to be kept secret from competitors, or as typical acts of public authority, or as a management prerogative.

In Quebec, as well as in the Canadian jurisdictions where privacy acts exist, we still rely on first generation laws enunciating 'fair information principles.' These laws, however, share three major flaws. First, they do not set operational criteria to determine what types of data banks and information systems are legitimate in our society. The laws assume that once the system is set, and in operation, its administrators will follow general and abstract rules related to such elastic concepts as 'relevance' or 'necessity.' The laws depend on privacy officials using individual complaints as the grounds to interpret such loose terms. This approach could rapidly become an exercise in futility in the face of growing, systemic attacks to privacy. The solution? Regulatory powers exercised by public authorities after extensive consultation with industries and consumers.

Second, the numerous exceptions and exemptions provided by these laws, especially those that facilitate exchanges of data between users, actually grant permission to act without the data subject's consent and expropriate informational self-determination. Thus, despite Quebec's privacy statutes applying to both the public and the private sectors, one can still hear official proposals to sell entire public information banks to the private sector or to use the information superhighway to allow any government official to amalgamate and retrieve all data on a given individual from the data banks of public bodies. One wonders if the next step would be to link this virtual information bank to those of private institutions, such as credit bureaus, banks, and insurance companies, to obtain a more extensive profile. This is just what the Quebec government resolved to do by amending the Social Welfare Act in 1996 to allow extensive data searches to check the eligibility of welfare applicants or recipients. Permission is thus officially granted to extend surveillance on whole sectors of the population. Manifestly, loopholes should be tightened, not widened.

This brings us to a third major difficulty, related to the discriminatory potential of information systems, left untouched by the privacy protection laws. The collective nature and stakes of privacy have been identified by some authors,[28] but they were never recognized in laws that presumed the formal equality of all citizens. Meanwhile governments routinely select the most vulnerable populations, like welfare recipients, as targets for technological experimentation and extended surveillance, thus attacking fundamental privacy rights. The concept of personal privacy clearly does not cope with the social problems of groups.[29] Yet the law does not generally recognize the rights of groups with one major exception: courts readily recognize the privacy rights of corporations. Even the national privacy rights of Canadians are hard to defend abroad in an era of transborder data flows. Much of the contemporary effort of North American and European privacy specialists is devoted to trying to determine the influence of an international instrument such as the European Union directive on the protection of personal data.[30]

Conclusion: The Future of Privacy

Let me conclude by first commenting briefly on the role of law. Two general paths of action are open to protecting privacy. The first is the insistence on second generation privacy laws. Such laws might help to determine more precisely for each economic sector what data banks should be set up, what types of information should be subject to collection, with what rules of disclosure, and what norms of security. In this approach, privacy-enhancing devices would be mandatory and systematically included in systems designs from the outset of a project. A second path would be radical public opposition from the outset to any new system that would jeopardize privacy. The strong positions taken by the objectors to a national identity card in Australia exemplify how public outrage and threats of civil disobedience can drive privacy-invasive projects into disrepute and abandonment, as Simon Davies recounts in his essay herein.

Law belongs naturally on the first path: it is concerned with security and consolidating vested rights; it is ill-adapted to change, especially rapid change brought by technological advances. Moreover, law is a means of social exclusion, protecting the haves from the have-nots. To use it as a tool fostering human rights against discrimination and abuse is a real challenge. The symbolic values of justice embedded in law may help promote fair information principles, but if the principles are not put into practice they simply mask the deeper penetration of surveillance and control in our societies at the risk of promoting rupture, refusal, and social unrest. Unless the 'powers that be' succeed in establishing a 'secure society,' the result could be an 'exclusive society' where law is merely a device protecting the privacy of a happy few against the claims of all others.

The dawn of the twenty-first century demands a deeper reflection on the relationship between the public and the private spheres and a corresponding redefinition of the role of privacy in society. The private sector has assumed an increasingly important role in the field of information, corresponding to a shift in the relative power of the business world in general at the expense of national governments and even international organizations. To counteract this privatization of social power, we must rejuvenate public controls, not those overseeing legitimate initiatives or putting the citizenry under general police or bureaucratic surveillance, but those ensuring that citizens' fundamental rights, including the right to privacy, are respected. Private power vested in the corporations, whatever their size and location, has superseded the authority of elected governments. At the same time, corporate actions tend to be invisible, often cloaked in secrecy, and they are devoted to the maximization of profits regardless of the social consequences.

The balance between private interests and public good must be restored. Pursuit of the citizen's interest must be the measure of all policy assessments, public and private. As the gap increases between the level of education, income, and opportunities of the happy few compared with the degrading conditions of living of the vast majority, and especially of the impoverished and ever-growing number of persons denied access to the labour market, the state has a special responsibility to enlarge the public sphere to restore equality or at least realize a more equitable redistribution of wealth and power. The role of citizens remains crucial at all levels, be it as electors, consumers, civil servants, shareholders, or even data subjects; it is on the basis of their vigilance and their action that public policies can be claimed, adopted, and implemented.

In this general context, privacy has a special role to play. Its protection should be reserved for physical persons, and not corporations, the idea of fundamental rights being to defend the citizens against powerful organizations, be they public, private, cooperative, or associative. As a fundamental right, privacy should be isolated from commerce to ensure that no person can be deprived of privacy, obliged to sell it out of economic need, or be forced to renounce exercising it because of cost. Conversely, 'free' personal information should not be used without public controls that delineate the interests of society in the free flow of information, the right of the public to adequate information, and the interests of individuals in the preservation of their private domain.

Privacy as a social value has defied many attempts at a definition, and that is good. A definition, especially in the legal field, is an exercise in power. It tends to limit the notion to the terms of the definition, whereas privacy should remain one of the last ramparts against the exercise of power on individuals. Privacy should not be separated from the social functions it is meant to perform. Its validity as a concept and as a right should be measured by the degree of effective protection it offers the citizenry in the exercise of its democratic rights and not by its capacity to oppose legitimate public scrutiny on individual activity. One cannot predict the long-term political evolution of our societies, but one can safely assert that privacy will remain a vital ingredient of democracy. It will retain its vitality by being regularly assessed, affirmed, and balanced against the imperatives of the public interest and according to the interests of society at large, depending on what type of regime holds the power to define and vindicate privacy rights.

NOTES

1 LQ 1993, c. 17.
2 1975, RSQ, c. C-12, a. 5.
3 LQ 1991, c. 64, a. 3 and 35–41.
4 RSQ, c. A-2.1.
5 Groupe de recherche informatique et droit (GRID), *L'Identité Piratée* (Montreal: Société québécoise d'informatique juridique, 1986).
6 André Ouimet, 'The Québec Privacy Solution: A Unique Model,' paper delivered to the Visions for Privacy Conference, Victoria, BC, 9–11 May 1996.
7 Paul-André Comeau, 'Privacy and Technology: A Common Sense Approach,' paper delivered to the Visions for Privacy Conference, 9–11 May 1996. For a thorough analysis of the act and some of its applications, see R. Côté and R. Laperrière, eds., *Vie privée sous surveillance: La protection des renseignements personnels en droit québécois et comparé* (Cowansville: Yvon Blais, 1994).
8 See David Lyon, *The Electronic Eye: The Rise of Surveillance Society* (Minneapolis: University of Minnesota Press, 1994); and Oscar Gandy, *The Panoptic Sort: A Political Economy of Personal Information* (Boulder: Westview Press, 1992).
9 For instance, police surveillance systems collect enormous quantities of information stored in huge databases. The Royal Canadian Mounted Police manages its own database, the Canadian Police Information Centre (CPIC), claiming that it only coordinates provincial and local police forces in Canada. Quebec also has its Centre de renseignements policiers du Québec (CRPQ). In addition, secret services and organizations, such as the Canadian Security Establishment, spy on Canadians and maintain data banks and information collection routines without public scrutiny. See David H. Flaherty, 'Protecting Privacy in Police Information Systems: Data Protection in the Canadian Police Information Centre,' *University of Texas Law Journal* 36 (1986), 116–48. A similar data bank, called the National Crime Information Center (NCIC) also exists in the United States. In the private sector, insurance companies have established a clearing-house of information on persons for life and health insurance purposes: the Medical Information Bureau, which collects huge amounts of very sensitive medical data (see GRID, *L'identité piratée*), causing many problems for consumers who have tried to correct errors. See Jeff Rothfeder, *Privacy for Sale* (New York: Simon and Schuster, 1992). Many large

financial institutions, such as American Express, maintain tracking systems on their customers' habits, and they feed nationwide credit bureaus maintaining credit profiles on millions of individuals and selling information for marketing purposes.

10 See, e.g., a technical definition given by R.A. Edmunds, *Prentice-Hall Standard Glossary of Computer Terminology* (Englewood Cliffs, NJ: Prentice-Hall 1984), under 'system design'; for the general meaning of the term, see *Webster's Third New International Dictionary* (1971), under the word 'design.'

11 [1993] 3 SCR 281.

12 Canada Act 1982, Sch. B, 1992, c. 11 (UK).

13 *R v Nikolovski* [1996] 3 SCR 1197.

14 In addition to the usual meaning of surveillance activities, refering to eavesdropping, video-camera surveillance, and the like, we adopt the broader social meaning of surveillance developed in David H. Flaherty's works, mainly *Protecting Privacy in Surveillance Societies* (Chapel Hill: University of North Carolina Press, 1989).

15 *R v O'Connor* [1995] 4 SCR 411.

16 Because of the ever-increasing memory capacities of computers and the multiplying telecommunication links between computers, real or virtual data banks develop allowing governments, businesses, or even individuals to retrieve and process huge amounts of personal data. The phenomenon is universal: for Quebec it was analysed in detail in GRID, *L'Identité Piratée*. This phenomenon extends beyond state borders: see R. Laperrière, R. Côté, G.A. LeBel, P. Roy, and K. Benyekhlef, *Crossing the Borders of Privacy* (Ottawa: Justice Canada, 1991).

17 The annual reports of privacy commissioners and general auditors often cite cases of lack of security, unauthorized accesses, and the like. For instance, the Quebec CSST, acting as a workers' compensation board and holding medical files on hundreds of thousands of beneficiaries, was given five years by the Quebec CAI to enhance security in its database access procedures. Insurance companies are particularly fond of gaining access to medical data held by hospitals and public automobile insurance schemes.

18 See R. Laperrière, H. Claret, and P. Péladeau, eds., *Une démocratie technologique?* Actes d'un Colloque Multidisciplinaire de l'ACFAS, coédition GRID-ACFAS (1988), particularly the contributions by G. Hottois and G. Métayer. There is a substantial body of literature in French developed by authors such as Jacques Ellul, *La technique ou l'enjeu du siècle* (Paris: A. Colin, 1954), and particularly, as far as computers are concerned, A. Vitalis, *Informatique, pouvoir et libertés*,(Paris: Economica, 1988). Space forbids us from initiating in these pages a polemic about contrary opinions of authors from

different cultural backgrounds, such as Shoshana Zuboff, 'New Worlds of Computer Mediated Work,' *Harvard Business Review* 60, no. 5 (1982), 142–52.

19 Practically any person working with a computer has experienced diverse bugs or breakdowns. The last public nuisance caused by a computer network failure in Quebec happened at the beginning of 1997, when a new mandatory medication insurance regime was implemented, causing hundreds of persons to pay cash for their covered medication or to be deprived of it.

20 'Prendre le virage technologique' was an expression used by the Quebec government in the 1980s to foster rapid technological change.

21 This is well illustrated by many recent developments in Quebec. See particularly, Michel Venne, 'L'autoroute des renseignements personnels,' *Le Devoir*, 8 Feb. 1993, A-1, and a series of five articles by the same journalist on the same question; 'Gestion des banques de données sur la santé: le projet d'une agence sème l'inquiétude,' *Le Devoir*, 11 April 1995, A-8; 'Québec songe à une carte d'identité électronique universelle,' *Le Devoir*, 16 April 1996, A-1.

22 See Michel Venne, 'Une agence privée pour gérer les données du réseau de la santé: les banques de données pourraient être vendues au secteur privé,' *Le Devoir*, 5 April 1995, A-10; M. Venne, 'La Commission d'accès à l'information réprouve la privatisation des services informatiques,' *Le Devoir*, 29 Aug. 1994, A-2.

23 Article 18.

24 Article 6.

25 Article 11.

26 Article 12.

27 This, in part, is the process envisaged under the Canadian Standards Association's *Model Code for the Protection of Personal Information* (Rexdale, ON: CSA, 1995). Codes are to be tailored to this overall standard within key sectors.

28 See Vitalis, *Informatique, pouvoir et libertés*; Priscilla Regan, *Legislating Privacy: Technology, Social Values and Public Policy* (Chapel Hill: University of North Carolina Press, 1995); Colin J. Bennett, 'The Public Surveillance of Personal Data: A Cross-National Analysis,' in David Lyon and Elia Zureik, eds., *Computers, Surveillance and Privacy* (Minneapolis: University of Minnesota Press, 1996), 237–59.

29 See Charles D. Raab and Colin J. Bennett, 'Distributing Privacy: Risks, Protection and Policy,' *The Information Society* (forthcoming).

30 See Priscilla Regan's essay in this volume; and Colin J. Bennett and Charles D. Raab, 'The Adequacy of Privacy: The European Union's Data Protection Directive and the North American Response,' *The Information Society* 13, no. 4 (June 1997), 245–63.

PART IV

GLOBAL CHOICES

10

American Business and the European Data Protection Directive: Lobbying Strategies and Tactics

PRISCILLA M. REGAN

During the early 1990s U.S. businesses watched with some trepidation as the European Union's Data Protection (or Privacy) Directive worked its way through the somewhat tortuous course of policy development and adoption required by the European Union. To achieve a unitary European market, the European Union is harmonizing national laws that affect the workings of the European economic market. Included among such proposals is one that requires the twelve countries in the European Union to harmonize their privacy or data protection legislation. The proposed 'Directive on the Protection of Individuals with Regard to the Processing of Personal Data and on the Free Movement of Such Data'[1] (hereafter referred to as the Data Protection Directive) provoked discussion not only among the members of the European Union, but also in countries that trade or deal commercially with those states. The proposed directive raised the prospect of a global solution to problems caused by the collection and exchanges of personally identifiable information. Talk of a global solution concedes that technological and market forces are beginning to frustrate the effectiveness of national privacy laws. At the same time, the proposed directive exposed the rationales for national variations and the particular interests of multinational firms.

Much discussion is occurring in the United States, which will be affected by the Data Protection Directive because of its extensive trade with the European Union and because many observers believe that the privacy laws of the United States do not provide the level of protection that the data protection directive requires. Somewhat early in the process of the development of the directive, it appeared that American business might support the establishment of some form of privacy or data protection commission in the United States, similar to the commissions found in European countries. Some analysts, including this author, believed that the proposed Data Protection Directive might open a 'policy window' leading to the strengthening of privacy laws in the United States and the establishment of some form of commission.[2] The establishment of a commission in the United States would provide a buffer against questions about the 'adequacy' or 'equivalency' of U.S. policy on privacy and data protection in comparison with European policies and to the requirements of the European directive.

The final Data Protection Directive was adopted by the European Parliament and the Council of Ministers of the European Union on 24 October 1995. Contrary to the initial projection of some commentators, the United States has not established a commission or strengthened its privacy legislation. As the process of approval in the European Union progressed, no real support for a privacy or data protection commission developed among U.S. businesses. Instead, the basic strategy that business adopted was to lobby abroad rather than to lobby for change in legislation at home. The essential reason for adopting this strategy was that the status quo at home represented business interests; the primary gain from changing U.S. policy was that changes would address European concerns. Instead of addressing these concerns indirectly, by lobbying for changes in U.S. policy, business addressed them directly, by lobbying for changes in European policy.

This essay examines the strategies that U.S. businesses adopted in response to the proposed Data Protection Directive, offers some explanation for why businesses adopted those strategies, and analyses why those strategies were successful. There are three primary reasons why the European-based strategy was successful. First was the timing of the European directive. The early 1990s saw the height of American business interest, as well as European interest, in the global marketplace. Second, the complexity of the European Union's process provided numerous decision points and hence access points at which decision makers could be influenced. Third, the European Union's process for approval of the directive was lengthy, allowing time for U.S. businesses to educate themselves about the implications of the directive, time to tutor European businesses, and time to organize on both sides of the Atlantic.

The essay concludes with some thoughts about the continuing influence of U.S. business in the European arena, the likelihood of U.S. interests placing a barrier to the realization of a truly global privacy standard, and the conditions under which a global solution to privacy and data protection is likely.

The Global Marketplace

The proposed data protection directive engendered a 'firestorm of criticism' in the U.S. and internationally because of concern that the requirements would increase business costs and hamper the development of a global marketplace.[3] Information systems, often containing identifiable personal information, provide the basic infrastructure of a multinational company. For a business to operate and be competitive in a global marketplace, computer and telecommunication systems operate as seamless networks across national boundaries exchanging billions of data including personnel records, customer information, supplier information, investor information, and information about competitors. At the same time, as Simon Davies argues in his essay in this volume, technological imperatives of the information revolution compromise the privacy of personal data being exchanged in these various systems.

From the perspective of a global firm, several aspects of the proposed directive were potentially problematic. In general, companies and trade associations raised four primary objections: *practical problems* with the directive, especially in the areas of banking, air travel, insurance, and direct marketing; *ambiguities in the directive*, which made it difficult to achieve the uniformity sought by the directive; *the business expense* associated with complying, which might lead some companies to forsake critical business activities involving the use of personal data; and, perhaps most importantly, *the restrictions on the export of personal data*, which were viewed as a step backward in terms of the globalization of business activity. More specifically, American companies were troubled by the requirements of 'informed consent' and 'adequate' or 'equivalent' protection.

To enable individuals to control the use of personal information, the proposed directive required that individuals give their 'informed consent' for secondary uses of information (that is, for a purpose other than that for which the information was collected). The goal was to prohibit organizations from trading and exchanging information about individuals without, at a minimum, the knowledge and, hopefully, the active consent of the individual. Early drafts of the directive required that information collected for one purpose not be used for another purpose without the 'specific informed consent' of the data subject. In effect, this

required that individuals 'opt in' to any new uses of exchanges of information. Businesses preferred a more passive 'opt out' requirement
whereby individuals would be informed of secondary uses and be given
an opportunity to object to or 'opt out' of having personal information
reused or exchanged. Giving individuals the ability to object to secondary uses of information is consistent, as Mary Culnan and Robert Bies
argue in their essay in this volume, with business interests in treating
customers fairly in order to develop trust and make customers willing to
disclose personal information. In this way, 'opt out' provisions help to
nurture a 'culture of privacy' that makes individuals more comfortable
with disclosing information.

From a business perspective, the draft Data Protection Directive
raised the possibility that businesses would have to adopt a more active
role in securing 'informed consent' from their customers. A key question
was whether an 'informed consent' requirement of the draft directive
was possible in an era of interactive data communications where transactions and manipulations take place routinely and immediately. Under
these conditions, industry officials argue that it is impractical to get permission from everyone in a database before financial and credit transactions can be processed. Customer and employer databases pose similar
problems. According to Kenneth B. Allen, senior vice president of the
Information Industry Association in Washington, DC, 'The major concern is that the draft is totally unrealistic and onerous.'[4]

To provide basically similar protection among the countries, of the
European Union and with countries trading with EU members, the proposed directive needed to establish a standard by which to judge
whether the laws and/or practices of countries were in harmony with
the level of protection they afforded. Business groups also knew that
harmonization was not going to be easy to achieve even within the
European Union. Several European countries, namely, Italy, Belgium,
Spain, and Portugal, at that time did not have data protection laws. The
laws of some European countries were not as restrictive as the commission's proposal, which was most influenced by German law. But, it
appeared probable that the policies of the United States, Japan, Australia, and Canada would not meet the standards set in the directive. The
United States has national legislation, the Privacy Act of 1974, addressing the personal information practices of federal agencies, some national
legislation addressing information practices for certain private sector
firms, and some state laws. But there are critical areas of personal information activities that are not addressed by national legislation. Strength-

ening existing laws and passing new ones, for example, in the area of health information, are not easy tasks as Robert Gellman demonstrates herein. And even where there is national legislation, it is quite questionable whether the American approach of individual rights and access to the courts would be regarded as being able to achieve a similar level of protection to that of the European countries. Joel Reidenberg discusses in more detail the complexity of assessing American practices in the following chapter.

Within the business community, most discussion focused on the standards of 'adequate' or 'equivalent' protection, with 'equivalent' protection requiring more similarity between a third country's laws and those of the European Union and 'adequate' protection requiring a lower level of comparability and protection. Although American business preferred the standard of 'adequate' protection, either requirement generated fear among American businesses operating in Europe because of the possibility that they would be prevented from transferring data to an EU country and that European companies would be prevented from transferring data to the United States if it did not ensure 'equivalent' or 'adequate' levels of protection for personal information. British Airways, for example, said that under a requirement of 'adequate' protection they would not be able to confirm the return flight of a passenger who flew from the EU to Chile (or any other number of countries, including possibly the United States). Additionally, if a traveller tried to use a credit card in that country, the European Union credit card firm would not be able to authorize the transaction.[5]

For information-intensive businesses that were considering expanding into global markets, the proposed Data Protection Directive created anxiety. For example, the American credit card industry was poised to enter Europe at the time the privacy directive was being discussed. By the early 1990s the credit card market in the United States was somewhat saturated, and the rate of growth had slowed appreciably. Two U.S. credit bureaus, Equifax and Trans Union Credit, were investigating the potential for expansion in Europe. Traditionally, Europeans held more conservative attitudes towards savings and more scepticism towards consumer credit. These attitudes were beginning to change, offering an enormous potential market for American credit card companies. As companies considered such expansion, they confronted several potential barriers or uncertainties, including questions about the draft EU Data Protection Directive. Indeed, Martin Abrams, director of policy analysis and consumer affairs at Experian Information Solutions, Inc., was quoted as saying that 'we won't do anything there until the European Commission makes some decisions about privacy laws.'[6] As one observer noted, 'Because of local custom and rigid privacy laws, the free-flowing credit information that fuels the U.S. consumer credit market just isn't available in Europe. That hinders credit judgments and makes it nearly impossible to aim marketing pieces at likely prospects.'[7] Although credit card companies had a need to expand and changing attitudes in Europe offered an opportunity, the possibility of restrictive policies within the European Union and between EU countries and other countries made Europe less attractive as a new market for credit company expansion than otherwise would have been the case.

Any information-intensive industry was likely to be affected by the proposed directive. A columnist in *Marketing News* in 1993 gave the following advice to U.S. marketing companies considering business opportunities in Europe: 'So, before venturing into direct marketing in Europe, do make sure you are familiar with the directive, which will not become law until 1995 at the earliest, and check whether registration of your organization in that European country is necessary. Also, ensure that your European suppliers of personal information about consumers guarantee the accuracy and integrity of their data. Finally, make sure they have complied with their home country's data protection agencies. Being forewarned must surely be the best insurance policy against usually expensive mistakes.'[8] Steve Metalitz, vice president of the Information Industry Association, argued that 'any company that does business in Europe, or that relies on information about individual Europeans, should anticipate and plan for the adoption of new and potentially onerous data protection regulations throughout the EC.'[9]

The spectre of onerous regulations imposing costs on business was not entirely unfounded. There have been instances where a European country's data protection legislation has prohibited exchange of personal information in the course of 'normal' business transactions. The case that received the most press attention, and provoked the most fears, was in 1991 when the French data protection agency prevented Fiat from electronically transferring information about French employees of Fiat to the home office in Italy until Fiat agreed to abide by the requirements of the French law on data protection. In 1992 a German bank refused to give its Hong Kong branch access to customer information regarding German citizens. In another decision, Sony Germany was denied permission to export German consumer data to the United States.

The U.S. International Trade Commission (ITC) took the position that the proposed EU directive would significantly affect any U.S. industry that did business in Europe and that the restrictions on transfer of data to third countries would be 'particularly onerous in light of the fact that 1990 exports of data processing services form the U.S. to the EC totaled approximately $319 million.'[10] The U.S. Council for International Business, based in New York, also lobbied against the proposed data protection regulations. And U.S. business looked for protection and intervention from the Department of State and the Office of the International Trade Representative.[11] In efforts to understand the issues and options regarding the proposed directive, several meetings of business, government, and academic representatives from the United States and Europe were sponsored by organizations such as the German Marshall Fund and the Annenberg Washington Program.

Titles of articles reflect the fear felt by business, as these examples illustrate: 'A one-way street: Fortress Europe may bar transfers of personnel and customer data to the U.S.'[12] and 'EC's new privacy proposals could hobble global nets.'[13] For those who were opposed to the directive, it was easy to come up with scenarios that played on this fear. In an article in the *Journal of European Business*, Steve Metalitz developed several 'unpleasant' scenarios involving U.S. business opportunities in Europe.[14] In one scenario a company is considering an acquisition of some European companies and orders a confidential research report on the companies, officers, and stockholders. The report yields little information on the individuals because of the necessity under the proposed directive for informed consent. In another scenario an American company with European retail operations wanted to compile a database to make special offers to preferred customers. The company is told it cannot do so because of limitations on profiling. Similarly, in an article in *American Business Law Journal*, Robert Boehmer and Todd Palmer developed comparable scenarios in which the personal information handling practices of the British office of an American firm are restricted by the requirements of the EU directive and suggest the directive may cause a 'nervous breakdown' in the information systems of multinational companies.[15]

The proposal of a Data Protection Directive coincided with an increased interest among American businesses in the global marketplace. This was especially true for service industries who also tend to be information-intensive industries. For these industries the proposed directive raised uncertainty about the development of the legal and trade environment. The uncertainty caused U.S. businesses to hesitate, which had negative effects on their potential European partners. Thus, American and European business interests about the proposed Data Protection Directive were harmonized because of their shared interests in the development of a global marketplace.

The Complexity of the EU Process and Access to Influence

The initial proposal regarding data protection was made by the European Commission in 1990, after several requests by the European Parliament for action on this issue. A second revised proposal was released in October 1992 following a number of changes suggested by the European Parliament. On 8 December 1994, the member states reached a political agreement on the framework Data Protection Directive, and in February 1995 it was adopted formally by the Council of Ministers. As someone who has worked closely in the European Commission on the passage of the directive said, 'The wheels of European Union law-making procedures can sometimes grind very slowly.'[16] This slowness has worked to the advantage of U.S. businesses and others opposed to the directive.

The process of policy making within the European Union is quite complex. First, the Commission of the European Communities (seventeen members appointed by common accord of the governments of the member states for a term of four years) initiates a proposal. After its approval is secured, the proposal generally goes for consultation to the European Parliament (518 members from member states based on a proportional representation system – ranging from Germany, France, Italy, and the United Kingdom with 81 members, to Luxembourg with six), as well as to the numerous committees of the Parliament, and to the Economic and Social Committee (189 experts). Then it goes to the Council of Ministers (twelve representatives, one from each of the member states, with weighted votes ranging from 10 for France, Germany, Italy, and the United Kingdom, to 2 for Luxembourg), which has the actual legislative power, for a first reading and amendment. The proposal goes through a similar process again for a second reading. Throughout this process, not only are there different groups and interests participating in decisions, but each point in the process offers countries an opportunity to modify their position. Moreover, each stage in the process allows opportunities for lobbying and influence by outside groups, including multinational corporations and other governments.

In October 1990 the European Commission released a draft proposal for a council directive 'concerning the protection of individuals in relation to the processing of personal data.' The directive's central principle was that individuals should control the use of personal information, and it required that individuals give their informed consent for secondary uses of information. The proposal prohibited the transfer of personal data to another country unless that country ensured an 'adequate' level of protection. The proposal also provided for the establishment of a European-wide 'supervision authority' with investigative and supervisory powers over files covered by the directive.

Some multinational firms responded with alarm to this proposal. Others were more cautious, recognizing that this was but step one of a long process that would be open to influence. The European Direct Marketing Association (EDMA) and other business groups spent over $50 million lobbying primarily against the 'opt in' requirement of the October 1990 Data Protection Draft directive and the restriction on transfer of data to third countries. Although early on in the process the EDMA was given indications that EC officials were likely to relax the most controversial provisions, the numerous layers of the European Community approval process and the sensitivity of European politicians to citizen concerns about privacy and human rights kept business on edge.[17]

In January 1992 the Legal Affairs Committee of the European Parliament recommended several changes to the proposed directive. In response to lobbying by European and U.S. business, some changes made the directive more flexible, workable, and understandable. But the committee supported the guideline that use of personal data be based on informed consent of the data subject and endorsed the principle of blocking the flow of personal information to countries that were not providing an adequate level of data or privacy protection. In October 1992, after deliberation and approval by the European Parliament, the European Commission adopted an amended Data Protection Directive, which somewhat weakened informed consent but contained the requirement for adequate protection, and sent it to the Council of Ministers.

The Euro-MP who was writing the European Parliament's report on the directive, Geoffrey Hoon, was lobbied by over a hundred companies and associations. He recommended to the European Parliament that the 'opt in' clause be changed to 'opt out,' that some profiling be permitted, that the rules on shifting data overseas be relaxed, and that the media be exempted. As the *Economist* reported, 'The howls of protest have embarrassed the commission, which admits that it neglected to consult interested parties before publishing its directive.'[18]

Observers pointed out that 'reaction to the Data Protection Directive from the European private sector has been voluminous and strongly negative'[19] and suggested that this may lead the commission to rethink some parts of the directive. Any rethinking, however, occurred within the framework of the fundamental principles of data protection. It was widely believed that private sector interests would not be successful at stopping the directive, but could seek to change some of the specific requirements. In commenting on the EU process, Michael Nugent of Citibank commented that the process was a 'good' one, 'almost like trade negotiations.'[20] The complex, slow process of the European Commission did indeed resemble the 'bargaining, negotiating, and compromise' that is typical of interest group politics in the United States. It is a process that U.S. business understands, and it is a process through which resoluteness often is undermined by the forces opposing change.

On 20 February 1995 the Council of Ministers of the European Union adopted a common position on a data protection directive. The European Parliament made only minor changes in the common position on 15 June 1995. Final adoption of the directive by the European Parliament and the Council of the European Union occurred on 24 October 1995. The directive is to be implemented by the member states by 24 October 1998.

Length of the European Union's Process and Organization of Opposition

For American businesses concerned about the requirements of the proposed data protection directive, the question was one of strategy. Should they seek changes in American policy, lobby directly for changes in the draft directive, or work through European counterparts to secure changes in the directive? G. Russell Pipe, deputy director of the Global Information Infrastructure Commission, recommended that 'changes in the directive are more likely to come from lobbying by European businesses that happen to share U.S. concerns, as well as from the conservative German and U.K. governments.'[21]

Many European businesses did share the concerns of American businesses. As the *Economist* reported in 1992, 'Businesses which depend on the manipulation of computer data-lists – such as direct-mail companies, charities, credit-reference agencies and financial-services firms – claim the commission's directive is so ham-fisted that it would hobble their industries.'[22] At the same time European businesses looked to American businesses for both financial and political support in influencing the commission. For example, Norman Vale, director general of the International Advertising Association, told attendees at a New York publishers conference in 1992 that direct marketers should develop a 'financial war chest within the Direct Marketing Association (DMA) and to direct the DMA to invest in FEDIM's [European Federation of Direct Marketing] lobbying efforts within the EC.'[23]

Most worried about the directive and most vocal in opposition was the European direct marketing industry. In response to the October 1992 Draft Directive on Data Protection, the U.K.'s Direct Marketing Association objected to three parts: first, the ambiguity of the requirement that uses of information must be 'compatible' with the purpose for which it was collected, the timing of the disclosure to the consumer about the data's possible uses, and the requirement that consumers be given an express opportunity to opt out from being included on a mailing list. The direct mail industry, including mail order and financial service firms, was concerned about the proposed directive's limitation on 'profiling,' or selection of people who share certain characteristics as the basis for a mailing. The British Direct Marketing Association argued that profiling, because it is selective, reduces the amount of junk mail that people receive and that the proposed limitations would increase mail and increase the costs to business and consumers. The association claimed that the average Briton gets forty-three pieces of junk mail a year, whereas the average German gets sixty-three pieces, even though German laws restrict profiling.[24]

In previous attempts to influence legislation, the European direct marketing industry used the European Advertising Tripartite (composed of European advertisers, agencies, and media) as its lobbying group. Concern about the implications of the proposed Data Protection Directive provoked the European direct marketing industry to establish in 1992 its own lobbying group in Brussels, the European Federation of Direct Marketing (FEDIM). It is comprised of seven national direct marketing associations and the European Direct Marketing Association (EDMA).[25]

Telemarketing and market research companies in Europe were most concerned about the Data Protection Directive's proposed stipulation that data subjects must give written consent for 'automated data processing' of data considered 'sensitive,' meaning political opinions, religious beliefs, health and sexual behaviour, and union membership. The European Society for Opinion and Marketing Research (ESOMAR) sent a delegation to lobby in Brussels for deletion of this proposal for fear that it would make most telephone surveys impossible.[26]

Many groups who use direct marketing as a technique to contact potentially interested persons reacted negatively to the directive, and they organized in response to it. Seventy charities set up a pressure group, called Charities and Non-profit Groups in Europe (CHANGE), to oppose the directive. The fear on the part of the charities was that the directive would reduce their mailing lists and hurt their fund-raising.[27] They were particularly concerned about the 'informed consent' requirement, which would mean that unless people 'opted into' a mailing list they could not be included.

Political parties who canvass voters and send direct mail to voters were also concerned that they would not be able to collect information about political beliefs or voters' preferences, without the prior written consent of the individual. This was reflected in a front page article in the London Guardian in 1993. A Labour MP was quoted as saying, 'If the directive as it presently stands were to be implemented, the political process would be thrown into absolute turmoil, with traditional techniques such as canvassing rendered illegal and new direct mail techniques universally used in elections outlawed.'[28] This concern arose when a clause allowing personal data in the public domain to be used for direct mailing was deleted from the privacy directive in October 1993 at the request of Sweden, Norway, and Denmark. The new clause said that no use can be made of information in the public domain unless it is compatible with the purpose for which the information was originally collected. Other research-oriented entities were also worried about the implications of the directive's requirements. European epidemiologists were concerned that the 'informed consent' requirement would reduce the number of patients willing to engage in research. The EU Council of Ministers of Health asked that the directive be changed.[29]

All information-intensive industries were concerned about the ramifications of the proposed Data Protection Directive. In response, eighteen credit bureaus formed an association to represent the interests of European suppliers of consumer credit data, the European Union of Consumer Credit Information Providers. The goal of the group was to achieve a balanced and workable data protection regime in Europe.[30] CCN Systems, the London-based unit of Great Universal Stores that provides more than half of all the U.K.'s credit-referencing services, reportedly was more concerned with the European Data Protection Directive than with U.S. companies taking away business.

Employers throughout Europe were also concerned about the proposed Data Protection Directive. The Union of Industrial and Employers'

Confederations of Europe (UNICE), the umbrella group of European employer confederations, warned that the proposed directive 'might have the effect of totally paralyzing some forms of activity which are necessary to the sound administration of the economy' and that restrictions on export of data 'will isolate the Community from third countries and will represent a handicap in its relations with them.'[31]

General business organizations throughout Europe also lobbied. The EU Committee of the American Chamber of Commerce, representing European companies with American owners, argued that the directive might increase differences among data protection standards within the EU and would result in 'reducing information availability, restricting its flow, and putting it out of the reach of many public and private entities now dependent upon its use.'[32] The Association of European Chambers of Commerce and Industry (EUROCHAMBRES), which represents twenty-four chambers of commerce and more than thirteen million companies in the EU, lobbied the European Commission for a data protection policy that would allow the member states to establish their own regulations. The International Chamber of Commerce (ICC) asked the EU Commission to allow intracorporate data transfers regardless of the level of data protection in the country to which data was being sent. Both EUROCHAMBRES and the ICC criticized the original proposed directive and the amended version (October 1992) because of the excessive compliance costs it would impose on businesses.[33] The Global Alliance of Information Industry Associations (GAIIA) questioned whether the proposed directive would lead to more harmonization, greater privacy protection, or a strengthened European and/or global information marketplace.

Conclusion: The Future with the EU Data Protection Directive

Now that the directive has been approved and member states are considering their legislative responses, observers are once again pondering whether this will provoke stronger legislation in the United States. David Banisar, of the Electronic Privacy Information Center, for example, said that approval of the EU directive brought 'good potential for seeing improved privacy legislation.'[34] On the other hand, Melanie Janin, a manager at the U.S. Council for International Business, took the position that there would be no effect on American legislation. Based on analysis of events leading up to approval of the directive, it is more likely that American businesses will continue to work through and with their European partners and counterparts, rather than lobbying for change in U.S.

laws. In pursuing this strategy business will find a number of options open that may satisfy the European Data Protection Directive in particular, but that, perhaps more importantly, will address the very real constraints imposed when multinational companies rely upon global information and communication systems. This places the question of regional privacy solutions, such as the directive, within the larger context of this volume. Will the European Data Protection Directive provide the potential for a global solution? In answering this question, it becomes clear that a 'global solution' cannot be viewed in isolation from other solutions. The role of data protection commissions, privacy-enhancing technologies, market-based solutions, and privacy advocacy are all part of the answer to the potential for a 'global solution.'

American business regards the application of market-based solutions as the appropriate alternative to legal solutions. The preference has been, and is likely to continue to be, for voluntary, self-regulation rather than regulation imposed by law. In response to threats of legislative action and to domestic consumer pressure, many American businesses have adopted 'Codes of Fair Information Use.' Such market-based codes may be relevant to the creation of a global solution. The Data Protection Directive requires that 'adequacy' of American data protection policy be evaluated in light of 'all circumstances surrounding a data transfer operation.' These codes will be used by business as evidence of the protection offered. Paul Schwartz pointed out that this may allow 'business practices in the receiving nation to be scrutinized in a potentially uncritical way and specifically permits contracts that add to the level of data protection available in a given country.'[35]

Events since the adoption of the directive make it appear less likely that these codes will be evaluated in an uncritical way. Because contractual arrangements do not have the force of law and are not entered into by two sovereign nations, some European Commission members do not find such arrangements to be politically acceptable. A less lenient attitude towards contractual arrangements is found in remarks regarding an arrangement between German Railway and Citibank by the Berlin Data Protection Deputy Commissioner to the 18th International Privacy and Data Protection Conference.[36] In this arrangement the German Railway cooperated with the German subsidiary of Citibank to issue a railway card with a VISA credit card function. After criticism by consumer groups and data protection authorities, German Railway and Citibank signed a data protection agreement that gave German Railway responsibility for protecting personal data collected for purposes of rail travel and fares, Citibank responsibility for protecting credit data, and both companies responsibility for name and address of card holders. Additionally, both German Railway and Citibank agree to apply the German data protection law to their handling of card holders' data, the German card customers have the same individual rights against the Citibank subsidiary that they have under German law, the Citibank subsidiary has to appoint data protection supervisors as required by German law, and the Citibank subsidiaries in the United States agree to on-site audits by the German data protection supervisory authority. The Berlin Data Protection Deputy Commissioner argued that this arrangement would meet the 'adequate protection' test required by the EU Data Protection Directive, but that this type of contractual solution cannot be regarded as a model because the rule required by Articles 25 and 26 of the EU directive is that the receiving country ensures an adequate level of protection. An *exception* to the rule would be a contractual arrangement, but an exception cannot provide a model. His conclusion was that 'contractual standard-setting by private corporations can only complement and support but never replace national legislation.'[37]

Although reliance on relevant business practices may serve to protect American businesses, some business representatives are currently in favour of the establishment of a data protection or privacy commission, but not the type of commission envisioned by privacy advocates in the United States. Instead, for example, Michael Nugent of Citibank advocated a 'data protection authority in the U.S. to *help* business in Europe.' (emphasis added).[38] He believed that help is needed in terms of understanding how to implement the directive, how to respond in a timely fashion, and how to figure out European expectations. If a data protection or privacy commission were established to negotiate with the European Union and to help with certification for U.S. business, as Rob Veeder pointed out, this could lead to ombudsman and advisory functions in the United States.[39] At this point much will depend on the implementation process throughout the member states. If European countries offer guidance themselves out of a desire to keep U.S. business, then intervention by a U.S. entity would not be necessary.

However, pressure for an American data protection or privacy commission is likely to continue from outside the United States. National governments prefer to deal with national governments, and representatives from data protection commissions prefer to deal with representatives from data protection commissions. Other essays in this book provide astute reflections on the problems and value of such commissions. Data protection commissions are not going to become extinct, although their roles may be modified to accommodate more global solutions, as reflected in the EU directive, and the technological changes brought about by the Global Information Infrastructure, as discussed by Janlori Goldman in her essay in this volume.

Analysis of the process of decision making of the EU Data Protection Directive reveals the influence and strategies of American, as well as European, business. Businesses have an interest in achieving privacy solutions with which they can continue to function and make profits. For multinational firms, global solutions to problems are often attractive. As in other areas, the details are critical. Rather than having global solutions imposed by national or regional organizations, businesses would prefer to develop such solutions themselves. Technological solutions and standards, especially along the lines of the Canadian Standards Association, may well be more attractive to business as a basis for a global solution than legal requirements.[40] Although business may not look with favour upon legal requirements, privacy advocates and data protection commissioners will continue to see the necessity of legal requirements as a way of holding business accountable and of motivating business to take actions to protect privacy.

The focus of action on the EU Data Protection Directive now shifts to the legislative arena of the member states who must harmonize their national laws with the directive's articles by 24 October 1998. American business representatives will monitor these national legislative processes and seek opportunities to influence outcomes. Although the directive itself imposes parameters on the scope of national decisions, questions of interpretation continue. For example, Article 7 of the final directive, rather than requiring 'informed consent,' requires, with some exceptions, that member states shall provide that personal data may be processed only if 'the data subject has unambiguously given his consent.' Whether the return to national decision-making forums provides American businesses with opportunities to weaken the protections in the directive is likely to depend on how the national business interests and the national government view the directive.

NOTES

1 The early drafts of the proposal (European Commission proposals of July 1990; the Economic and Social Committee of April 1991) were entitled 'Council Directive Concerning the Protection of Individuals in Relation to the Pro-

cessing of Personal Data.' The European Parliament amended the proposal in March 1992, and the proposal approved by the European Commission and submitted to the Council of Ministers is entitled 'Council Directive on the Protection of Individuals with Regard to the Processing of Personal Data and on the Free Movement of Such Data.' COM (92) 422 final – SYN 287 (Brussels, 15 Oct. 1992).

2 Priscilla M. Regan, 'The Globalization of Privacy: Implications of Recent Changes in Europe,' *The American Journal of Economics and Sociology* 52, no. 3 (July 1993), 258–9.

3 James Kobielus, 'EC's New Privacy Proposals Could Hobble Global Nets,' *NetworkWorld* 9, no. 4 (27 Jan. 1992), 27.

4 Mitch Betts, 'A One-Way Street: Fortress Europe Bars Transfers of Personnel and Customer Data to the U.S.,' *Computerworld* 24, no. 52, 53 (24 Dec. 1990 / 1 Jan. 1991), 10.

5 'Brussels v Big Brother,' *Economist* 322, no. 7745 (8 Feb. 1992), 72.

6 Wanda Cantrell, 'Europe's Siren Song for U.S. Bureaus,' *Credit Card Management* 5, no. 1 (April 1992), 89.

7 Katherine Morrall, 'Prying Eyes Still Aren't Welcome in Europe,' *Credit Card Management* 4, no. 3 (June 1991), 55.

8 Allyson L. Stewart, 'Direct Marketing in Europe Is Not as Direct as It Sounds,' *Marketing News* 27, no. 3 (1 Feb. 1993), 17.

9 Steven J. Metalitz, 'The Proposed Data Protection Directive: At What Price Privacy?' *Journal of European Business* 2, no. 6 (July/Aug. 1991), 14.

10 Susanne Meier Robinson, 'Privacy vs Profit,' *Journal of European Business* vol. 4, no. 6 (July/Aug. 1993), 9.

11 David Flaherty, 'Telecommunications Privacy: A Report to the Canadian Radio-Television and Telecommunications Commission' (Ottawa: CRTC, 1992).

12 Betts, 'One-Way Street,' 8.

13 Kobielus, 'EC's New Privacy Proposals,' 27.

14 Metalitz, 'Proposed Data Protection Directive,' 13–14.

15 Robert G. Boehmer and Todd S. Palmer, 'The 1992 EC Data Protection Proposal: An Examination of Its Implications for U.S. Business and U.S. Privacy Law,' *American Business Law Journal* 31, no. 2 (Sept. 1993), 265–6.

16 Nick Platten, 'The Impact of New EU Rules on Data Protection,' *Marketing and Research Today* 23, no. 3 (Aug. 1995), 147.

17 Harry Chevan, 'Privacy Battles Overseas,' *Catalog Age* 9, no. 3 (March 1992), 49.

18 'Brussels v. Big Brother.'

19 Metalitz, 'Proposed Data Protection Directive,' 16.

20 'The EC Privacy Directive and the Future of U.S. Business in Europe: A Panel Discussion,' *Iowa Law Review* 80, no. 3 (March 1995), 675.
21 Betts, 'One-Way Street,' 10.
22 'Brussels v Big Brother.'
23 Alastair Tempest, 'Top Issues on Europe's Data Laws,' *Target Marketing* 15, no. 4 (April 1992), 34.
24 'Brussels v Big Brother.'
25 Tempest, 'Top Issues,' 33.
26 Jack Honomichl, 'Legislation Threatens Research by Phone,' *Marketing News* 25, no. 13 (24 June 1991), 4.
27 'Brussels v Big Brother.'
28 David Hencke, 'Canvassing Ban Looms,' *Guardian* (15 Nov. 1993), 1.
29 Cori Vanchieri, 'New EC Privacy Directive Worries European Epidemiologists,' *Journal of the National Cancer Institute* 85, no. 13 (7 July 1993), 1022.
30 Morrall, 'Prying Eyes,' 57.
31 Metalitz, 'Proposed Data Protection Directive,' 16.
32 Ibid.
33 Robinson, 'Privacy v Profit,' 10.
34 Neil Munro, 'Foreign Privacy Law Shields U.S. Consumer,' *Washington Technology* 10, no. 10 (24 Aug. 1995), 64.
35 Paul M. Schwartz, 'European Data Protection Law and Restrictions on International Data Flows,' *Iowa Law Review* 80, no. 3 (March 1995), 485.
36 Alexander Dix, 'Case Study: North America and the European Directive – The German Railway Card, A Model Contractual Solution of the 'Adequate Level of Protection' Issue?' Presented at the 18th International Privacy and Data Protection Conference, Ottawa, 18–20 Sept. 1996.
37 Ibid., 7.
38 'The EC Privacy Directive and the Future of U.S. Business in Europe,' 673.
39 Ibid., 679.
40 Canadian Standards Association, *Model Code for the Protection of Personal Information* CAN/CSA-Q830–96 (Rexdale, ON: CSA, 1996).

11

The Globalization of Privacy Solutions: The Movement towards Obligatory Standards for Fair Information Practices

JOEL R. REIDENBERG

Varying jurisdictional approaches as well as different standards for the treatment of personal information will pose conflicts for the interrelated and international data processing arrangements of the twenty-first century. The European Union's directive on data protection (the 'EU directive')[1] coupled with the Global Information Infrastructure (GII) raise the stakes for global solutions to the universally recognized need to maintain fair information practices in an information society. Yet, at the same time, the nature of twenty-first century information-processing arrangements will be complex and ill-suited for a single type of solution. This essay argues that data protection norms in Europe will promote obligatory standards for fair information practices in the United States as a consequence of the provisions found in European law and in the EU directive.

The European Pressure

The EU directive establishes a comprehensive legal foundation throughout Europe for the fair treatment of personal information and subjects international data flows from Europe to restrictions if the destination does not assure an 'adequate' level of protection.[2] It therefore exerts significant pressure on information rights, practices, and policies in North America.

Over the past twenty years, U.S. law has provided sporadic legal rights and remedies for information privacy.[3] Most regulatory efforts have constrained the government, while existing private sector standards derive largely from company-specific practices.[4] In essence the U.S. approach means that the existence and non-existence of meaningful data protection will be specific to particular circumstances.[5] The EU directive and the GII, thus, present critical challenges for U.S. policies and practices. Against this divergent structural background, the imposition by the EU directive both of harmonized European legal requirements for the fair treatment of personal information and of limitations on transborder data flows outside of Europe forces the U.S. government to recognize that American standards will be examined in Europe and forces U.S. companies to recognize that they will have to respect European legal mandates. Although there is uncertainty regarding the long-term application of the EU directive to particular contexts, multinational companies and the U.S. government will by necessity follow closely the implementation of the EU directive.

Although the EU directive provides an impetus for introspection by the United States as well as other countries outside Europe, the GII is also forcing American scrutiny of the treatment of personal information. Public opinion polls show that Americans care about privacy and are concerned about the treatment of personal information. This concern is noted particularly with respect to the development of online services. Similarly, companies are increasingly fearful of becoming the subject of the next data scandal and are beginning to see pro-active data protection policies as a commercial strategy. Businesses also express a critical need for confidence and security in the treatment of network information.

Nevertheless, the United States is not likely to adopt a comprehensive data protection law similar in content to the EU directive at the beginning of the new millennium. The ad hoc, reactive legal approach in the United States combined with an ingrained distrust of government are both unlikely to change without a major shift in political culture. For the foreseeable future, such a shift appears highly improbable. Instead, a proliferation of legal and extra-legal mechanisms are beginning to converge in a way that will proliferate the rules for the treatment of personal information within the United States. The nascent response, thus, to the twin pressures of the EU directive and the GII is a movement towards obligatory standards of fair information practice within the United States and a globalization of respect for mandatory principles of fair information practice.

Scrutiny and 'Adequacy'

The initial source for the extension within the United States of respect for mandatory principles of fair information practice will be the required European scrutiny of U.S. data protection. Because the EU directive is now law, comparisons between European data protection principles and U.S. standards of fair information practice must be made.[6] The EU directive requires that American standards of fair information practice be 'adequate' in order to permit transfers of personal information to the United States.[7] In the absence of directly comparable, comprehensive data protection legislation in the United States and the lack of explicit criteria for the determination of 'adequacy,' the assessment of the data flows to the United States is by necessity complex. Any general comparison would not be meaningful, as the context of information processing must be considered. More recently, the working party, created under the directive to advise the European Commission and composed of representatives from the European data protection agencies,[8] prepared a preliminary guidance note on the interpretation of 'adequacy' that similarly took a contextual view for future assessments.[9] A study of U.S. data protection conducted for the European Commission argued that the comparison should be made on the basis of 'functionally similar' treatment.[10] This approach matches an aggregation of targeted legal privacy rights, non-specific legal rights that have an impact on the treatment of personal information as well as the actual practices of data collectors in the United States against a core set of European standards. The result offers important points of convergence as well as divergence.[11]

In the context of the GII, data protection authorities will have significant difficulty applying European standards to trans-Atlantic data flows. As a practical matter, the diversity of activities, participants, and information-processing arrangements obscure clear analysis. The GII crosses sectoral and national regulatory boundaries, and crucial aspects of the treatment of personal information depend on esoteric technical characteristics. Even if a data protection authority wanted to investigate all contexts in each sector, the specialized expertise and the necessary resources are unlikely to be available.

Unless the European Union seeks to withdraw from international information flows, data protection authorities will face unexpected legal obstacles to export prohibitions. The relatively new world trade agreements embodied in the Final Act of the Uruguay Round, also known as the GATT 1994, include a sectoral accord on services, the General Agreement on Trade in Services (GATS). Because transnational information processing qualifies as a 'service,' the GATT 1994 provisions are likely to be a restraining force on European data export prohibitions. Restrictions on data flows applied against an entire country or against a specific sector within a country may violate these accords. Consistent with international trade agreements, GATS requires 'most-favoured nation treatment' that obligates signatory members to accord other signatories 'treatment no less favourable than it accords to like services and service suppliers of any other country.'[12] Article 14 of the GATS expressly allows signatories to adopt measures for the protection of the privacy of individuals and the protection of confidentiality.[13] However, any such measures are still subject to the most-favoured nation clause. Similarly, the GATS Annex on Telecommunications allows signatories to take measures necessary to ensure 'security and confidentiality of messages' provided that such measures are not discriminatory.[14]

Any European restrictions on the flow of personal information must, thus, satisfy the tests of non-discrimination among third countries. For member states in the European Union to block information flows to one country with 'inadequate' privacy protection and not violate the principles of 'most-favoured nation' and non-discrimination, the member states must, at the same time, block information flows to all countries with similarly lacking privacy protection. In other words, to single out the information flows to a particular country without taking comparable action against other countries with similar privacy deficiencies is likely to constitute an impermissible discrimination.

By contrast, a focus on particular contexts, such as the treatment of caller identification information or the processing of particular information by a specific corporation, would be less likely to violate the non-discrimination obligation. The contextual analysis significantly diminishes any claim to discriminatory action on transborder data flows or to violations of 'most-favoured nation' status because the narrower the examination, the less likely it will be to find a comparable case treated in a more favourable way. Politically, the least problematic restrictions will thus come from case-by-case analysis and assessment.

Regardless of pressure from the EU directive, fair information practices in the United States face increasing public examination. Data protection scandals continue to attract attention. For example, within the past few years, NYNEX, one of the major American telephone companies, was publicly exposed for failing to implement customer subscriptions for number blocking on its caller identification service. The direct marketing industry has been criticized in the press for surreptitious data gathering activities on the Internet and for designing web sites to collect personal information from children. And Netscape was revealed to contain features that allow Internet web sites to read browsing patterns from the user's own hard drive.

At the same time, businesses are also concerned with privacy issues. Industry wants certainty of standards for the fair treatment of information. And, business needs confidence in the integrity of information.[15] Data protection around the world will be an essential element of 'good business practice' because the treatment of personal information is now an issue of business competitiveness. Already in Belgium, financial institutions have fought each other over the use of bank payment records to cross-sell products of affiliated companies.[16]

Companies based in the United States have also begun to recognize this key aspect of data protection. For example, Citibank has developed a data protection arrangement among affiliates for worldwide information processing that establishes a high competitive standard. Citibank implemented among its affiliates a series of contractual standards in the United States for the processing of railway card data originating in Germany.[17] Internet software providers are, likewise, seeking to incorporate privacy preferences in products. Microsoft, for example, has implemented filtering software for web sites in the Explorer 3.0 browser software. In essence, the sufficiency of standards of fair information practice within the United States is now on the political and business agenda.

The Confusing Governmental Response in the United States

The U.S. governmental reaction, however, to the twin pressures from the EU directive and the GII is confusing. Despite the EU directive and the GII, the American regulatory philosophy remains wedded to targeted sectoral rules adopted in reaction to particular issues. The prospects for a comprehensive data protection law in the United States remain low. The U.S. government, particularly the federal government, has tried to give fresh thought to fair information practice issues, but the messages from policy decisions are neither coherent nor consistent.

In 1993, while the EU directive was still in draft form, Vice President Gore and the Clinton Administration launched the National Information Infrastructure initiative and created the Information Infrastructure Task Force (IITF). As part of the initiative, the IITF attempted an ambitious effort to define American standards of fair treatment of personal information for the information infrastructure. Because of the likelihood of increased foreign scrutiny of transborder data flows, the IITF examined the standards from the Council of Europe convention, the OECD guidelines, and the drafts of the EU directive with the intent to develop an American position consistent with global norms. By the end of 1995 the IITF issued a series of reports, non-binding policy statements, and guidelines that appear to compete with one another and result in the preservation of the federal regulatory status quo.[18] In 1996 and 1997 the Federal Trade Commission even took a brief foray into privacy policy and held widely publicized hearings that resulted in another government rehash of the debate over the effectiveness of self-regulation. Then, in fear of waning influence, the NTIA issued yet another explanation of self-regulation.[19]

More recently, individual states have begun to grapple with information infrastructure issues, and there is a growing movement to increase legal standards of fair information practice, particularly with respect to marketing uses of personal information. Interestingly, the EU directive is having an influence on the direction and drafting of proposals at the state level, as legislative staff consult the EU directive to find ideas and to strengthen support among representatives. In this election year, however, privacy issues are not likely to be a high priority.

Another more concrete response to the EU directive and the GII may be a centralization of privacy policy within the federal government. The IITF presented a white paper in 1997 to address the issue of a data protection board.[20] The white paper presents a set of options for the institutional structure of privacy policy making, including the centralization of decision making. Because of the scrutiny of U.S. treatment of personal information, industry has a new incentive to seek international assistance from the U.S. government. If European regulators take the transborder data flow provisions seriously, the dispersion in the United States of jurisdiction for privacy issues coupled with inter-agency rivalries will ultimately encourage businesses to push for the creation of an executive branch data protection office. Otherwise, foreign data protection authorities will continue to have no appropriate U.S. counterpart with which to engage in problem solving and constructive dialogue. However, between budget pressures and ideological beliefs, a new independent agency with full regulatory powers has little chance of adoption. Instead, a consolidation of the dispersed functions in a single executive branch office is more likely to occur, and any powers for the private sector are likely to be limited to an ombudsman role.

In the likely event that European data protection authorities begin to block flows of personal information to the United States, a more specific American response can be expected. The U.S. government and industry groups will certainly raise initial objections to the principle of actual data transfer prohibitions. Some will strongly disagree with any foreign judgments of U.S. law and practice. Yet the American public reaction, and consequently the political pressure, will be much harder to anticipate. A data transfer prohibition that discloses a lack of fair treatment of personal information within the United States could greatly assist privacy advocates seeking additional U.S. protections. In addition, such decisions may split industry cohesion, as those companies with strong global data protection will have a commercial incentive to see businesses with poor practices thwarted in their international activities. Alternatively, the restraints may not be perceived within the United States as an appropriate level of response by European regulators to any identified problem with American data protection, and U.S. business positions against regulatory protections for privacy may be strengthened politically.

For the long run, bilateral negotiations between the United States and the European Commission may assist the development of consistent U.S. government policies. Although the U.S. government has little to offer initially, given that domestic politics keep comprehensive data protection legislation off the negotiating table, the discussions themselves force the U.S. government and industry to confront the need to satisfy international privacy standards.

Globalizing Fair Treatment in Transborder Data Flows

The ambiguous state of fair information practice policy in the United States and the impending evaluation of U.S. processing activities, as required by the EU directive, together force data protection regulators, global companies, and their respective constituencies to achieve a workable consensus on satisfying fair information practice obligations for international data flows. In the global environment, the legal requirements of the EU directive will set the agenda; the treatment of personal information in Europe must conform to its mandates, and the personal information is not geographically constrained. As a result, two strategies may be offered to minimize conflicts over transborder data flows: (1) a new contractual model based on the liability of data exporters,[21] and (2) a technological approach based on the development and deployment of privacy conscious technical standards.

The contractual strategy offers a way to sustain European standards on the GII without the complexities of intensive regulatory intervention in a world of globally distributed information processing. Under the EU directive, an exporter of personal information could be held to violate the requirement of 'fair and lawful' processing if the exporter fails to assure that adequate information practices follow the data.[22] This means, for example, that a French data exporter would be liable in France under the standards imposed by French law for the treatment of the exported personal information regardless of where the data are processed. Under this interpretation, if an exporter cannot show that European standards are applied to the foreign processing, the exporter does not comply with the 'fair and lawful' processing requirements. Contractual arrangements, then, become the key for data exporters to minimize the risk of European liability; data exporters will need to develop contracts that assure protection by data recipients.[23] This contractual strategy avoids the problems associated with enforcement of intercorporate agreements by individuals because it shifts the focus of contracts from protection of the individual to protection of the corporation itself.[24] At the same time, the liability approach maintains corporate responsibility and preserves local recourse for individuals against data exporters, rather than attempting to create rights against remote processors that will be hard to enforce.

This type of contractual strategy forces companies to assure fair treatment of personal information without the need for data protection regulators to make direct complex evaluations of foreign law. In the absence of contractual arrangements, data exporters will be unable to show 'fair and lawful' processing. To meet the burden of liability, companies will impose data protection obligations privately on data recipients. In practice, the legal strategy will require a serious commitment to supervision of foreign processing activities by data exporters. Without supervision, the data exporter remains widely exposed to liability at the place of export. This suggests an important role for codes of conduct both as a device to define contractually imposed standards for specific contexts and as a benchmark to measure compliance.[25] With this strategy 'information audits' become a critical self-preservation device for companies, while simultaneously avoiding the difficulties of extraterritorial inspection by data protection authorities and costly duplication of supervision by multiple data protection agencies. European data protection authorities may, for example, decide that an information audit certified by a trusted third party is the only way for a company to demonstrate 'fair and lawful' processing when personal data are exported. In any case, with this contractual strategy, European data protection authorities might accomplish the goal of assuring adequate treatment of personal information without many of the difficulties inherent to the assessment of foreign law.

The second strategy, a technological approach based on the development and deployment of privacy conscious technical standards, also offers an opportunity to embed fair information practices in the GII.[26] Technological choices establish default rules. For example, Netscape browser software allows Internet web sites to log visits on the user's computer hard drive and access that traffic information for profile purposes.[27] The feature is not publicized by Netscape, though technically savvy users can disable the logging capability without impeding their use of the Netscape browser.

The use of 'technologies of privacy' is essentially a business-driven solution that can be used to promote data protection goals and implement European obligations. Standards and architecture planning may in effect create binding privacy rules. For example, Internet web pages may adopt a common opt-out protocol, such as a small green box that can be clicked to erase a visitor's traffic data and thus preclude its use for secondary purposes. Similarly, protocols may be developed that anonymize personal information whenever possible.

The significance of technical protocols cannot be underestimated as a policy tool to develop binding standards of fair information practice. Two particularly noteworthy endeavours reflect complementary technical approaches. The Canadian Standards Association has elaborated a standard for fair information practice. The CSA model code integrates privacy as a technical quality standard. This standard emphasizes business policy and becomes a robust instrument as pressure mounts on the private sector to use the standard as a reference point in contracts. The CSA has sought to expand this approach by proposing a privacy quality standard at the International Organization for Standards (ISO). From Europe, data protection officials have endorsed the contribution to privacy that this standards initiative can offer.[28]

In the United States, however, the private sector has been more ambivalent; any such standard would require enforcement mechanisms against companies, mechanisms that do not presently exist within the U.S. framework. American industry has, instead, invested heavily in the promotion of architectural standards that would seek to incorporate privacy policies within Internet transmission protocols. Labelling and filtering technologies along with standard formats for data profiles present possibilities for the assurance of fair information practices. If implemented, the choices and structure of such architectural mechanisms will offer binding rules for participants. The proper design and implementation, thus, raise critical issues for data protection.[29] Nevertheless, as in the case of the CSA model code, European data protection authorities do see possibilities for the labelling and filtering approach.[30] The recognition and implementation of new technical strategies can reduce the potential regulatory conflicts for international information flows.

Conclusions

As information becomes the key asset of the twenty-first century, the treatment of personal information and the verification of compliance with fair standards become critical for public confidence in network activities.[31] In spite of the confusing U.S. government response to the GII and the EU directive, the possible solutions for international information flows exert a tremendous pressure towards obligatory standards. Liability coupled with contractual arrangements and network architecture impose significant rules on information processing. Narrow developments in U.S. government policy, greater corporate attention to fair information practices, new contractual arrangements, and network system default rules will collectively decrease the divergent characteristics of fair information practice standards in the United States from those of the EU directive. Yet the more seriously European data protection authorities take international data flows and the more extensively the public debates the GII, the greater the pressure will be towards these obligatory standards in the United States.

NOTES

1 European Union, *Directive 95/46/EC of the European Parliament and of the Council on the Protection of Individuals with Regard to the Processing of Personal Data and on the Free Movement of Such Data* (Brussels: Official Journal L281, 24 Oct. 1995).
2 Ibid., Article 25–6.
3 See Paul Schwartz and Joel R. Reidenberg, *Data Privacy Law: A Study of U.S. Data Protection* (Charlottesville: Michie, 1996)
4 Ibid.
5 Ibid.
6 European Union, *Directive 95/46/EC*, Article 25.
7 Ibid.

8 See European Union *Directive 95/46/EC*, Article 29.

9 Working Party on the Protection of Individuals with Regard to the Processing of Personal Data, *Discussion Document: First Orientations on Transfers of Personal Data to Third Countries – Possible Ways Forward in Assessing Adequacy* (26 June 1997).

10 See Schwartz and Reidenberg, *Data Privacy Law*.

11 Ibid.

12 See *General Agreement on Tariffs and Trade*, Annex 1B: General Agreement on Trade in Services (GATS) (MTN/FA II-A1B), Article 2.

13 Ibid., Article 14 (c)(ii).

14 Ibid., Annex on Telecommunications, Article 5.4.

15 Encryption controversies reflect this critical aspect of standards for fair information practices. In Congress recent proposals seek to confront the encryption issues.

16 See Aff. OCCH c. Générale de Banque, Trib. de comm. de Bruxelles, Chbre. des actions en cass., slle des référés, 15 sept. 1994 (Belgium) reprinted in *Droit de l'informatique et des télécoms* (1994–4), 46–50; Aff. Feprabel et Fédération des courtiers en Assurance c. Kredietbank NV, Trib. de comm. d'Anvers, 7 juillet 1994 (Belgium), reprinted in *Droit de l'informatique et des télécoms* (1994–4), 51–5. Significantly, individuals did not bring these cases. Instead, the bank competitors successfully sued, based in part on the data protection prescriptions against secondary use of personal information.

17 See Alexander Dix, *The German Railway Card: A Model Contractual Solution of the 'Adequate level of Protection' Issue*, Proceedings of the 18th International Conference of Data Protection Commissioners, Ottawa, 1996.

18 See, e.g., U.S. Department of Commerce, NTIA, *Privacy and the NII: Safeguarding Telecommunications-Related Personal Information* (Washington, DC: Department of Commerce, Oct. 1995); IITF, *Report of the Privacy Working Group, Privacy and the NII: Principles for Providing and Using Personal Information* (Oct. 1995); U.S. Advisory Council, *First Report: Common Ground* (1995) (containing section on 'Privacy and Security').

19 See U.S. Department of Commerce, *Privacy and Self-Regulation in the Information Age* (Washington, DC: U.S. Department of Commerce, NTIA, 1997) (available at: http://www.ntia.doc.gov/reports/privacy/privacy_rpt.htm).

20 U.S. National Information Infrastructure Task Force, *Options for Promoting Privacy on the National Information Infrastructure* (April 1997) (available at: http://www.iitf.nist.gov/ipc/privacy.htm).

21 For an extended discussion, see Schwartz and Reidenberg, *Data Privacy Law*; see also Joel R. Reidenberg, 'Setting Standards for Fair Information Practice in the U.S. Private Sector,' *Iowa Law Review* 80: (1996), 497, 545–50.

22 See Schwartz and Reidenberg, *Data Privacy Law.*

23 Ibid.

24 Ibid.

25 For a discussion of the usefulness of codes of conduct and standards, see Colin Bennett, *Implementing Privacy Codes of Practice: A Report to the Canadian Standards Association* (Rexdale, ON: Canadian Standards Association, 1995).

26 See Joel R. Reidenberg, *Governing Networks and Rule-Making in Cyberspace, Emory Law Journal* 45 (1996), 911, 927–8.

27 Usually the data are stored in the Netscape directory in a file <cookies.txt>.

28 See Working Party on the Protection of Individuals with Regard to the Processing of Personal Data, *Opinion 1/97 on Canadian Initiatives Relating to Standardization in the Field of Protection of Privacy Set Up by Directive 95/46/EC of the European Parliament and of the Council of 24 October 1995,* (29 May 1997), stating that the Canadian and ISO initiatives 'significantly contribute to the protection of fundamental rights and privacy on a world-wide basis.'

29 See Joel R. Reidenberg, 'The Use of Technology to Assure Internet Privacy: Adapting Labels and Filters for Data Protection,' *Lex Electronica* I:1, available at: http://www.lex-electronica.org/reidenb.html.

30 In both the April and September 1997 meetings the International Working Group on Data Protection in Telecommunications examined the Platform for Internet Content Selection and the Platform for Privacy Preferences technologies being developed by the World Wide Web consortium.

31 See Joel R. Reidenberg and Françoise Gamet-Pol, *The Fundamental Role of Privacy and Confidence in the Network, Wake Forest Law Review* 30 (1995), 105.

PART V

CHOICES FOR PRIVACY ADVOCATES

12

Life in the Privacy Trenches: Experiences of the British Columbia Civil Liberties Association

JOHN WESTWOOD

The British Columbia Civil Liberties Association (BCCLA) has not been nearly as successful as we would have liked in securing privacy protection for citizens.[1] Our experiences are not unique; other privacy advocates in Canada have also found their task heavy sledding, and I suspect advocates around the world have too. In this essay I will analyse four cases in which the BCCLA tried to secure or influence privacy protection and discuss the lessons privacy advocates can learn from these experiences.

First, I will offer some comments about the world facing privacy advocates. The difficulty in getting public and private sector institutions to respect privacy stems from two major sources: first, the strong pressures on these institutions to act in ways that invade our privacy; and, second, the distressingly weak citizens' response to privacy invasions. Institutions invade privacy for two main reasons: money and power. In both the public and private sectors, there is intense pressure on agencies to operate efficiently. If they believe that they can save resources and exercise their power more effectively by not duplicating the collection of personal information or by collecting more of it, by adopting new technologies to more carefully monitor the behaviour of individuals, or by compiling denser and more complete profiles of citizens, then there is almost a biological imperative to do so. At the management level, all the instincts run in the same direction. If a proposal looks like it will save money or increase what is thought to be a legitimate exercise of power, the fact that it invades privacy is rarely if ever an important consideration. It is not the job of management to balance what is good for the institution against what is good for individuals, or for society at large.[2]

At the governing level – whether in the boardroom or at the Cabinet table – the situation is slightly different, but no less difficult. Corporate CEOs and boards of directors are at the bidding of the shareholders, who in turn are almost solely concerned with bottom-line profitability. When questions about the ethics of a business practice are raised, it is more often as window dressing at an annual general meeting than as real consideration of the day-to-day running of the corporation. To persuade a corporation that it should move towards respecting privacy it is almost always necessary either to show that doing so makes business sense (in terms of better client or public relations), because it opens doors previously closed, or because not doing so runs afoul of the law.[3] There have been many arguments made recently about the expanding role of ethics in business decision making – some large corporations have retained or hired their own ethicists – but we should be sceptical about the fate of ethical considerations when bottom-line profitability is at stake.

In the political sphere, government ministers and their Cabinet colleagues are acutely attuned to the direction of the political winds and aware of the political costs and benefits involved in any proposal. For example, saving taxpayers dollars, punishing criminals, and exposing cheaters usually earn political favour. Only an even stronger political current running in the other direction, or (more rarely) a heartfelt belief that the proposal is morally wrong, will persuade our political masters to forego the benefits of invading personal privacy. In fact, it is rare that the political downside of invading privacy is strong enough to outweigh clear political advantages.

Let me illustrate these general considerations by describing several cases in which the BCCLA has been closely involved.

The PharmaNet Issue

PharmaNet is a data bank containing the complete prescription profiles of every citizen in the province of British Columbia. It is run by the Ministry of Health, although the data on it are nominally under the control of the province's College of Pharmacists. Every pharmacist must by law query the database to check a patient's record for unusual dosages, conflicting or contraindicated prescriptions, and evidence of multidoctoring, before filling any prescription.[4]

PharmaNet has been in operation since September 1995. It was conceived and substantial resources put into its development long before the BCCLA read about it in the press. The collection of such sensitive information in one data bank, its widespread access, and its mandatory use by pharmacists set off alarm bells. The BCCLA wrote to the Minister of Health setting out our concerns, and asked that PharmaNet's implementation be stopped until wider consultation on the privacy issues was carried out.

In March 1994 the ministry organized a meeting of ministry officials, health industry representatives, the BC Information and Privacy Commissioner, and two public interest groups. PharmaNet was portrayed by the ministry and the College of Pharmacists as a 'magic bullet,' a technology that would protect people (especially seniors) from drug interactions, and catch drug abusers who are multidoctoring. It would save lives and save money.

After reviewing the system's design and proposed use at length, the Information and Privacy Commissioner recommended better security measures and urged wider consultation before the project went ahead.[5] He also questioned whether the benefits of collecting this information outweighed the risks to personal privacy. His concerns, echoed by the BCCLA, were that:

- The potential for 'browsing' the data bank was great
- The completeness of the information made it very valuable to parties other than pharmacists (such as employers, the police, and litigants in court)
- Access to the data bank was bound to expand over time.

The BCCLA held the view that the risk–benefit judgment should be left up to citizens, not made by the ministry. We also felt strongly that the mandatory nature of access by pharmacists violated citizens' privacy rights. The ministry responded by promising wide public consultation before proceeding with the project.[6]

During the summer of 1994 the ministry conducted what it called 'public information sessions' in seven communities across British Columbia. The 'information' panel consisted of three PharmaNet supporters and myself. Even though publicity for these 'town hall' meetings was adequate, the turnout was depressingly small. Most of the people who did turn up understood and supported the BCCLA's concerns.

At the same time as it was conducting its 'information sessions,' the ministry secretly commissioned a public opinion poll on people's attitudes towards PharmaNet. In 1995 the BCCLA obtained a copy of the polling results under the Freedom of Information and Protection of Privacy Act. Despite the fact that the poll glossed over the most important privacy issues, fully 42 per cent of the respondents thought that Pharma-Net should be a voluntary system. However, the poll also showed that the twin goals of saving health care dollars and catching those bilking the Pharmacare system won almost unanimous support. Given these levels of support, the campaign to stop the system was all downhill from there. We met with the minister in the fall of 1995, but he refused to alter any aspect of the data bank. When told of our concerns about the privacy implications, he responded with words to the effect that PharmaNet is not the most serious privacy problem in the world and that it would go ahead as planned.

What can be learned from the BCCLA's failed attempt to stop or alter PharmaNet? First, there were clearly powerful internal forces behind the system: ministry bureaucrats who wanted to save money, the pharmacists who wanted to enhance their reputation as professionals (that is, as more than 'pill pushers'), and the physicians, who supported it on the understanding that they would ultimately get access. The health industry is a powerful lobby in BC's capital. Second, a lot of time and money had been spent on its development before the public had any inkling of what was going on. We entered the fray too late. Third, being seen to save lives and money was too potent a political pay-off to be resisted. Fourth, it was cost-effective: the ministry had to buy a new computer system anyway and building PharmaNet into it was relatively cheap.

Most important, there was no groundswell of public opposition to PharmaNet. The reasons for the lack of public concern likely were:

- The complex nature of the privacy issues – the principle of meaningful consent to the collection and disclosure of personal information, the extraordinary value of a complete prescription profile, and the prospect of 'function creep'
- The fact that most people would grant access to a pharmacist even if it were optional, and so they did not readily see what the fuss was about
- The long term privacy concerns did not weigh heavily enough in peoples' minds given the easy-to-understand and powerful health and cost advantages.

The Videotaping of Police Calls

Several years ago the BCCLA received a complaint from a woman who had called 911 because her brother was drunk and threatening her and her children. The police arrived with a cameraman from *To Serve and Protect* (a local 'reality-based' cop show) in tow. The woman was frantic, and she did not think to refuse the cameraman permission to enter her house. A couple of months later, the details of her family crisis were broadcast. The woman was terribly embarrassed, and her children were taunted at school.

We advised her to lodge a police complaint, which she did. The police responded that they could not act on the complaint because the department had no policy about camera ride-alongs, and so the officers involved had contravened no policy. We then suggested a civil suit under the provincial Privacy Act, and offered to find *pro bono* counsel.[7] The woman was initially enthusiastic, but subsequently changed her mind, mainly because she did not want to put her family through the same privacy invasion all over again in court. She was also unable to sustain her anger about the incident over the year or so that it would take to get the case heard.

The BCCLA took it upon itself to complain to the BC Police Commission about the lack of policy in this area. The commission responded positively, producing a well-argued discussion paper that recommended that all police forces have a policy, that all identifying information be fuzzed out before broadcast, and that police have veto power over the contents of tape made with police assistance. Over the next year or so, most municipal police forces and the RCMP agreed to abide by these recommendations. The producer of the show was livid, blamed the police, complained to the Information and Privacy Commissioner, and took his concerns to the press, but to no avail. The program, *To Serve and Protect* was eventually abandoned.

This case was an easy win for the BCCLA. The idea that there is something drastically wrong with the unfortunate moments of one's life being taped and broadcast on television for public entertainment was one that both the public and police were quick to grasp. Any one of us could well find ourselves in the woman's situation. The images of a camera operator recording the details of a personal tragedy for posterity, and a television program airing the tape for entertainment, are powerful images. To do nothing in response to this type of complaint would place law enforcement agencies in a bad light. In addition, there were institutional factors acting in our favour. The police are naturally concerned about protecting their own information, as well as the way they are portrayed on television. And the Police Commission saw an opportunity to respond positively to a citizen's complaint on an issue that did not put it in conflict with the police. The invasion of privacy in this case was obvious and powerful, and there were no strong institutional or political forces acting in the opposite direction.

Drug Testing in the Workplace

The BCCLA has received numerous complaints from employees in the private sector who have been forced to undergo drug testing as a condition of employment. We have been only moderately successful in addressing these complaints. The arguments against drug testing are well known and include:[8]

- The tests are invasive.
- The results are often unreliable.
- The tests can reveal tangential information that the employer has no business learning.
- The tests impose on employees who are engaged in drug use.
- The problem of drug use in the workplace can be better addressed in other ways.

Despite these criticisms, employers have generally ignored workers' and the privacy advocates' concerns. They believe that workplace drug use has heavy costs, such as sloppy and dangerous workplace behaviour, theft, and sick time. In addition, some senior managers view drug use as a scourge in our society and have taken up an American-style 'war on drugs.' They see drug testing of their employees as not only a prudent policy in business terms, but as well an opportunity to sit on the right side of the moral fence. Interestingly, one of the cases where we were successful involved a U.S. firm doing business in Canada. We told the firm that there is a different attitude towards drug testing here in Canada[9] and appealed to their acceptance of local employment standards.

One of the difficulties in addressing drug testing is the lack of legal protection for employees. Drug testing for railroad engineers has been held by the courts not to unduly invade privacy, and drug testing of bank employees has been held by a human rights commission not to unfairly discriminate on the basis of disability.[10] In unionized workplaces the strength of an employer's right to manage the workplace under union contracts has determined whether drug testing is permitted; for non-union workplaces there is no protection against drug testing under provincial employment standards legislation. Drug testing in provincial or federal government workplaces would, of course, come under the scrutiny of the privacy commissioners.

The fight against drug testing in the workplace runs into three major stumbling blocks:

- The view that drug abuse is morally wrong – with the concomitant adage 'if you're not taking drugs, you've nothing to hide'
- The desire to cut business costs believed to be associated with employee drug use
- Employers' assumption that they have a right to pry into the private lives of employees whenever those private lives could affect performance in the workplace.

Moral suasion on a case-by-case basis has proven virtually useless. Legal protections are needed in this area. Even where employees do not receive direct protection under privacy law or Canada's Charter of Rights and Freedoms, legal precedents would signal to employers the extent to which drug testing is permissible. The BCCLA has begun preparing a constitutional challenge to the drug-testing policy of a provincial commission in an effort to create some jurisprudence in this area.

Criminal Record Checks

The BCCLA does not oppose in principle criminal record checks for those in a position of trust or authority over vulnerable people, such as children, the elderly, and the handicapped. Provincial government employees have had to undergo criminal record checks since 1987; they are sporadically used in the private and volunteer sectors. Our main concerns are that:

- Only those in a need-to-know position should have access to a person's criminal record
- The protection of the vulnerable should be the only use made of such checks
- Employees have due process protections
- The information be securely kept and destroyed when no longer needed.

In 1995 the provincial government introduced legislation that mandated criminal record checks for all government employees in positions of trust or authority over children, all employees of government-funded child care centres, and a host of professionals, including physicians, dentists, nurses, teachers, physiotherapists, and lawyers.[11] At the time the Information and Privacy Commissioner commented (this time more privately) that the huge invasion of privacy involved was not warranted by the infinitesimal gain in protection of children. The BCCLA's concerns were:

- The large number (64) of criminal offences considered 'relevant' for the purposes of the legislation (many of which have only a remote connection with child abuse)
- The fact that potential employers would be notified of a 'relevant' criminal record before it had been determined that a candidate posed a risk to children
- The lack of due process for persons deemed to pose a risk to children.

We took the usual steps – expressed our concerns in a letter to the Attorney General, discussed them with senior officials, and held a press conference. Again, our efforts were for naught. Fear and loathing of pedophiles, the protection of children, and 'hang 'em high' attitudes towards criminals are strong currents in Western Canada. Despite acknowledging that criminal record checks address only a tiny portion of the child abuse problem, the government judged rightly that it had overwhelming public support in introducing sweeping legislation that included coverage of vast numbers of employees for a broad range of criminal offences.

There is a 'zero tolerance' attitude towards child abuse. Restricting the scope of child protection legislation, even when the privacy invasion is widespread and the hope of gain in the level of protection extremely remote, is an idea that has a very short life span. Our opposition to sections of this law ran counter to virtually all the political winds and was a hopeless cause from the start.

Data Matching by Ministry of Social Services

In 1995 the BC government amended welfare legislation to give the provincial Ministry of Social Services carte blanche to share personal information about welfare recipients with other federal, provincial, and local government agencies. The purpose is to cut down welfare fraud by matching client files against other databases. Although the BCCLA is not, in principle, opposed to all such information sharing, we are concerned that there are no restrictions or reporting requirements on the ministry's use of its power. We fear that, left alone, the government will almost always view its own objectives as overriding.

We wrote to the minister asking that the legislation be changed to require that the ministry notify the Information and Privacy Commissioner in advance of any proposed data matching. Even though the commissioner would have no order-making power (because the data sharing was authorized by statute), his assessment whether an appropriate balance was being struck between legitimate government objectives and the privacy rights of welfare recipients could act as a check on government abuse of its powers. When we received an inadequate response, we wrote again to the minister, voiced our concerns in the press, and alerted the commissioner. I am sure it is no surprise that these efforts proved fruitless.[12]

Welfare recipients receive little sympathy from the majority of citizens, especially those suspected of bilking the system. The government rightly judged that it would not receive strong public opposition to checking welfare recipients' files to weed out those who are also receiving aid from other provinces, are in jail, or are also receiving unemployment insurance. Despite the fact that almost all those whose files are matched are legitimately receiving aid, the public was unmoved. The BCCLA's concern about the lack of oversight of government data matching was met with a deafening silence.

British Columbians have a short fuse when it comes to unnecessary drains on the public purse. People forget they too could find themselves in the unfortunate position of having to accept welfare. Thus, the real potential for invasion of privacy did not strike a responsive chord. The protest against a proposal that would save scarce public resources, catch cheaters, and affect only those 'different' from the rest of us was doomed from the start.

Conclusion – Lessons and Solutions

Advances in technology – from cheap video-surveillance systems to enhanced data matching and retrieval systems to genetic mapping – have vastly increased the capability of public and private sector institutions to collect, use, and disclose information about citizens. The genie is out of the bottle, and it is impossible to put it back. The only real hope for securing some measure of privacy for ourselves is to make the downside of using these technologies more expensive than the benefits. That means (a) making illegal the misuse of personal information by the private sector as well as the public sector and (b) generating an awareness on the part of citizens about privacy invasions and translating that awareness into a political force. Even (a) is not likely to occur until (b) is a reality.

It is difficult to get people stirred up about privacy invasions or motivated to protest or take political action. There appear to be three constraining factors. First is the lack of empathy. Few people are aroused to protest when it is someone else's privacy that is being invaded, unless they can readily imagine themselves falling into a similar predicament. This is especially true when those whose privacy is invaded are different in important ways (for example, welfare recipients). This perception is but an example of a more widespread problem, namely, many people's lack of concern for the plight of those not of their family, their neighbourhood, their race, or their 'kind.' However, I do not see this lack of empathy as an excuse for doing nothing. We might as well address it here as in any of its other manifestations. We must therefore be more creative in portraying the effects of privacy invasions, so that more people will care about the plight of others. We need a modern Dickens.

A second constraint is that interests and values other than privacy are often seen as more powerful, or more pressing, than privacy interests. In fact, the proposition, 'Privacy is what's left over when all other interests are satisfied' fairly accurately describes many people's attitude, and government's and business's behaviour, when privacy is at stake. In this way, privacy shares a feature with freedom of expression. When asked, virtually everyone expresses a strong belief in freedom of speech, but these same people will readily retreat from this commitment as soon as they view the ideas in question as offensive or dangerous. Similarly, most people say that they value privacy highly – except of course when another interest conflicts, such as better protecting their children or saving taxpayers' dollars.

We must, therefore, do a better job of presenting privacy as a positive good, in terms of the benefits that control over access to ourselves has for our psychological, social, and political lives. We need to follow up on the analysis provided thirty years ago in Alan Westin's seminal work *Privacy and Freedom* and encourage research on the consequences that a lack of privacy has on people's lives and their ability to cope with a rapidly intruding world, and we need to see to it that the results are widely publicized.[13]

Finally, invasions of privacy are often complex, abstract, or cumulative in effect, and so they do not readily fire people's imaginations. The fact that PharmaNet creates a new kind of information (complete prescription profiles), and the likelihood that as time goes by more and more uses will be found for these profiles, fell on deaf ears during the consultation sessions at which I spoke. The few who showed up nodded in sage agreement that this was indeed dangerous, then went home to cut the lawn. Privacy issues that are simple, concrete, and immediate are most likely to move people to protest. For example, many in British Columbia are indignant about photo radar, and they yell long and loud about the junk mail 'invading' their homes, but they are indifferent to the proliferation of data matching schemes in both the public and private spheres.

We must create images or icons that bring the issues to a more simple, concrete, or immediate level. In this vein, Orwell's *Nineteen Eighty-Four*, the expression 'Big Brother,' and the adjective 'Orwellian' have done more for privacy than any other single factor. Simultaneously, Orwell gave us images we can use to focus on privacy issues and a vivid portrayal of the devastating effects of invasions of privacy on human beings. We need fresh images, better tailored to illustrate and animate the dangers presented by data sharing and manipulation, by the concentration of personal information in the hands of the already powerful in our society, and by the lack of data protection in the private sector.

Lobbying institutions in the public and private sectors to better protect privacy, educating the media about privacy issues, and using the law when the opportunity arises are actions worth continuing. But given the power of the forces aligned against privacy advocates, and the lure of the technology, I am convinced that we are fighting a losing battle unless we can somehow create vivid and forceful images. They must have the power to stir people up about the more complex and far-reaching threats to our privacy that today draw a yawn. We need to create a greater and opposite force to the pressures on public and private institutions to invade citizen's privacy, so that the political cost to governments is too great to pay and the cost to corporations' bottom lines too great to ignore.

NOTES

1 The efforts of the BCCLA have included the publication by Erin Shaw, John Westwood, and Russell Wodell of *The Privacy Handbook: A Practical Guide to*

Your Privacy Rights in British Columbia and How to Protect Them (Vancouver: BCCLA, 1994), and 'Drug Testing in the Workplace' (1996), an informational pamphlet for employees and employers.

2 See Charles Raab's arguments, in this volume, about the ambiguity of the notion of 'balance.'

3 This relates to Mary Culnan's and Robert Bies's arguments herein about the strong relationship between fair information principles and the building of consumer trust and loyalty.

4 Legislation giving the government control over expansion of the use of the data bank was passed in 1997, and the government announced its intention to include emergency room physicians as users of PharmaNet, and eventually all physicians.

5 'Information and Privacy Commissioner Calls for Public Consultation on PharmaNet,' Press Notice of 17 March 1994 (available at: www.oipcbc.org).

6 It is worth noting here that although the BC Information and Privacy Commissioner has order-making power with respect to the collection, use, and disclosure of personal information by government bodies in the province, he was powerless to stop PharmaNet. The province's Freedom of Information and Protection of Privacy Act allows public bodies to collect, use, and disclose personal information at will so long as the collection, use, or disclosure is authorized by statute. Thus, whenever the provincial government sees the political pay-offs as strong enough and wants to subvert the letter or the spirit of the law, it need only introduce legislation authorizing it to do whatever it wants to do. The commissioner can act privately and publicly chastise the government for its information practices, but he cannot prevent it from invading privacy.

7 This tort law dates from 1979 and allows an independent cause of action for a privacy invasion. Privacy Act RSBC 1979, c. 336.

8 See Privacy Commissioner of Canada, *Drug-Testing and Privacy* (Ottawa: Minister of Supply and Services, 1990).

9 Whether that is actually true is another matter.

10 The drug-testing program of Toronto Dominion Bank was litigated before the Canadian Human Rights Council in 1994 by the Canadian Civil Liberties Association; 22 CHRR D/301 (HRT). The commission essentially declared that the program did not violate Canadian human rights law because its random nature did not discriminate against any one category of employees, an interpretation that was later upheld by the Federal Court in 1996; 25 CHRR D/373 (FCTD).

11 Bill 26, Criminal Records Review Act, Fourth Session, Thirty-Fifth Parliament, Legislative Assembly of British Columbia, 1995.

12 In 1996 the government introduced legislation giving similar powers to the ministers of finance. This time we were successful in having the legislation amended to reduce the scope of allowable data sharing and in securing a written undertaking by the ministers to consult the Information and Privacy Commissioner in advance of any data sharing program.

13 Alan F. Westin, *Privacy and Freedom* (New York: Atheneum, 1967).

13

Spanners in the Works: How the Privacy Movement Is Adapting to the Challenge of Big Brother

SIMON DAVIES

Since the birth of the modern privacy movement in the late 1960s, the goals and tactics of privacy activists around the world have demonstrated an extraordinary diversity. As with the environmental movement that paralleled it, some privacy strategies have been designed along institutional lines, while others involved varying degrees of civil disobedience and non-violent direct action (NVDA). Promotion of privacy concerns has ranged from intellectual expression through to physical violence against technology.

Privacy organizations and campaigns have varied from country to country, and from time to time. Some were quasi-industry initiatives that worked 'within the system.' Others were overt campaigning groups that worked primarily within the mass media, using high-profile campaigning tactics. Despite this diversity, some clear patterns have emerged within the privacy field. In the late 1960s and early 1970s, at the height of public concern over the emergence of a Big Brother society, privacy activism shared features in common with some of the hard-line environmental campaigns of the 1990s. Street marches, industrial sabotage, civil disobedience, and violence against machinery were sporadic, but common. In many countries it is clear that the concept of privacy has in previous decades been interpreted as a political idea fuelled by issues of sovereignty, techno-phobia, power, and autonomy.[1] Citizens in all industrialized countries looked forward with trepidation to the impending Orwellian dystopia of *1984*. One influential thinker of the time described the prevailing mood as 'profound distress.'[2] Technology was viewed widely as a threat to privacy, employment, and cultural identity. Actions against the technology reflected this view.

With the advent of new information-gathering techniques, a strong anti-census movement evolved throughout Europe. The protest in the Netherlands was so widespread that it achieved a critical mass that finally made the census entirely unworkable. A substantial number of Dutch citizens simply refused to supply information to the census authority. A little over a decade later, in 1983, Germans responded to their national census in the same fashion, resulting in a landmark Constitutional Court decision protecting personal information rights.[3]

Since the late 1970 the environment of privacy activism changed substantially. Privacy protection in more recent years has been widely perceived as constituting a set of technical rules governing the handling of data. A scan of privacy-related publications in the two decades from 1970 indicates a steady decrease in polemical works and a corresponding increase in technical and legal works.

Ironically, while this change of focus paralleled an unprecedented variety of privacy codes, conventions, and legislation, more data are being collected by more powerful systems on more people and for more purposes than at any time in history. Despite the evolution of technologies that were the subject of 'nightmare' dystopias in the 1960s, resistance to their introduction since 1985 has been minimal. The technology had become familiar to people. By the late 1970s the 'information society' was well and truly part of common language. The popular vision of the future changed almost overnight, and the world economy went through a transformation.

The Big Brother society imagined by the world in 1970 depended on coercion and fear. This vision for the developed world is largely redundant, and the view of many observers is that society now appears to be more Huxley-like than Orwellian. It is a Brave New World dominated not so much by the tyranny of technology, but by a disempowering political and cultural phenomenon that Ralph Nader calls 'Harmony Ideology.'[4]

As privacy activism became mainstream throughout the 1980s, so too did the organizations that were the vehicles of the privacy movement. Most came to depend on institutional funding, particularly from philanthropic trusts and companies. Increasingly, as the issues became more sophisticated, representatives from commerce and government were invited to join the movement. After the 1970s the uncomplicated motivation of 'state power versus the individual right' gave way increasingly to discussions of specific technologies and specialist legal questions. The emergence of such complex fields as encryption, biometrics, data matching, smart cards, and data warehousing became a challenge to the ability of privacy organizations to strike a popular message in their campaigns.

After the 1970s the idea of 'Big Brother in a bunker' was clearly more of a popular myth than a genuine threat. Consequently, the privacy movement matured into a highly specialized field that was expected to provide constructive solutions to privacy problems.

The Archetypal Privacy Organization

Since the early 1970s national non-governmental privacy and data protection organizations have been formed in several countries. These include the:

- United States Privacy Council
- Australian Privacy Foundation
- Stichting Waakzaamheid Persoonsregistratie (The Netherlands)
- ArgeDaten (Austria)
- Electronic Privacy Information Center (USA)
- Canadian Privacy Network
- New Zealand Privacy Foundation
- Infofilia (Hungary)

In addition to these, a global group – Privacy International – was formed in 1990.

Such organizations have, generally, come about through one of two processes. The most common process, as with the case of Hungary and Canada, is the orderly establishment of a coalition of academics and specialists coming together in response to a general need for a non-government organization. The Canadian privacy initiative, for example, came about through a breakfast meeting in Washington of a dozen specialists and activists in the privacy field. Although Canada has federal and provincial privacy laws, the participants felt there was an urgent need for a non-government group as privacy issues in Canada continue to attract considerable public attention. The U.S. Privacy Council (USPC) is more broadly based, but still a specialist initiative which brought together many recognized experts from all quadrants of the privacy movement.[5] The initiative was particularly important in view of the high level of cooperation within commercial circles to dissuade Congress from enacting privacy legislation.

The second process can be seen, for example, in Australia and New Zealand, where an issue of national concern sparked the random formation of a broad spectrum group. The New Zealand Privacy Foundation was launched in 1991 at a stormy public meeting in Auckland of three hundred people protesting about the government's proposed 'Kiwi Card.' The Australian Privacy Foundation, formed during 1987 in response to the proposed 'Australia Card,' had a membership comprising people from divergent political positions, many of whom had no prior interest or involvement in privacy.[6]

The structure of privacy organizations varies widely. The majority of privacy organizations fall into one of three categories:

- *A foundation* governed by a deed of trust and headed by a number of trustees – usually eminent public figures. The trustees are vested with the responsibility to ensure that public funds are dealt with properly.
- *An incorporated body or charity* registered with the relevant government agency and having a board of management and ordinary public membership.
- *A private organization* in which there is no or very limited public involvement and with a single-tiered management structure. Privacy councils, in which all members are voting members of a closed group, fall into this category.

It would be a difficult and imprecise task to judge which structure has been the most suitable to the interests of privacy. An expert group in the form of a council is an excellent mechanism to respond to specific threats to privacy. Such bodies can provide the sort of input that is necessary to amend legislation and attract institutional support. One problem with expert bodies is that they can be technocratic or legalistic by nature, and they may lack the motivation to use populist language and imagery.

A more broadly based organization has the dual advantage of being able to more accurately express the public pulse, and it can have the potential to draw a broad spectrum of support and resources. The disadvantage is often that internal politics can all but destroy such organizations. A coalition of ideologies that comes together to oppose a government initiative may soon fall apart when private sector surveillance is criticized. An example of this phenomenon is found in Australia, where libertarian groups supported the Australian Privacy Foundation in its campaign against the identity card, but withdrew on ideological grounds when the foundation mounted a campaign for credit reporting legislation.

Most broadly based privacy organizations aim to be seen as both experts and advocates. In such cases the membership generally comprises a number of people from diverse backgrounds, typically data protection, freedom of information, computer and data security, consumer advocates, journalists, political scientists, social scientists, members of such professions as law, accountancy, and medicine, civil rights advocates, and computer professionals.

The Objectives of Privacy Organizations

The constitutional aims of many privacy organizations are quite similar. Most organizations have the aim of education, critical analysis, support for legal protections, and opposition to surveillance measures. Most specify their aim to encompass all the generally held data protection principles (fair use, finality, collection limitation, and access).

U.S. privacy organizations have a particularly difficult mandate, having to overcome the effect of a well-organized industry lobby and a Congressional culture which has been hostile to omnibus privacy regulation. The USPC specifies in its aims the establishment of legislative protections that many Europeans take for granted. Its aims also include:

- To educate all people and organizations about the importance of privacy protection, the ethical implications of the misuse of personal information, and what they can do about it personally
- To oppose restrictions on privacy-enhancing technology such as encryption and to encourage the development and deployment of technologies for privacy protection
- To oppose the creation of a national identification card and to restrict the use of personal information numbers such as the Social Security Number.[7]

Organizations in many other countries are able to express non-specific goals. The Australian Privacy Foundation has among its aims:

- To support legal and other limits being placed on the development and operation of surveillance techniques as a means of social control
- To provide a means of communication among privacy advocates and between privacy advocates and other organizations with similar interests in the protection of privacy
- To support the work of international privacy protection bodies in relation to privacy issues of international scope.[8]

Privacy International, while not being a national body, chose an amalgam of objectives, many of which were based on the defence against surveillance. These include:

- To assess the impact of new technologies on the privacy and freedom of the individual
- To assess the nature, extent, and implications of transborder flows of information between countries
- To seek ways through which information technology can be used in the attainment of the protection of privacy.

One of the aims that consistently features in the manifestos of more recent non-government privacy groups is the promotion of privacy-enhancing technologies (PET). PET are encryption-based technologies that can be used as a mechanism to achieve basic privacy protections such as preservation of anonymity and access to data.

New Model Privacy Organizations

From the early 1990s the privacy movement commenced a new phase in its evolution. The growth of the Internet had rekindled ideas of sovereignty, state power, and autonomy. These concepts no longer resided within legal and specialist circles, as was the case in the privacy movement of the 1980s, but were reinterpreted for the broad mass of Internet users. Inspired in particular by Computer Professionals for Social Responsibility (CPSR) and the Electronic Privacy Information Center (EPIC) a new generation of groups emerged to champion the privacy cause. Many had abandoned the now unruly expression of privacy in favour of the broader concept of liberty.

Nevertheless, privacy and liberty had always been inseparable. Indeed, autonomy and informational self-determination were key planks in privacy protection in several countries, particularly Germany. In the new equation liberty also encompassed freedom from intrusion, control, and censorship. But whereas the old generation of privacy advocates had measured privacy in terms of legal protections, the new generation were more suspicious of law and authority. A strong element of libertarianism ran through many organizations. The spirit of the Internet – anarchy, atomization, and resistance to regulation – pervaded the campaign for liberty. Ironically, although the nature of the Internet prevented many legislative controls (and protections) it was the commercial sector that began to impinge most on the rights of users. The clear failure of both the government and the market to protect privacy is a contributing factor to the anarchist nature of new privacy organizations.

Recognizing the international nature of the Internet, many of these organizations joined forces at the 1996 annual meeting of the Internet Society in Montreal to form the Global Internet Liberty Campaign (GILC). The Association des Utilisateurs d'Internet, CypherNet, Fronteras Electrónicas España, and NetAction were among the newer organizations, but such was the presence of the issues surrounding the Internet (particularly censorship and surveillance) that traditional organizations such as the American Civil Liberties Union, Human Rights Watch, and Amnesty International also joined. The coalition thus formed continued the long-standing nexus between privacy and mainstream human rights that was forged in the 1970s.

GILC's statement of principles embodied some traditional privacy concepts, but reflected the privacy landscape that is likely to prevail until the second decade of the new millenium:

1 Prohibiting prior censorship of online communication
2 Requiring that laws restricting the content of online speech distinguish between the liability of content providers and the liability of data carriers
3 Insisting that online free expression not be restricted by indirect means such as excessively restrictive governmental or private controls over computer hardware or software, telecommunications infrastructure, or other essential components of the Internet
4 Including citizens in the Global Information Infrastructure (GII) development process from countries that are currently unstable economically, have insufficient infrastructure, or lack sophisticated technology
5 Prohibiting discrimination on the basis of race, colour, sex, language, religion, political or other opinion, national or social origin, property, and birth or other status
6 Ensuring that personal information generated on the GII for one purpose is not used for an unrelated purpose or disclosed without the data subject's informed consent and enabling individuals to review personal information on the Internet and to correct inaccurate information
7 Allowing online users to encrypt their communications and information without restriction.

This document makes no mention of either privacy or surveillance. It does, however, augment the spirit and intent of more conventional privacy bodies. Individual rights, freedom of expression, openness, and equal access had rarely been directly expressed in the constitutions of other bodies, yet clearly were necessary components in any society that respects privacy. The key element in the GILC constitution is not its commitment to human rights or to opposition to censorship, but its expression that opposes any restriction on encryption. This bold assertion challenges one of the key planks of the national security and law enforcement communities worldwide. That is, to establish a licensing system for encryption that will ensure that government has the ability to easily intercept all electronic communications.

Marc Rotenberg of EPIC has described the encryption issue as 'the future battleground for privacy.' Encryption is crucial because it holds the key to authentication, privacy, security, trust, and anonymity in electronic communications. It establishes the technical means to set limits on intrusion by government and commercial organizations. It provides the mechanism to ensure that anonymity and authentication can work in parallel. It is likely that the battle over encryption policy will be the most important privacy issue in modern times, and it is equally likely that the new generation of privacy organizations will face unprecedented challenges from both government and commercial organizations.

The cyber-rights groups encompass a wide range of traditional values, but their campaigning tactics have been confined almost exclusively to lobbying via electronic media. Some of these tactics have been very successful. In early 1994 the Electronic Privacy Information Center and Computer Professionals for Social Responsibility circulated an electronic petition opposing the government's proposed Clipper Chip wiretapping initiative. Despite very little lead time, the petition garnered fifty thousand signatures and received considerable publicity. [9] In another initiative, EPIC mounted an electronic mail campaign against the Lotus organization which had planned to release a CD-ROM containing the financial details of a hundred million U.S. households. The chairman of the company received forty thousand protest E-mail messages over three weeks and consequently withdrew the product.

The 1995 battle over Senator Exon's Communications Decency Act brought both the campaigning potential and the campaigning deficits of the Net community into sharp focus. For months, as the Exon proposal slowly worked its way through Congress, Net users – while apparently unanimous in their condemnation of the initiative – were unable to coordinate a national campaign. Meanwhile, the Christian Coalition, which supported the bill, was organizing letter-writing campaigns, lobbying Congress, and controlling the spin of the mainstream media by fashioning its censorship proposals as essential measures to protect children from online pornography.[10]

In December 1995, after a House conference committee had finally agreed to adopt the 'indecency' language contained within the Exon Senate bill, the Net community devised a series of campaigns. Voters' Telecommunications Watch organized an Internet Day of Protest by urging its readers to phone or write their representatives in Washington. Meanwhile, protest rallies were held in San Francisco, Seattle, and New York City. This rare crossover between traditional protest tactics and 'new' campaign tactics was reported widely in the media, but failed to stop the passage of the bill.

The Exon bill became law, prompting *Wired*, in its 'Cyber Rights Now' page, to observe: 'Netizens seem incapable of defending themselves. Time and time again, repressive proposals concocted by clueless lawmakers have failed to raise more than a whimper from the online community. Congress and the White House have come to believe that the Net is useless as a political weapon – and that its users are incapable of organized political resistance. If netizens want to stem the hemorrhage of remaining freedoms, this passive stance must change – and fast. We must seize every tool at our disposal to bash Congress and make our voices heard.'[11] The criticism was justified to the extent that the Net community tended to be inward looking. This was not the case for the more enlightened watchdog groups, a small number of which were emerging as a potent and skilful force against surveillance and censorship. These groups combined a range of lobbying tactics and articulated the privacy position across many levels.

A superb example of this combination of skills was enacted in late 1996 when EPIC staged a one-day 'summit' on the development of encryption guidelines by the Organization for Economic Cooperation and Development (OECD). The U.S. government had exerted strong pressure on the OECD to pass prescriptive guidelines that would favour the discredited 'Clipper' escrow system. EPIC had fought to make the OECD aware that this would be a retrograde step. On 26 September the OECD was to hold a key meeting of its members to determine the basis of the encryption policy, and EPIC had decided that a non-government meeting on the doorstep of the OECD in Paris would be crucial to get the message across. According to one publication:

While EPIC had initially thought of staging a sort of anti-conference some smart lobbying enabled it to win recognition from the OECD. Held in the luxurious official setting of the International Conference Center on the Avenue Kleber, the OECD conclave was opened by the Australian magistrate Norman Reaburn, chairman of the OECD group of experts, and John Dryden of the OECD Science, Technologies and Communications division. The moderators of all the debates that followed were also members of the group of experts. Still, sitting side by side were four cryptographers who, between them, added up to a singular nightmare for western intelligence agencies.[12]

Most of the speakers found systems based on trusted third parties (the encryption key system most favoured by the United States) to be pointless and ineffective. As a result, a new draft of the OECD guidelines was unexpectedly tabled before the group of experts the next day, this one stressing respect for individual freedoms.[13]

The second stage of EPIC's strategy was to use the Internet as a means of communicating its success at the OECD. By combining a knowledge of the technical weaknesses of the opposition, with a strong and well-reasoned alternative position, the organization was able to foster a dialogue across the Net community that moved quickly into the political arena via mainstream media.

The New Luddism in Britain

Both the archetypal privacy movement of the 1980s and the cyber-rights movement of the 1990s have been strongly pro-technology. Most privacy activities have been aimed at either the creation of regulation or the adoption of privacy-enhancing technologies. However, between 1995 and 1997 a series of highly publicized actions against technology inspired a new wing to the privacy movement in the United Kingdom.

In 1995 a group of women peace campaigners broke into a British Aerospace facility in Lancashire and caused £1.5 million damage to a Hawk jet that was destined for export to Indonesia. The women justified their action on the basis that all the normal democratic steps had been exhausted in their campaign against the genocide in East Timor. Evidence was presented in their trial which indicated that there was a significant threat that the Hawk jet would be used against the East Timor population. The women argued that they were merely disarming an aggressor. The technology was responsible in the final phase for destruction of life and was thus anything but neutral.

In a landmark decision the jury at Liverpool Crown Court accepted the women's argument that their action was legal under British and international law because they were using reasonable force to prevent a greater crime.[14] Such actions have taken place on more than sixty occasions since 1980, when the Ploughshares movement began in Pennsylvania, USA. This was the first occasion that the British defence had been accepted by a court.

On 12 January 1997 protesters at the site of the Newbury road bypass in Devon set light to road-making machinery, destroying a dump truck.[15] This simple but spectacular action had the effect of splitting the environmental movement. Traditional campaigners were of the view that non-violent direct action included technology as well as people. Other campaigners argued that technology was exempt from the ethics of direct action. One protester observed that 'the more we hit the contractors in their pockets the more reluctant other companies will be to bid for new road schemes in the future.'[16]

Actions against surveillance technology have also increased. This is true particularly in the field of visual surveillance. In recent years the use of closed circuit television (CCTV) in the United Kingdom has grown to unprecedented levels. Between £150 and £300 million per year is now spent on a surveillance industry involving an estimated two hundred thousand cameras. According to the British Security Industry Association more than three-quarters of these systems have been professionally installed. Most towns and cities are moving to CCTV surveillance of public areas, housing estates, car parks, and public facilities. Growth in the market is estimated at 15 to 20 per cent annually.[17]

The central business districts of most British cities are now covered by surveillance camera systems involving a linked system of cameras with full pan, tilt, zoom, and infrared capacity. Their use on private property is also becoming popular. Increasingly, police and local councils are placing camera systems into housing estates and red light districts. Residents associations are independently organizing their own surveillance initiatives. Tens of thousands of cameras operate in public places, in phone booths, vending machines, buses, trains, taxis, alongside motorways, and inside automatic teller machines. Urban centre systems involve sophisticated technology. Features include night vision, computer-assisted operation, and motion-detection facilities that allow the operator to instruct the system to go on red alert when anything moves in view of the cameras. Camera systems increasingly employ bulletproof casing and automated self-defence mechanisms.[18] The clarity of the pictures is usually excellent, with many systems being able to read a cigarette packet at a hundred metres. The systems can often work in pitch blackness, bringing images up to daylight level.

Although it appears that a majority of people tentatively support this technology, opposition is becoming more vocal and more vehement. Claims that the technology has substantially reduced levels of crime have been discredited by several studies. However, the cameras have been used increasingly as a tool to enforce public order and morals, and in most cities to monitor protesters and street demonstrators. This has had the effect of fuelling opposition throughout the mainstream direct action community. Environmental organization, roads protesters, animal rights groups, and other campaigning bodies began from the mid-1990s to view the cameras as a threat to their freedom of movement and to their privacy. Young people, gays, and blacks had often expressed concern that the technology would be used as a tool of oppression. People in more than a dozen cities took it into their own hands to destroy or damage the cameras. In an environment in which CCTV has been introduced without debate or legal protection, these direct actions helped fuel a broader campaign against the technology.

In April 1997 the British campaign group 'Justice?' together with Privacy International announced a day of direct action against cameras in Brighton. The campaign initially involved three hundred activists from around the country and had been sparked by the introduction of four new cameras in the city centre. Residential areas were to be next in line. When the council erected a twenty-foot steel camera pole in the North Lanes conservation area in March of that year, local environmentalists decided to work with civil rights and privacy groups to bring the issue into the mainstream.

The tactics used by the campaign coalition were colourful and dynamic. They included a campaign of disinformation using CCTV warning stickers in public toilets, changing rooms, trains, and buses. More direct tactics used microwave jamming transmitters, pseudo-emergency radiation teams, and tracking mirrors aimed at the cameras. Street theatre, helium balloons, and various other stunts, including two surplus army tanks, covered the whole of Brighton's network of seventeen cameras.

These actions were intended to destabilize public confidence in the cameras, rather than shut them down by force or criminal damage. Alongside the highly effective campaign of disinformation, which included stickers on each camera that read 'Danger: radiation,' a second series of tactics was aimed at destabilizing the relationship of trust between the camera operators and the police. This involved several weeks of subtle and widespread street theatre including mimmickry of drug taking, theft, fighting, alcohol consumption, car theft, shoplifting, and harassment. The process resulted in a great many false call outs to police and a corresponding decline in the relationship of trust that had existed.

These innovative actions marked a change of direction for the protest movement and could become a template for direct action in the future. Groups of community organizations in Bradford and Manchester decided to organize similar actions later in 1997.

Old Wine in New Bottles – The Alinsky Factor

Three clear trends are emerging within the privacy movement. The most important of these is the shift to direct activism – a trend that is substantially different to the more moderate legalistic approach of the 1980s. The second trend is towards hard-line, high-standard lobbying techniques. The third is a trend to amalgamation. Privacy groups, are increasingly working with environmental groups, consumer organizations, anarchist groups and a wide spectrum of single-issue lobbies.

These trends embody a great many tactics and principles of the social justice movements of previous decades. Astute political methodologies have been borrowed from the civil rights campaigns of the 1950s and 1960s. The most important influence appears to be from U.S. rights campaigner Saul Alinsky, and it is his legacy that appears, increasingly, to be the engine room of the new privacy movement.

Saul Alinsky began his career as a Chicago sociologist. His work at the Institute for Juvenile Research included studies into 'organized crime' and the reasons behind it. Using census data, court records, and school reports, Alinsky began to see a correlation between crime and the urban environment. In Chicago, particularly on the west side, juvenile delinquency was endemic in the industrial areas such as the Union Stock Yards and the South Chicago steel mills.[19] It was in the immigrant stockyards of Upton Sinclair's *The Jungle* that Alinsky took the bland notion of community organization and turned it into a rallying call for social justice and equality. In 1939 he formed the Back of the Yards Neighbourhood Council. This was the starting point for the radical notion of 'People's Organizations.'

People's organizations worked to pull together diverse factional interest groups from local business, religious communities, race, labour divisions, and commercial interests. Alinsky's interest was in 'uniting all of the organizations within the community ... in order to promote the welfare of all residents ... so that they may all have the opportunity to find health, happiness and security through the democratic way of life.'[20] *Reveille for Radicals* was written to inspire an alternative to 'monopolistic capitalism and organized labour.'[21] Alinsky launched a firebrand at the union leadership of the day, which he claimed had failed the workers.

To Alinsky, the radical organizer was an outsider, and his goal was to create a platform from which people could experience and express self-worth, power, and dignity. Over the course of the mid-1950s and 1960s Alinsky integrated the civil rights movement with housing and urban planning. Chicago was, at the time, one of the most segregated cities in the North. He challenged existing urban renewal projects aimed at the wealthy and worked towards community integration, social welfare, and education. In taking on the slum landlords, the banks, and council leaders, Alinsky paved the way for a major housing project on the South Side in1961.

Alinsky confronted the counterculture, anti-establishment posturing of the hippies and the yippies, and told them to 'go away and get organized.' His dying thoughts when he wrote *Rules for Radicals* were focused on the 1960's revolution and where it had gone wrong. He sought to find the means of addressing this deficiency through tactics and organization. One of the last actions Alinsky organized, but did not live to see into victory, was the campaign against rising pollution levels in Chicago and the proposed billion dollar Crosstown Expressway.[22]

Saul Alinsky died on 12 June 1972. In his final book *Rules for Radicals* he observed: 'There are no rules for revolution, any more than there are rules for love or rules for happiness, but there are rules for radicals who want to change their world; there are certain central concepts of action in human politics that operate regardless of the scene or the time. To know these is basic to a pragmatic attack on the system.'[23]

These rules were themselves condensed from the likes of Tom Paine, Thomas Jefferson, and the 'founding fathers.' They also had strong military campaign parallels. They included:

- Information warfare and disinformation: Power is not only what you have, but what the enemy thinks you have.
- Wherever possible, go outside the experience of the enemy.
- Make the enemy live up to their own book of rules.

- A constructive alternative should always accompany a successful attack.
- Identify the target, isolate it, personalize it, and polarize it.[24]

Conclusions

The privacy movement is facing an interesting irony. On the one hand, the nightmare vision of Big Brother portrayed by the founding fathers of privacy advocacy is becoming partially evident – even if not in as blatant a form as Orwell had predicted. Globalization, privatization, commodification, convergence, and a trend to perfect human identification are eliminating traditional boundaries of private life. Surveillance is a core component of most forms of information technology.

On the other hand, privacy advocates have never been in such a strong position to accomplish reform. Advocates and experts from all backgrounds and geographic areas are now in regular communication with each other. Common experiences and ideas are strengthening the foundation of privacy advocacy.

There is, in domestic politics, a recognition of privacy that underscores the sensitivity of the subject. The growth of the Internet has created fertile ground for campaigners who strive to raise public awareness of emerging threats to privacy. The recent passing of the European Data Protection Directive offers new opportunities to promote privacy.[25] Media organizations routinely appoint specialist correspondents on technology issues. In the 'quality' media these people are often keenly aware of the range of privacy concerns flowing from the technologies they report on.

Privacy campaigners are, however, unlikely to agree on any single formula for dealing with the perils of the information age. Some have taken a legalistic route, while others are pursuing such ideas as civil disobedience and non-violent direct action against technology. Yet it seems increasingly that many campaigners agree on a set of common positions. Most are moving to the view that industry codes of practice are without merit. Many campaigners now support civil disobedience as a legitimate and often necessary tool. Almost all practising privacy advocates have lost faith in the ability of business to demonstrate a commitment to privacy reform. Meanwhile, the privacy movement speaks almost with one voice in its condemnation of 'opt out' business practices, data protection exemptions in privacy law for national security agencies, and such technologies as biometrics, data matching, 'cookies,' and covert visual surveillance.

Opponents of privacy reform are keen to point out occasional differences of opinion in the privacy movement. Nevertheless, it would be fairer to say that such different views are a result of specialization, rather than fissuring. Privacy in the 1990s is a complex business that requires a vast knowledge of law, politics, and technology. An activist working on, for example, a campaign against a national identity card system will need to be familiar with a maze of interconnecting concepts. It is not unusual for a privacy advocate to be called on to debate issues of law, science, international relations, domestic politics, organizational reform, and human rights. Little wonder that people in the field are fine-tuning their skills. Networking among advocates makes this a logical and very positive step.

The Alinsky factor, which I discussed in the preceding section, is an indication of just how sophisticated the privacy movement has become. Focused campaigns employing a strong intellectual foundation have achieved results for privacy reform. Astute tactics, historical perspective, good contacts in media and politics, and a broad general knowledge of technology and law are ensuring that privacy campaigns are noticed.

Some younger activists in the realm of electronic privacy are still some distance from developing these strengths, but these shortcomings are more than compensated by the renewed passion that this new generation of advocates brings to the movement. With the modern campaigns for Internet rights came a vital renewal of the fusion between the concepts of privacy and liberty.

It is in the international realm where the privacy movement faces its greatest challenge. The idea 'Think global, act local' has become a *modus operandi* for the privacy community, but it is an approach that may ultimately undermine privacy reform. Most of the deals struck at the international level – even those in the European Union – are largely outside the experience of activists, most of whom are occupied fighting fires on domestic turf.

A recent 'memorandum of understanding' between the European Union and the FBI on wiretapping is fundamental to privacy, and yet the deal, obliging telecommunications technology suppliers across the world to supply equipment that is 'wiretap friendly,' occurred without public input. International standards meetings, likewise, are rarely troubled by privacy activists. Most intergovernmental mechanisms that are responsible for producing global conventions and agreements give little or no opportunity for direct external input.

These are difficult challenges for the privacy movement, but there is evidence that progress is being made. Recent interventions in international deals by EPIC, Privacy International, and GILC have taken some intergovernmental bodies by surprise. The largely domestic focus of privacy groups is changing. Only time will tell whether the pace of change in the privacy movement can match the speed and convergence of anti-privacy interests.

NOTES

1 Simon Davies, 'Re-engineering the Right of Privacy: How Privacy Has Been Transformed from a Right to a Commodity,' in *Technology and Privacy: The New Landscape*, Phil Agre and Marc Rotenberg, eds. (Cambridge: MIT Press, 1997).
2 Alan F. Westin, *Privacy and Freedom* (New York: Atheneum, 1967), vii.
3 David H. Flaherty, *Protecting Privacy in Surveillance Societies* (Chapel Hill: University of North Carolina Press, 1989), 45–6.
4 Cited in Simon Davies, *Big Brother: Britain's Web of Surveillance and the New Technological Order* (London: Pan Books, 1996), 53. Harmony Ideology is described as the coming together of opposing ideologies and beliefs into a manufactured consensus.
5 See Simon Davies, 'Non-Governmental Privacy and Data Protection Organizations: Formation, Aims and Activities,' *International Privacy Bulletin* 1, no. 4 (Oct. 1993), 22–3.
6 Davies, *Big Brother*, 130–9.
7 See Davies, 'Non-Governmental Privacy and Data Protection Organizations,' 22.
8 Ibid.
9 Simon Davies, 'Don't Mourn – Organize,' *Wired* 4, no. 3 (March 1996). 86.
10 Ibid.
11 Ibid.
12 'The World-Wide Encryption Battle,' *Intelligence Newsletter* (3 Oct. 1996).
13 Ibid.
14 'Peace Women Cleared over Hawk Attack,' *Statewatch London* 6, no. 4 (July–Aug. 1996), 8.
15 John Vidal, 'Unhappy Birthday Ends in Fire and Tears,' *The Independent*, (13 Jan. 1997), 3.
16 Camilla Berens, 'Are You Fluffy or Spikey?' *The Big Issue* (10–16 Feb. 1997).
17 Davies, *Big Brother*, 173–205.
18 Ibid.

19 Sheridan Hough, 'Saul Alinsky: An Anniversary of Radicalism and Social Change' (published on the web-site of Privacy International, 1997, at www.epic.org).
20 Sanford Horwitt, *Let Them Call Me Rebel* (New York: Knopf, 1989), 79.
21 Ibid., 169.
22 Ibid., 533.
23 Saul Alinsky, *Rules for Radicals* (New York: Vintage, 1971).
24 In the lead-up to the twenty-fifth anniversary of Alinsky's death in 1997, the rules for radicals were widely disseminated around British campaign groups. The Brighton CCTV action was the first of several privacy actions to overtly adopt these rules in the form of a charter.
25 See the essay by Joel Reidenberg in this volume.

Conclusion

COLIN J. BENNETT AND REBECCA GRANT

Times change, technology changes, and we move inexorably into the twenty-first century. Advances in database technology reduce the cost of data collection and management, even as increased competition for profitable niche markets increases the economic value of that same data. Businesses and governments spend more and more money on data and reap ever greater return from such expenditures. Citizens decry Big Brother watching them, but applaud governments that merge databases to ferret out 'welfare cheats' and child molesters. Consumers report being increasingly concerned about the erosion of personal privacy, which they attribute to new technologies. At the same time, they volunteer extensive information about themselves in return for coupons, catalogues, and credit. Attitudes towards privacy remain one of life's paradoxes.

There is clearly an imbalance in the information marketplace. Classic economic theory would contend that an imperfect marketplace can be rectified by two mechanisms. First, one can give a value to personal information so that the costs and benefits of transactions are allocated more appropriately. James Rule and Lawrence Hunter have demonstrated how an explicit market scheme might be implemented. Mary Culnan and Robert Bies, on the other hand, have presented an argument that personal information already has an implicit value. Consumers might recognize this value only rarely. Nevertheless, it may become apparent in a negative sense: A company that demands too much personal information may lose business, implying that the collection of such data costs at least the value of the lost business. Proposals to use market-based solutions ultimately rely on schemes to give individuals some property rights over their personal data with compensation mechanisms and monitoring.

The second mechanism is regulatory intervention to redress the marketplace imbalances. David Flaherty has been, from his perspective as a privacy watchdog, a vocal supporter of expanded *statutory* intervention. The province of Quebec has gone farther than any other government in legislating privacy protection. René Laperrière described the need to regulate the private *and* public sectors. Quebec has, perhaps, recognized that the implicit cost of personal information to business may not be high enough to trigger voluntary protective policies. One can well question whether economic theory should play a role in the protection of a fundamental human right. Nonetheless, the market and regulatory arguments remain appealingly straightforward and easy to envision.

On the other hand, societies have been slow to adopt comprehensive market or regulatory mechanisms, as our privacy advocates and commissioners have illustrated. With the exception of Quebec, the personal information practices of the private sector in North America remain largely uncontrolled and show little voluntary movement towards a different future. Perhaps the solution lies in the technology itself. Technology changes make it easier to gather and track data. They also improve the opportunity to limit access, enhance data security, and reduce the frequency with which we must reveal extraneous data in the course of working, shopping, and interacting with government. Ann Cavoukian described the positive impact that technology can have on our medical privacy. No longer must we have manual medical records, readily visible to all and sundry; computer-based files protected by passwords and access restrictions can ensure that only those with the expertise and need to interpret the data ever see them. Electronic wallets combine the ease of credit cards and banking networks with the anonymity of cash transactions. Anonymous remailers, such as those highlighted by the Center for Democracy and Technology, protect the identity of Internet users, and enhancements to browser software enable readers to refuse 'cookies' or other invasive probes from sites visited. Yet using technology to protect privacy often calls for significant effort on the part of the individual who seeks the privacy. Low privacy protection remains the default condition in much modern technology.

Economic and moral suasion come together in the global approach, as they often have in issues related to ecology, human rights, and economic development. One can see the potential for countries and international alliances to exert pressure on would-be economic partners to meet the higher privacy standards and expectations of the alliance or lose out on significant opportunities for trade. Such is the potential of the European

Union's directive to force North American compliance with broader and tougher European standards, in a scenario where failure to comply could close off the appealing European consumer and labour markets. At the same time, negotiations among partners or outright refusal to comply *or* capitulate could minimize the impact of such global mechanisms. These are the issues Priscilla Regan and Joel Reidenberg wrestle with, and their insights have enlarged our understanding of the direction the future may take.

Privacy advocates uphold the traditions of an earlier time, keeping the issue ever in the public mind, and raising consciousness of potential threats to privacy that might otherwise remain unreported or unanalysed. It is instructive that most of the issues fought within the 'privacy trenches' are often not those that are driven by the latest technologies. At a time when the majority of North Americans report being concerned about potential threats to personal privacy, advocates are commonly among the very few who actively seek to do something about those threats in response to the genuine fears of ordinary people. They confront, cajole, and campaign. They have won some impressive victories, yet they have often suffered depressing defeats, as both Simon Davies and John Westwood attest. In the end, they are loud but often lonely.

As we approach the end of the millenium, we foresee four possible futures for privacy. The first is the *surveillance society*, in which the individual would have little or no control over the collection and circulation of personal information. Information could be collected through a range of surreptitious and intrusive means. It could be matched, profiled, traded, and communicated at will by public and private organizations. This is not, however, an Orwellian vision of a centralized data bank society. It is rather the logical result of a multitude of decentralized institutions, each making pragmatic and incremental judgments that a specific loss of privacy is a price worth paying for the more effective pursuit of government efficiency, safer societies, higher profits, and so on. To the extent that the instruments for data protection existed, they would constitute a symbolic and perfunctory attempt to manage this inexorable drift. They would have no substantial effect on relentless progress towards a globalized system of surveillance.

The second possibility is one of an *incoherent and fragmented patchwork* of privacy protection. The pressures towards surveillance would continue, but would be punctuated by periodic and unpredictable victories for the privacy value. This scenario captures a more chaotic future in which the instruments of privacy would occasionally succeed in building real safeguards into new information systems. Privacy-enhancing technologies would be applied in a variety of contexts and succeed in building in anonymity. Consumer pressure would force the corporate sector to continue to develop codes of practice, and the efforts to develop certifiable standards would force privacy audits in some organizations. However, the victories would have little permanence. The spotlight would focus on a particular practice for a brief period and would then move on.

A third vision sees a world of *privacy haves and have-nots*. Some societies would apply instruments for privacy protection comprehensively and vigorously. The default would become privacy, rather than surveillance. The issue would be politicized, with citizens aware and informed. Data protection agencies would occupy a central role in national administrative systems. Privacy-enhancing technologies would be applied extensively. Consumers would constantly pressure businesses to implement fair information practices. In the terms of the EU Data Protection Directive, there would be an 'adequate level of protection.' Other societies would continue to drift and react to privacy issues as they emerge. Further efforts to globalize international standards would meet with stiff resistance in societies whose economies have benefited from the existence of 'data havens.'

A final vision is one of *global privacy standards*. Under this scenario instruments of privacy protection spread as a process of 'ratcheting up' to the European standard. No public or private organization could transfer data on the global information networks unless it followed the fair information principles. The imperative to secure consumer confidence as the networks are increasingly used for electronic commerce produces a widespread economic incentive to be privacy friendly and be seen as such. The policy instruments would include law, codes of practice, certifiable standards, and privacy-enhancing technologies.

The essays in this volume make it clear that any of these futures is possible. Each author has emphasized the uncertainty that will confront us in our search for solutions to privacy dilemmas. Each essay also makes a compelling argument for a particular approach to privacy protection, even as it makes it clear that no single solution holds all the answers. None would, we think, deny that different conditions will demand different solutions, none of which are mutually exclusive. The mosaic of solutions does not need to be a default position bred out of a confusion and desperation in the face of overwhelming technological, political, and economic pressures. It can also be an explicit policy choice.

There is then nothing to stop us from applying the principles, building privacy in, factoring privacy into business practices, thinking privacy globally, and protesting surveillance out. All are necessary and none is sufficient.

Appendix

Key Internet Sites on Privacy

General Sites

Electronic Privacy Information Center: http://www.epic.org/
Electronic Frontier Foundation: http://www.eff.org/
Politics of Information: http://www.cous.uvic.ca/poli/456/ index.htm
Hotwired: http://www.hotwired.com/
Center for Democracy and Technology: http://www.cdt.org/
Data Surveillance and Information Privacy Webpage: http://www.anu.edu.au/
   people/Roger.Clarke/DV/

Privacy and Data Protection Commissioners' Sites

Office of the Privacy Commissioner (Canada): http://infoweb.magi.com/
   ~privcan/
Office of the Information Commissioner (Canada): http://infoweb.magi.com/
   %7Eaccessca/
Ontario Information and Privacy Commissioner: http://www.ipc.on.ca/
Information and Privacy Commissioner (British Columbia): http://
   www.oipcbc.org
Alberta Freedom of Information and Protection of Privacy Commissioner:
   http://www.gov.ab.ca/foip/
Australian Privacy Commissioner: http://www.austlii.edu.au/hreoc/privacy/
   privacy.htm
Berlin Data Protection Commissioner: http://www.datenschutz-berlin.de/
   ueber/aktuelle/inheng.htm
Office of the Privacy Commissioner for Personal Data, Hong Kong:
   http://www.pco.org.hk

U.K. Data Protection Registrar: http://www.open.gov.uk/dpr/dprhome.htm

New Zealand Privacy Commissioner: http://www.knowledge-basket.co.nz/
privacy/welcome.html

Privacy Rights Clearinghouse: http://www.privacyrights.org

Isle of Man Data Protection Registrar: http://www.odpr.org/

Bibliography

Alderman, Ellen, and Caroline Kennedy. 1995. *The Right to Privacy*. New York: Knopf.

Alpert, Sheri. 1993. 'Smart Cards, Smarter Policy: Medical Records, Privacy and Health Care Reform,' *Hastings Center Report* 23: 13–23.

Agre, Philip E., and Marc Rotenberg (eds.). 1997. *Technology and Privacy: The New Landscape*. Cambridge, MA: MIT Press.

Bennett, Colin J. 1992. *Regulating Privacy: Data Protection and Public Policy in Europe and the United States*. Ithaca, NY: Cornell University Press.

– 1995. *Implementing Privacy Codes of Practice: A Report to the Canadian Standards Association*. Rexdale, ON: Canadian Standards Association, PLUS 8830.

– 1996. 'The Public Surveillance of Personal Data: A Cross-National Analysis,' in David Lyon and Elia Zureik (eds.) *Computers, Surveillance, and Privacy*. Minneapolis: University of Minnesota Press.

– 1997a. *Prospects for an International Standard for the Protection of Personal Information: A Report to the Standards Council of Canada*. Ottawa: Standards Council of Canada (at www.cous.uvic.ca/poli/iso.htm).

– 1997b. 'Convergence Re-visited: Toward a Global Policy for the Protection of Personal Data?' in Agre and Rotenberg (eds.) *Technology and Privacy: The New Landscape*, 99–123.

– 1997c. 'Adequate Data Protection by the Year 2000: The Prospects for Privacy in Canada,' *International Review of Law, Computers and Technology* 11: 79–92.

Bennett, Colin J., and Charles D. Raab. 1997. 'The Adequacy of Privacy: The European Union's Data Protection Directive and the North American Response,' *The Information Society* 13: 245–63.

Bies, Robert J. 1993. 'Privacy and Procedural Justice in Organizations,' *Social Justice Research* 6: 69–86.

Bloustein, Edward J. 1964. 'Privacy as an Aspect of Human Dignity: An Answer to Dean Prosser,' *New York University Law Review.* 962–1007.
– 1978. 'Privacy Is Dear at Any Price: A Response to Professor Posner's Economic Theory?' *Georgia Law Review* 12: 429–53.
Boehmer, Robert G., and Todd S. Palmer. 1993. 'The 1992 EC Data Protection Proposal: An Examination of Its Implications for U.S. Business and U.S. Privacy Law,' *American Business Law Journal* 31(2): 265–311.
Bok, Sissela. 1984. *Lying: Moral Choice in Public and Private Life.* New York: Pantheon.
Canadian Standards Association (CSA). 1996. *Model Code for the Protection of Personal Information.* CAN/CSA-Q830–96. Rexdale: CSA (at http://www.csa.ca).
Cavoukian, Ann, and Don Tapscott. 1995. *Who Knows: Safeguarding Your Privacy in a Networked World.* Toronto: Random House.
Chaum, David. 1992. 'Achieving Electronic Privacy,' *Scientific American* Aug.: 96–101.
Clarke, Roger. 1998. 'Information Technology and Dataveillance,' *Communications of the ACM* 31:(5), 498–512.
Côté, Réné, and Réné Laperrière. 1994. *Vie Privée sous Surveillance: La Protection des Renseignements Personnels en Droit Québécois et Comparé.* Cowansville: Yvon Blais.
Council of Europe. 1981. *Convention on the Protection of Individuals with Regard to Automatic Processing of Personal Data.* Strasbourg: Author.
Culnan, Mary J. 1993. 'How Did They Get My Name?: An Exploratory Investigation of Consumer Attitudes toward Secondary Information Use,' *MIS Quarterly* 17: 341–64.
– 1995. 'Consumer Awareness of Name Removal Procedures: Implications for Direct Marketing,' *Journal of Direct Marketing* 2: 10–19.
Culnan, Mary J., and Priscilla M. Regan. 1995. 'Privacy Issues and the Creation of Campaign Mailing Lists,' *The Information Society* 2: 85–100.
Culnan, Mary J., and H. Jeff Smith. 1995. 'Lotus MarketPlace: Households – Managing Information Privacy Concerns,' in D.C. Johnson and H. Nissenbaum (eds.) *Computers and Social Values.* Englewood Cliffs: Prentice-Hall.
Culnan, Mary J., H. Jeff Smith, and Robert J. Bies, 'Law, Privacy and Organizations: The Corporate Obsession to Know Versus the Individual Right Not to Be Known,' in S.B. Sitkin and R.J. Bies (eds.) *The Legalistic Organization.* Thousand Oaks: Sage.
Davies, Simon. 1996. *Big Brother: Britain's Web of Surveillance and the New Technological Order.* London: Pan Books.
– 1997. 'Re-engineering the Right to Privacy: How Privacy Has Been Trans-

formed from a Right to a Commodity,' in Agre and Rotenberg (eds). *Technology and Privacy*, 143–65.

Equifax, Inc. 1996. *The 1996 Harris–Equifax Consumer Privacy Survey*. New York: Louis Harris and Associates, Inc.

European Union. 1995. *Directive 95/46/EC of the European Parliament and of the Council on the Protection of Individuals with regard to the Processing of Personal Data and on the Free Movement of Such Data*. Brussels: Official Journal of the European Communities No. L281/31, 24 Oct. 1995.

Flaherty, David H. 1972. *Privacy in Colonial New England*. Charlottesville: University Press of Virginia.

– 1979. *Privacy and Government Data Banks: An International Perspective*. London: Mansell.

– 1986. 'Protecting Privacy in Police Information Systems: Data Protection in the Canadian Police Information Centre,' *University of Texas Law Journal* 36: 116–48.

– 1989. *Protecting Privacy in Surveillance Societies*. Chapel Hill: University of North Carolina Press.

– 1991. 'On the Utility of Constitutional Rights to Privacy and Data Protection,' *Case Western Reserve Law Review* 41: 831–55.

Foucault, Michel. 1977. *Discipline and Punish: The Birth of the Prison*. New York: Vintage.

Gandy, Oscar H., Jr. 1993. *The Panoptic Sort: A Political Economy of Personal Information*. Boulder: Westview.

Goffman, Erving. 1958. *The Presentation of the Self in Everyday Life*. New York: Doubleday.

Groupe de récherche informatique et droit (GRID). 1986. *L'Identité Piratée*. Montreal: Société québécoise d'informatique juridique.

Hagel, John III, and Jeffery F. Rayport. 1997. 'The Coming Battle for Customer Information,' *Harvard Business Review*. 75: 53–65.

Harris, Louis, and Associates. 1993. *Health Information Privacy Survey*. New York: Author.

– 1994. *Interactive Services, Consumers, and Privacy*. New York: Author.

– 1995. *Mid-Decade Consumer Privacy Survey*. Atlanta: Equifax.

Harris, Louis, and Alan F. Westin. 1990. *The Equifax Report on Consumers in the Information Age*. Atlanta: Equifax Inc.

– 1992. *The Equifax Canada Report on Consumers and Privacy in the Information Age*. Ville d'Anjou: Equifax Canada.

– 1995. *The Equifax Canada Report on Consumers and Privacy in the Information Age*. Ville d'Anjou: Equifax Canada.

– 1996. *Equifax–Harris Consumer Privacy Survey*. Atlanta: Equifax.

Inness, Julie C. 1992. *Privacy, Intimacy, and Isolation.* New York: Oxford University Press.

Laperrière, Réné, Réné Côté, G.A. LeBel, R. Roy, and K. Benyekhlef. 1991. *Crossing the Borders of Privacy.* Ottawa: Justice Canada.

Laudon, Kenneth C. 1986. *The Dossier Society: Value Choices in the Design of National Information Systems.* New York: Columbia University Press.

– 1996. 'Markets and Privacy,' *Communications of the ACM* 39: 92–104.

Lyon, David. 1994. *The Electronic Eye: The Rise of Surveillance Society.* Minneapolis: University of Minnesota Press.

Lyon, David, and Elia Zureik, (eds.). 1996. *Computers, Surveillance and Privacy.* Minneapolis: University of Minnesota Press.

Madsen, Wayne. 1992. *Handbook on Personal Data Protection.* New York: Stockton Press.

Marx, Gary. 1988. *Undercover: Police Surveillance in America.* Berkeley: University of California Press.

– and Nancy Reichman. 1984. 'Routinizing the Discovery of Secrets: Computers as Informants,' *American Behavioral Scientist* 27: 423–52.

Metalitz, Steven J. 1991. 'The Proposed Data Protection Directive: At What Price Privacy?' *Journal of European Business* 2(6), 13–17.

Miller, Arthur R. 1971. *The Assault on Privacy: Computers, Data Banks and Dossiers.* Ann Arbor: University of Michigan Press.

Organization for Economic Cooperation and Development (OECD). 1981. *Guidelines on the Protection of Privacy and Transborder Data Flows of Personal Data.* Paris: Author.

Packard, Vance. 1964. *The Naked Society.* New York: David McKay.

Prosser, William. 1960. 'Privacy,' *California Law Review* 48: 383–98.

Raab, Charles D. 1997. 'Privacy, Democracy, Information,' in Brian D. Loader (ed.). *The Governance of Cyberspace.* London: Routledge.

– and Colin J. Bennett. 1994. 'Protecting Privacy across Borders: European Policies and Prospects,' *Public Administration*, 72: 95–112.

– 1996. 'Taking the Measure of Privacy: Can Data Protection be Evaluated?' *International Review of Administrative Sciences* 62: 535–56.

Radin, Margaret. 1986. 'Property and Personhood,' *Stanford Law Forum* 34: 957–1015.

Regan, Priscilla M. 1993. 'The Globalization of Privacy: Implications of Recent Changes in Europe,' *American Journal of Economics and Sociology* 52: 257–73.

– 1995. *Legislating Privacy: Technology, Social Values and Public Policy.* Chapel Hill: University of North Carolina Press.

Reich, Charles. 1990. 'The Liberty Impact of the New Property,' *William and Mary Law Review* 31: 295–306.

Reidenberg, Joel R. 1993. 'Rules of the Road for Global Electronic Highways: Merging the Trade and Technical Paradigms,' *Harvard Journal of Law and Technology* 6: 287–305.

– 1995. 'Setting Standards for Fair Information Practice in the U.S. Private Sector,' *Iowa Law Review* 80: 497–551.

– and Françoise Gamet-Pol. 1995. 'The Fundamental Role of Privacy and Confidence in the Network.' *Wake Forest Law Review* 30: 105–25.

Rothfeder, Jeffrey. 1992. *Privacy for Sale: How Computerization Has Made Everyone's Life an Open Secret*. New York: Simon and Shuster.

Rule, James B. 1974. *Private Lives and Public Surveillance: Social Control in the Computer Age*. New York: Schocken.

– 1980. *The Politics of Privacy: Planning for Personal Data Systems as Powerful Technologies*. New York: Elsevier.

Schoeman, Ferdinand D. (ed.). 1984. *Philosophical Dimensions of Privacy: An Anthology*. Cambridge: Cambridge University Press.

Schwartz, Paul M. 1995. 'European Data Protection Law and Restrictions on International Data Flows,' *Iowa Law Review* 80: 471–96.

– and Joel M. Reidenberg. 1996. *Data Privacy Law: A Study of United States Data Protection*. Charlottesville: Michie.

Seipp, David J. 1978. *The Right to Privacy in American History*. Cambridge MA: Harvard University Program on Information Resources Policy.

Shaw, Erin, John Westwood, and Russell Wodell. 1994. *The Privacy Handbook: A Practical Guide to Your Privacy Rights in British Columbia and How to Protect Them*. Vancouver: British Columbia Civil Liberties Association.

Sieghart, Paul. 1976. *Privacy and Computers*. London: Latimer.

Simitis, Spiros. 1987. 'Reviewing Privacy in an Information Society,' *University of Pennsylvania Law Review* 135: 707–46.

Smith, H. Jeff. 1994. *Managing Privacy: Information Technology and Corporate America*. Chapel Hill: University of North Carolina Press.

Smith, H. Jeff, Sandra J. Milberg, and Sandra J. Burke. 1996. 'Information Privacy: Measuring Individuals' Concerns about Organizational Practices,' *MIS Quarterly* 20(2), 167–95.

U.S. Department of Commerce. 1995. *Privacy and the NII: Safeguarding Telecommunications-Related Personal Information*. Washington, DC: Author.

– 1997. *Privacy and Self-Regulation in the Information Age*. Washington, DC: Author.

U.S. Department of Health, Education and Welfare (HEW). 1973. *Computers, Records and the Rights of Citizens*. Report of the Secretary's Advisory Committee on Automated Personal Data Systems. Washington, DC: Author.

U.S. Office of Technology Assessment. 1993. *Protecting Privacy in Computerized Medical Information*. Washington, DC: Author.

U.S. Privacy Protection Study Commission. 1977. *Personal Privacy in an Information Society.* Washington, DC: Government Printing Office.

Vitalis, André. 1988. *Informatique, Pouvoir et Libertés.* Paris: Economica.

Warren, Samuel, and Louis Brandeis. 1890. 'The Right to Privacy,' *Harvard Law Review* 4: 193–220.

Westin, Alan F. 1967. *Privacy and Freedom.* New York: Atheneum.

Contributors

Colin J. Bennett is Associate Professor of Political Science at the University of Victoria, Victoria, BC. His research interests focus on the comparative analysis of public policies to protect personal data. He is author of *Regulating Privacy: Data Protection and Public Policy in Europe and the United States* (1996), as well as articles in a variety of policy and technology journals. Dr Bennett holds Bachelor's and Master's degrees from the University of Wales and a PhD from the University of Illinois at Urbana-Champaign.

Rebecca Grant is Associate Professor in the Faculty of Business at the University of Victoria, Victoria, BC. Dr Grant's research focuses on Internet business and information privacy. She is the author of articles in information technology and management journals, as well as the book *Silicon Supervisors* (1990). Dr Grant holds a PhD in business administration from the University of Western Ontario, an MBA from McGill University, and a BS in computer science from Union College in Schenectady, NY.

Robert J. Bies is Associate Professor of Management in the School of Business, Georgetown University, Washington, DC. His research interests include the delivery of bad news, revenge in the workplace, privacy, and organizational (in)justice. Dr Bies holds a PhD in Business Administration (organizational behavior) from Stanford University, as well as an MBA and a BA from the University of Washington in Seattle.

Ann Cavoukian joined the Information and Privacy Commission of Ontario in 1987 and was appointed commissioner in 1997. As commissioner, she oversees the operations of Ontario's freedom of information and protection of privacy laws. She speaks globally on the importance of privacy and is the author of *Who Knows: Safeguarding Your Privacy in a Networked World* (1996). Dr Cavoukian received her PhD and MA in psychology (specializing in criminology) from the University of Toronto.

Mary J. Culnan is Associate Professor in the School of Business, Georgetown University, Washington, DC, where she teaches courses in electronic commerce and information systems. Her current research addresses the privacy issues raised by electronic marketing, and during 1997 she served as a commissioner on the U.S. President's Commission on Critical Infrastructure Protection. She received her PhD in Management (information systems) from the Anderson School of the University of California, Los Angeles.

Simon Davies is Director General of Privacy International, a Visiting Fellow in the Computer Security Research Centre of the London School of Economics, and a Visiting Fellow in the Department of Law of the University of Essex. He has written five books, including *Big Brother – Britain's Web of Surveillance and the New Technological Order* (1996), and he contributes regularly to newspapers, journals, and periodicals. He has campaigned on privacy issues from identity cards to military surveillance in twenty countries and consults to numerous government, professional, and corporate bodies.

David H. Flaherty has served since 1993 as the first Information and Privacy Commissioner for the province of British Columbia (Canada). He is on leave from the University of Western Ontario, where he has taught history and law since 1972. Dr. Flaherty is the author of *Protecting Privacy in Surveillance Societies* (1989), as well as a host of articles and other books. He holds a PhD and MA in history from Columbia University and a BA (Honours) in history from McGill University.

Robert Gellman is a Privacy and Information Policy Consultant in Washington, DC. Former chief counsel to the Subcommittee on Government Information of the U.S. House of Representatives, he is currently a Fellow of the Cyberspace Law Institute. Mr Gellman is a graduate of the Yale Law School.

Janlori Goldman is Director of the Health Privacy Project at Georgetown University's Institute for Health Care Research and Policy in

Washington, DC. She co-founded the Center for Democracy and Technology, a public interest group dedicated to preserving and enhancing free speech and privacy on the Internet. Ms Goldman worked for more than ten years with the American Civil Liberties Union and directed the ACLU's Privacy and Technology Project from 1988 to 1994. She is a law graduate of Hofstra University and holds a BA from Macalester College.

Lawrence Hunter is a computer scientist at the (U.S.) National Library of Medicine, where he conducts basic research in machine learning and molecular biology. He has written about social issues and computing for the *New York Times*, *Technology Review*, *Washington Monthly*, *Whole Earth Review*, and other publications. Dr Hunter holds a PhD in computer science, MSc and MPhil in computer science, and a BA in psychology, all from Yale University.

René Laperrière is a professor and member of the Law, Science and Society Research Group (GRID), Université de Québec à Montréal (Canada). Among his recent works on privacy are *Private Sector Privacy* (1994), *Privacy under Surveillance*(1994), *The Pirated Identity* (1986), and 'Le droit des travailleurs au respect de leur vie privée,' (1994). Dr Laperrière holds an LLL, DES and LLD from the Université de Montréal.

Gary T. Marx is Professor of Sociology at the University of Colorado at Boulder (U.S.A.)and currently a research fellow at the Woodrow Wilson International Center for Scholars. He is Professor Emeritus at the Massachusetts Institute of Technology and the author of *Protest and Prejudice* and *Undercover: Police Surveillance in America*. His current research and writing focus on new forms of surveillance and social control across borders. Dr Marx received his PhD from the University of California at Berkeley.

Charles D. Raab is Reader in Politics at the University of Edinburgh (U.K.). He conducts research and teaches in the fields of data protection, public access to information, and the implications of information technology, with particular regard to regulatory policy. He has published extensively, including co-authoring *Policing the European Union* (1995). He is currently collaborating on a study of the British data protection system and holds a grant from the Economic and Social Research Council (UK) to study the virtual society. Mr Raab holds an MA degree from Yale University and a BA from Columbia University.

Priscilla M. Regan is an Associate Professor of Government and Politics in the Department of Public and International Affairs at George Mason University, in Fairfax, Virginia (U.S.A.). Her primary area of research involves the development of technological changes, especially communication and information technologies, and their effects on society, organizations, and individuals. She is the author of *Legislating Privacy: Technology, Social Values, and Public Policy* (1995). Dr Regan received her PhD from Cornell University in 1981 and her BA from Mount Holyoke College in 1972.

Joel R. Reidenberg is a Professor of Law at Fordham University School of Law, where he teaches courses in Information Technology Law, International Trade, Comparative Law, and Contracts. He writes extensively on fair information practices and is the co-author of the book *Data Privacy Law* (1996). He is a consultant for the European Commission on a study of data protection and electronic commerce. Professor Reidenberg received an AB degree from Dartmouth College, a JD from Columbia University and a DEA from the Université de Paris I (Panthéon-Sorbonne).

James Rule is Professor of Sociology at the State University of New York, Stony Brook (U.S.A.), where his research includes political sociology and technology. An editor of *Dissent* magazine, he has published widely on personal data systems and other information issues. Dr Rule has taught at the Massachusetts Institute of Technology, Oxford University, and the University of Bordeaux in France. He received his PhD and AM from Harvard University, as well as a BA at Brandeis University.

John Westwood joined the staff of the British Columbia (Canada) Civil Liberties Association in 1987 and was appointed its executive director in 1988, a position he still holds. He has pursued research under a Social Sciences and Humanities Research Council of Canada Private Scholar's Fellowship and taught several courses in Philosophy at the University of British Columbia and Kwantlen College, in addition to doing volunteer work with Amnesty International. He speaks and publishes widely on civil liberties issues and is the author of *AIDS Discrimination in Canada*. Dr Westwood received his PhD in Philosophy from the University of Waterloo and his BA in Economics and MA in Philosophy from the University of Windsor.

Index

advocacy: evolution of, 244–6; experiences, 117, 231–41, 244–58; future of, 258–60; on Internet, 251–3; need for, 241; obstacles to, 231; opposition to surveillance technologies, 258; promoting privacy-enhancing technologies, 253; promoting regulation, 253; reasons for failure of, 234; role of advocates, 13–14, 27, 81, 82, 241, 265; trends in, 256–8
Agre, Philip, 5
Alinsky, Saul, 256–8, 259, 261n
Allen, Kenneth, 202
American Chamber of Commerce, 211
American Civil Liberties Union, 250
American Society of Composers, Authors and Publishers, 172
American Express, 151, 195n
Amnesty International, 250
Annenberg Washington Program, 205
anonymity: in health information systems, 119–20, 127; historic, 20; loss of, 28–9, 32, 123; privacy-enhancing technologies and, 122–3; threats to, 23–4
anonymous identifiers, 119–20

anonymous remailers, 98, 264
ArgeDaten, 246
Armstrong, Pamela, 156
Association des Utilisateurs d'Internet, 250
Association of European Chambers of Commerce and Industry, 211
asymmetric cryptosystem, 123
Australia, 7, 192, 247
Australian Privacy Foundation, 246
autonomy, 63, 101, 102, 153, 249

balancing: concept of, 69–71, 76–9; conflicting objectives, 90n, 169; fundamentalist vs pragmatist interests, 73–4; individual vs commercial interests, 58, 76, 98, 159, 175–6, 163, 231; individual vs societal interests, 9, 24, 71–2, 153, 169, 240; means vs ends, 58–60; models of, 79–83; objectives of EU directive, 70–1; paradox of, 73–6, 169; in Puritan society, 20; right to privacy vs right to use information, 150–3; right to privacy vs societal interests, 9, 68–83, 169, 232, 240; right to privacy vs transborder dataflows, 70